Ireland: Authority and Crisis

Reimagining Ireland

Volume 70

Edited by Dr Eamon Maher
Institute of Technology, Tallaght

PETER LANG

Oxford • Bern • Berlin • Bruxelles • Frankfurt am Main • New York • Wien

Carine Berbéri and Martine Pelletier (eds)

Ireland: Authority and Crisis

PETER LANG

Oxford • Bern • Berlin • Bruxelles • Frankfurt am Main • New York • Wien

Bibliographic information published by Die Deutsche Nationalbibliothek.
Die Deutsche Nationalbibliothek lists this publication in the Deutsche
Nationalbibliografie; detailed bibliographic data is available on the Internet at
http://dnb.d-nb.de.

A catalogue record for this book is available from the British Library.

Library of Congress Control Number: 2015952228

ISSN 1662-9094
ISBN 978-3-0343-1939-3 (print)
ISBN 978-3-0353-0770-2 (eBook)

Cover image: *Our Lady of the Mobile Phone* © Mags Harnett,
www.magsharnett.com

This publication has been peer reviewed.

Printed in Germany

In memory of our colleague Bernard Escarbelt, who worked tirelessly and selflessly to advance the cause of Irish Studies in France and beyond and to whom so many of us owe so much. The SOFEIR conference in Tours is the last he attended before he passed away in November 2012.

Contents

Abbreviations

AIB	Allied Irish Bank
ASU	Active Service Unit
BBC	British Broadcasting Corporation
BOI	Bank of Ireland
CEO	Chief Executive Officer
CICA	Commission to Inquire into Child Abuse
DAAD	Direct Action Against Drugs
DUP	Democratic Unionist Party
EBS	Education Building Society
ECB	European Central Bank
GPO	General Post Office
IFSC	International Financial Services Centre
ILP	Irish Life and Permanent
IMF	International Monetary Fund
INBS	Irish Nationwide Building Society
IRA	Irish Republican Army
ISPCC	Irish Society for the Prevention of Cruelty to Children
MEP	Member of the European Parliament
MLA	Member of the Legislative Assembly (Northern Ireland Assembly)
NAMA	National Asset Management Agency
NGO	Non-governmental Organization
NSPCC	National Society for the Prevention of Cruelty to Children
OECD	Organization of Economic Co-operation and Development
OED	Oxford English Dictionary
OIRA	Official Irish Republican Army
PIRA	Provisional Irish Republican Army
PSNI	Police Service of Northern Ireland
RAAD	Republican Action Against Drugs

RIC   Royal Irish Constabulary
RTE   Raidió Teilifís Éireann
RUC   Royal Ulster Constabulary
STDs   Sexually Transmitted Diseases
TD   Teachta Dála (Member of Dáil Éireann)
UN   United Nations
UNRWA   United Nations Relief and Works Agency
US   United States
USC   Ulster Special Constabulary
UUP   Ulster Unionist Party

CARINE BERBÉRI AND MARTINE PELLETIER

Introduction: Authority and Crisis, Authority in Crisis

> In every crisis a piece of the world, something common to us all, is destroyed. The failure of common sense, like a divining rod, points to the place where such a cave-in has occurred.[1]

> The cynics may be able to point to the past. But we live in the future.[2]

> Practically as well as theoretically, we are no longer in a position to know what authority really is.[3]

In her influential and still highly relevant 1954 essay, 'What is Authority?' Hannah Arendt discusses what she calls the 'constant, ever-widening and deepening crisis of authority [that] has accompanied the development of the modern world in our century.' Her contention that 'authority has vanished from the modern world'[4] and the theoretical framework provided by

1   Hannah Arendt, 'The Crisis in Education', *Between Past and Future: Eight Exercises in Political Thought* (New York: Viking Press, 1961), 178.
2   An oft-quoted and much-derided statement by Taoiseach Bertie Ahern at the Fianna Fail *Ard-Fheis* in 1998; quoted in Roy F. Foster's *Luck and the Irish. A Brief History of Change 1970–2000* (Harmondsworth: Penguin Books, 2008), 1. Bertie Ahern unwittingly echoes the title of Arendt's collection of essays, *Between Past and Future*, leaving the present with little authority indeed.
3   Hannah Arendt, 'What is Authority?', *Between Past and Future: Eight Exercises in Political Thought* (New York: Viking Press, 1961) <http://la.utexas.edu/users/hcleaver/330T/350kPEEreadings.html> accessed 7 July 2015.
4   *Ibid.*

her collection of essays published in 1961 under the title *Between Past and Future* have inspired a number of the contributors to the present volume, and offer the theoretical framework for this introductory chapter. It is worth noting that when discussing authority Arendt often invokes the idea of a crisis, whether of education, of culture or indeed of authority itself. While many contributors have sought to define 'authority', often turning to Arendt's seminal and, dare we say, authoritative essay on the subject, the other key concept, that of crisis, has generally been left to speak for itself, as it were. The *OED* defines crisis as 'the point in the progress of a disease when an important development or change takes place which is decisive of recovery or death; the turning-point of a disease for better or worse; also applied to any marked or sudden variation occurring in the progress of a disease and to the phenomena accompanying it'; it is also, by extension 'a vitally important or decisive stage in the progress of anything; a turning-point; also, a state of affairs in which a decisive change for better or worse is imminent; now applied especially to times of difficulty, insecurity, and suspense in politics or commerce.'[5] In recent years the word crisis has been much used and abused in Ireland and beyond.[6] Turning once more to Hannah Arendt, this time her essay 'The Crisis in Education' also collected in *Between Past and Future*, we may ponder the opportunities paradoxically afforded by such moments of crisis:

> And that is the opportunity, provided by the very fact of crisis – which tears away facades and obliterates prejudices – to explore and inquire into whatever has been laid bare of the essence of the matter [...] A crisis forces us back to the questions themselves and requires from us either new or old answers, but in any case direct judgments. A crisis becomes a disaster only when we respond to it with preformed judgments, that is, with prejudices. Such an attitude not only sharpens the crisis but makes us forfeit the experience of reality and the opportunity for reflection it provides.[7]

5   *OED*, online edition.
6   For a valuable discussion of crisis in the context of contemporary Ireland see Eamon Maher and Eugene O'Brien, eds, *From Prosperity to Austerity. A Socio-Cultural Critique of the Celtic Tiger and its Aftermath* (Manchester: Manchester University Press, 2014).
7   Hannah Arendt, 'The Crisis in Education', 174–5.

The starting point for this volume – and for the French Association of Irish Studies conference where the various contributions were initially delivered – was a desire to analyse the ways in which a situation of crisis could challenge and transform various forms of authority whose efficacy and legitimacy thus became liable to rejection or renewal. In terms of cultural, social and political practices, the analysis of possible relationships between authority and identity is framed differently today: from Cultural Studies, Gender Studies and Postcolonial Studies to political multiculturalism and what is commonly referred to as 'Identity Politics', the critique of specific types of social, cultural and political authority is usually linked to particular definitions of 'identity' and has proved most relevant within the framework of Irish studies.

In all parts of the island of Ireland, the ambiguous relation with a political authority which was long seen as illegitimate, hegemonic and contested by virtue of a colonial past is a moot point. The strategies used over time by advocates of Irish autonomy and independence to fend off the ruling authorities and destabilize the colonial regime certainly offer a wide scope for investigation. From a historiographical perspective, the discourse that was seen to define and legitimize the nation has frequently been challenged in its claims to be authoritative. In the Republic of Ireland the crisis of the mainstays of the modern state is manifest when looking at the advent of the Celtic Tiger and the ensuing recession with the emerging critique of the prevailing liberal economic model; the declining influence of traditional political parties; the evolution of legislation in the fields of private morality (divorce, homosexuality) as a rapid process of secularization got underway; the challenge to the authority of the Catholic Church following various scandals and the publication of the Ryan Report. To what extent did the 2008 crisis that so badly affected Ireland – and many would argue still affects it today – act as a catalyst, showing various structures of authority giving way under pressure? The Good Friday Agreement (1998) has led to major changes for Northern Ireland as well as for the Republic: new authorities endowed with legislative and executive powers have been set up, entailing a radical transformation for the forces of law and order, as a result of the replacement of a military-type authority by civilian authorities striving to win the support and trust of both communities.

Beyond the somewhat simplistic 'authority versus liberty' dichotomy – after all Arendt has argued quite forcefully that 'we are in fact confronted with a simultaneous recession of both freedom and authority in the modern world'[8] and that 'authority implies an obedience in which men retain their freedom'[9] – looking at authority in a context of crisis enables a rethinking of the relationships between the known and the new, between primary and secondary sources, and the ways in which these come to be articulated. In literature and the arts a reappraisal of the authority of canonical authors, traditional forms, paradigms and critical discourses mostly revolves around intertextuality and rewriting, as well as the wider crisis of – authoritative – representation. It is worth engaging with those moments when the authority of an artistic form or a discursive mode, or the central position of the figure of the author comes to be challenged through the emergence of new paradigms claiming in their turn to be 'authoritative'. Models and their reproduction or critique, rewriting and translation issues all presuppose an analysis of how underlying mechanisms operate to legitimize or undermine a previously acknowledged, or already failing, authority.

The first part of the volume is entitled 'Crisis, Authority and Literature' and collects essays that discuss crisis and authority from a range of complementary perspectives in literature. What is the authority of an author? Of a text? Of literature itself? Is their authority in crisis? How do works of fiction represent, generate or resolve crises on their own aesthetic, stylistic and representational terms?

In the opening essay, Nicholas Grene considers 'the authority of English English as a standardized form of the written language and its subversion by the oral in Irish English writing' arguing that 'this subversion of the authority of the written by the spoken comes to carry with it a claim to another form of authority, the authority of the literary.' Moving from Boucicault's comic use of Irish-English speech to the tactics of the national theatre movement and the Literary Revival, Grene shows how Synge's

8   Hannah Arendt, 'What is Authority?', 6.
9   *Ibid.*, 9.

language succeeded in transvaluing 'the previously mocked Irish English dialect forms into a style to be perceived as poetic' and thus endowed with its 'own sort of literary authority.' James Joyce, Roddy Doyle and Seamus Heaney provide further instances of the ability of many Irish writers to forge a language that, through the 'subversion of more correct, proper English actually carries its own sort of authority.'

Where does authority lie in the matter of translation? Does a double transfer, from written translation to oral interpretation and from one language to another, create a possible conflict of allegiance or potential crisis? Brigitte Bastiat and Frank Healy recount the circumstances which led them to translate Owen McCafferty's play *Mojo Mickybo* into French. Discussing the authority of translation and translators they note that 'the concept of the functional authority of the source text has been undermined as the translator now seeks to respect and show linguistic, cultural and historical otherness'. Using the work of Lawrence Venuti, and in particular his 1995 book *The Translator's Invisibility*, they claim for their own translation the right not to defer wholly 'to the authority of the source text' and argue that 'in a translation for the theatre, the stage and the oral performance should have authority over the written score', thereby concurring with Nicholas Grene's earlier analysis which finds itself validated by the translators' practice.

The next two chapters, by Bertrand Cardin and Audrey Robitaillié, share a concern with intertextuality and an interest in Colum McCann's fiction. Bertrand Cardin wonders: 'Does the author actually have power and authority?' The question is further complicated when there may be several 'authors': 'isn't the authority of the quoting author put in the shade by that of the quoted author or vice versa?' The chapter convincingly explores the possibility that intertextual practice may be 'a sign that authority is in crisis.' Before focusing on Colum McCann's novel, *Let the Great World Spin,* and revealing its intertextual playfulness and indebtedness, Cardin reminds us that intertextuality came to prominence in critical discourse in a context of crisis and rejection of authority – 1968 – and is inextricably linked to the 'death of the author' theory as authority for the production of meaning in a text shifted from the author to the reader.

Audrey Robitaillié further teases out the possibilities and complexities of intertextuality by looking at the ways in which Colum McCann and

Keith Donohue have revisited and appropriated the traditional motif of
the changeling story. McCann's short story, 'Stolen Child', and Donohue's
first novel, *The Stolen Child*, explicitly share an intertextual reference to
Yeats's poem. She reads their work as 'challenges to Yeats's canonical use
of the motif in an attempt to (re)define their own Irishness'. In choosing
to position themselves in a tradition that stretches back to Irish folklore,
McCann and Donohue acknowledge Yeats's authority while working also
to subvert it through a form of parody that may suggest a crisis of his literary authority. What is more, they 'appropriate Yeats's canonical motif, by
relating it to themes that are significant for them such as exile and identity'.

John Banville's fiction provides fertile ground for Mehdi Ghassemi's
investigation into 'authorial and perceptual crises.' In Banville's novels,
the authority of the narrators is undermined at the level of personal experience, that is, their most immediate and intimate interiority. Banville's
2002 novel *Shroud* is read 'in relation to Paul de Man's "history" as well
as his theory of representation' and Ghassemi traces the consequences of
introspection for the narrator's subjectivity, arguing that what could first
appear as 'a crisis of authenticity' may really be 'a crisis of authorial (as well
as authoritative) perceptions in which Vander's very sense of self as well as
his grip over reality are undermined.'

Virginie Girel-Pietka's essay is devoted to the playwright Denis
Johnston and the ways in which the characters in his plays keep 'challenging authority, disowning the collective images put forward by the communities they belong to, and undoing canonical stage characters'. Writing
in the turbulent period leading from the Irish War of independence to the
aftermath of the Second World War, Johnston was 'concerned about authority, laws, national policies and traditions as both conditions for and threats
to individual freedom and self-expression'. When society is in turmoil, as
it was all too often in those tragic decades, authorities face a crisis 'when
their subjects are led to question or overthrow them, either because they are
too weak and can no longer be taken seriously, or when they overstep their
power and impose normative and actually crippling rules on individuals'.
Johnston is of interest in Irish theatre history not only because he staged
individuals challenging authority but also because of his own relentless
rejection of the dominant theatrical mode in Ireland at the time, realism,

and his exciting – though not always popular or successful – quest for new forms to better express the complexities of the time. Virginie Girel-Pietka concludes by calling for Ireland's theatre, in these times of crisis, to rediscover an artist who was on a permanent quest for 'an authoritative stage'.

Chantal Dessaint's '"Suffer the little children...": Éilís Ní Dhuibhne's Strategies of Subversion' approaches Ní Dhuibhne's fiction from the angle provided by the crisis brought about by the loss of authority of the Catholic Church in the wake of the various scandals over child abuse. Using 'mainly indirect and subversive strategies that range from irony, the use of a colloquial language, to tropic transfer', the writer is able to delve with great delicacy and occasional gusto into the hidden emotional depths of characters who suffered from and resisted the puritanical excess of an educational programme promoted by Church and State and aiming, ludicrously, 'to eliminate sex from the Irish way of life.' Her female protagonists and narrators challenge authority and Dessaint analyses how the writer empowers those submerged, often silenced female voices as they 'resist the insidious indoctrination operated by Church and State, particularly in matters of language and sexuality.' Thus *The Dancers Dancing* 'is more than just a bildungsroman about adolescent girls: it also proposes a subversive message where the linguistic and cultural program contrived by Church and State in order to tailor those teenagers into good Catholic citizens turns out to be their very means of liberation and provides them with the opportunity to challenge the figures of authority that endorse it.'

The closing chapter of the first part also acts as a bridge towards the second part of this volume in terms of its central theme of an increasing resistance towards the authority of Church and State in the Republic echoing Arendt's contention that: 'The crisis of authority in education is most closely connected with the crisis of tradition, that is with the crisis in our attitude toward the realm of the past.'[10]

The second part of the volume is entitled 'Society in Crisis: Challenges to Authority/ies' and its organization is both thematic and chronological.

---

10   Hannah Arendt, 'The Crisis in Education', 193.

The first chapters all address the challenges to authorities in a range of fields in contemporary Ireland: Church, State, government and the financial sector. The next two take us north of the border with investigations of how the political instability of the 'ill-founded state' of Northern Ireland has led to a situation in which the Irish Republican Army (IRA) has taken over the role of the discredited security forces and established its own authority, as Michel Savaric points out, while Fabrice Mourlon through his analysis of the BBC TV drama, *You, Me and Marley* points to a lost generation, that of the children born in the midst of a violent crisis that has discredited all the available figures of authority. The final two chapters move back in time with a focus on the second half of the nineteenth century, addressing respectively the use of cartoons against the backdrop of the Home Rule crisis and the Anglo-Irish writing of Irish history between 1840 and 1910.

Mathew D. Staunton and Nathalie Sebbane in their 'Authority and Child Abuse in Ireland: Rethinking History in a Hostile Field' argue that writing the history of child abuse in Ireland in the light of recent scandals raises the issue of determining who has the authority to decide if abuse took place or not. Much of this essay hinges not so much on the crisis that the revelations of widespread child abuse generated for the Roman Catholic Church as on the wider issue of authorizing a historiographical framing of those stories. Arendt's essay 'The Crisis of Education' does come to mind, notably her reminder that 'we have been accustomed in our tradition of political thought to regard the authority of parents over children, of teachers over pupils, as the model by which to understand political authority.'[11]

In the last few years the word 'crisis' has become broadly synonymous with 'economic' or 'financial' crisis, though that may in itself be the symptom of a wider crisis, of meaning and politics… Defining authority through the prism offered by Max Weber and Michel Crozier, Valerie Peyronel warns that: 'authority is likely to be irreparably undermined by any lack of skills, as its exercise rests in the trust of those it is exercised over'; she goes on to offer a persuasive reading of the banking crisis and the failures or strengths in the responses of the authorities, political and financial who have had to

11   Hannah Arendt, 'The Crisis in Education', 190.

deal with this exceptional situation, analysing 'the intricate confusion of authorities that prevailed in the remediation processes'.

Further probing the limits of the Irish Government's authority in another area, in foreign affairs and not on the home front, Marie-Violaine Louvet looks at the ways in which the initiative of pro-Palestinian activists came to challenge the authority of the Irish Republic, focusing on a confrontation relating to the so-called two 'Gaza flotillas' in 2010 and 2011. The resulting 'cacophony of voices claiming to express Irish foreign policy gave rise to a crisis and a challenge to the authority of a state confined to the role of mediator between the activists and Israel'.

Hannah Arendt is clear that authority should not, as it often is, be confused with coercion:

> Since authority always demands obedience, it is commonly mistaken for some form of power or violence. Yet authority precludes the use of external means of coercion where force is used, authority itself has failed! Authority, on the other hand, is incompatible with persuasion, which presupposes equality and works through a process of argumentation. [...] If authority is to be defined at all, then, it must be in contradistinction to both coercion by force and persuasion through arguments.[12]

She is equally adamant that authority is closely connected with foundation. Without a shared sense of foundation, authority can never be secure. For both Michel Savaric and Fabrice Mourlon, the crisis in Northern Ireland is at least partly the result of the failure of foundation, an initial flaw going back to the creation of a political entity nobody really wanted and which was either rejected – by Republicans and Irish Nationalists – or seized upon and appropriated with sectarian vengeance by those who had lost twenty-six of the thirty-two counties for the Union and were keen to hang on to the remaining six. The result has been a Northern Irish state that was founded without the necessary authority and was thus contested from the start before falling prey to a violent crisis with the 'Troubles' from the late 1960s onwards. The 1998 Good Friday Agreement has sought to reinvent institutions along power-sharing lines, following the route of argumentation

---

12 Hannah Arendt, 'What is Authority?', 1–2.

and persuasion, as an alternative to what was felt to be not the legitimate authority exercised by a state but the violent imposition of majority rule on a powerless and despised minority community.

Michel Savaric's chapter covers the period since 1969 and charts 'the origins of the undertaking of law and order by the republican movement' in Northern Ireland. The contention is that to some degree at least this 'endeavour was thought through and justified as a challenge to the authority of the State and an attempt at asserting itself as an alternative power', ultimately enabling 'the leaders of the republican movement to enter the State apparatus itself.' In his discussion of *You, Me and Marley*, a 1992 TV fiction broadcast by the BBC and located in Belfast against a backdrop of violence and political crisis, Fabrice Mourlon draws attention to the power of fictional TV/screen representation to capture the deleterious effects of the troubles on the younger generation. The film, based on a script by Graham Reid, tries hard not to take sides but paints a terrifying picture of a world in which teenagers reject authority and are drawn further and further into violence and confrontation with a range of failed authority figures, ultimately leading to tragedy. Once more, Hannah Arendt's essay on education comes to mind: 'Therefore by being emancipated from the authority of adults the child has not been freed but has been subjected to a much more terrifying and truly tyrannical authority, the tyranny of the majority. In any case the result is that the children have been so to speak banished from the world of grown-ups.'[13]

The final two essays are invitations to broaden the historical perspective, returning to the rise of the Nationalist discourse and movement in the nineteenth century, and forms of historiographical resistance to Anglo-Irish/Unionist authority. Claire Dubois turns to 'a series of chromolithographs published between 1880 and 1910 in Irish nationalist newspapers such as the *Weekly Freeman*, the *Nation*, or *United Ireland* the aim of which was to challenge the derogatory representation of Ireland in British satirical newspapers'. She thus engages both in a discussion of the appropriation and subversion of a popular form and the political uses it was put to in

---

13   Hannah Arendt, 'The Crisis in Education', 181–2.

what she reads as 'a visual strategy [which] played a critical role in shaping Irish public opinion and mobilizing the people for the nationalist cause, closely linking the visual arts and patriotism in a nationalist construct aimed at subverting British authority in the context of the Home Rule crisis.'

Ciaran Brady's final essay allows us to delve further back into a foundational moment – to borrow from Arendt's vocabulary once again – and to look at traditional history writing in the light of a contest to establish and preserve the authority of an Anglo-Irish discourse on Ireland as pressure from alternative Nationalist rhetoric kept mounting after the Act of Union was passed in 1801. Like Staunton and Sebbane but from a different vantage point, Ciaran Brady focuses on the role and authority of historians, selecting the writings of Lecky, Prendergast and Froude for analysis and seeking to understand 'the unwillingness of Irish scholars and intellectuals to participate overtly in the absorption of the widespread conviction that the study of history could be transformed into an authoritative scientific discipline'. His reading of the appeal of Augustin Thierry's conquest theory to Ireland's Anglo-Irish historians is persuasive and provides a useful lead into the writings of those who saw their role as 'mediating between the natives and new conquerors'. Within such a context, the Act of Union could not but present Irish historians with challenges as the authority of the official archive was 'intrinsically problematic' since it touched on the issue of foundation – here that of an Irish nation-state – which Arendt has consistently argued is crucial to understand both the nature and the limits of authority. Ciaran Brady's essay brings to a close this foray into the crisis of authority in Ireland, leaving us with the conviction that far from having exhausted the subject, the volume may hopefully have opened up a rich and varied field of investigation for further research and analysis.

PART I

Crisis, Authority and Literature

NICHOLAS GRENE

Irish English as a Literary Language: Authority and Subversion

ABSTRACT

The literary use of Irish English is often seen as part of the postcolonial phenomenon of the empire writing back, marginalized dialects challenging the hegemony of the metropolitan forms of language. This paper explores a somewhat different if related pattern: the way the authority of standard forms of written English are subverted by an Irish oral demotic. Beginning with the 'blarney' of Dion Boucicault's comic heroes, it is concerned with orality in the language of Synge and Joyce at the period of the Revival, and goes on to consider the very different later practice of Roddy Doyle and Seamus Heaney. In each case it can be argued that the subversion of the authority of correct print forms is a claim instead for the authority of the literary.

What is probably the most famous passage in all literature on the relationship between Irish English and English English is the exchange between Stephen Dedalus and the English Dean of Studies in *A Portrait of the Artist as a Young Man* on the subject of the peculiar use of the word 'tundish' for 'funnel' in Ireland. These are Stephen's inner reflections:

> He felt with a smart of dejection that the man to whom he was speaking was a countryman of Ben Jonson. He thought:
> — The language in which we are speaking is his before it is mine. How different are the words *home, Christ, ale, master*, on his lips and on mine! I cannot write or speak these words without unrest of spirit. His language, so familiar and so foreign, will always be for me an acquired speech. I have not made or accepted its words. My voice holds them at bay. My soul frets in the shadow of his language.[1]

---

1 James Joyce, *A Portrait of the Artist as a Young Man* (Harmondsworth: Penguin, 1960 [1916]), 189.

It is the *locus classicus* of postcolonial anxiety, the sense that the Irish speaker of English is always voicing a learned language, a speech that is for him derivative. And the strategy of many postcolonial authors, as we know from the influential book of Bill Ashcroft, Gareth Griffiths and Helen Tiffin, has been to 'write back', to challenge the authority of the metropolitan language of the colonizer by abrogation and appropriation.[2] There has of course been a debate as to whether Ireland, Britain's oldest colony, should or should not be included with other more recently colonized, more remote countries as comparably postcolonial: the authors of *The Empire Writes Back*, one notices, never use Irish writers as examples. The purpose of this essay is not to re-open that debate but to consider the authority of English English as a standardized form of the written language and its subversion by the oral in Irish English writing. My argument is that this subversion of the authority of the written by the spoken comes to carry with it a claim to another form of authority, the authority of the literary. Starting back with Boucicault and his comic use of Irish-English speech, I aim to show how that is transformed into the literary in the Revival period in the work of Synge and Joyce, before concluding at the other end of the twentieth century with some examples from Roddy Doyle and Seamus Heaney.

Boucicault

From very early on, Irish speakers of English were associated with fluency, the gift of the gab, 'blarney'. The word 'blarney' seems already to have settled into the language at the beginning of the nineteenth century. But it was an eloquence specifically associated with deception and dishonesty: 'a cajoling tongue and the art of flattery or of telling lies with unblushing effrontery' according to one *OED* citation. At the same time the peculiarities of

---

2   Bill Ashcroft, Gareth Griffiths and Helen Tiffin, *The Empire Writes Back* (London: Routledge, 2nd ed. 2002), 37.

pronunciation, idiom and vocabulary by Irish speakers were used to mark off their ignorance, their class subordination, or at best their whimsical charm. This was the tradition of Irish bulls and blunders, obvious grammatical or logical absurdities. The combination of oral proficiency and formal ineptitude could be exploited for great comic set pieces. The genre can be illustrated by Conn the Shaughraun in Boucicault's melodrama, defending himself against the charge of having stolen Squire Foley's horse:

> Well, here's a purty thing, for a horse to run away with a man's charachter like this! Oh, wurra! May I never die in sin, but this was the way of it. I was standing by ould Foley's gate, when I heard the cry of the hounds comin' across the tail end of the bog, and there they wor, my dear, spread out like the tail of a paycock, an' the finest dog fox you'd ever see sailing ahead of them up the boreen, and right across the church-yard. It was enough to raise the inhabitants. Well, as I looked, who should come up and put his head over the gate beside me but the Squire's brown mare, small blame to her. Divil a thing I said to her, nor she to me, for the hounds had lost the scent, we knew by their whelp and whine as they hunted among the grave-stones, when, whish! the fox went by us. I leapt on the gate, an' gave a shriek of a view holloo to the whip; in a minute the pack caught the scent again, an' the whole field came roarin' past. The mare lost her head, an' tore at the gate. 'Stop', ses I, 'ye devil!' and I slipped the taste of a rope over her head an' into her mouth. 'Come home now', ses I, 'asy' and I threw my leg across her. Be gabers! No sooner was I on her bare back than whoo! Holy rocket! She was over the gate, an' tearing like mad afther the hounds. 'Yoicks!', ses I, 'Come back the thief of the world, where are you takin' me to?' as she went through the huntin' field an' laid me beside the masther of the hounds, Squire Foley himself. He turned the colour of his leather breeches. 'Mother of Moses!' ses he, 'Is that Conn the Shaughraun on my brown mare?' 'Bad luck to me!', ses I 'It's no one else!' 'You sthole my horse', says the Squire. 'That's a lie!', ses I, 'For it was your horse sthole me!'[3]

This is typical in its use of Irish-derived exclamations – 'Oh, wurra' from the vocative 'Mhuire' an invocation of the Virgin – characteristically Irish pronunciations – 'baste' for 'beast' – and Irish idioms – 'Divil a thing I said to her' – not to mention obvious solecisms like the shift in gender of the personal pronouns – 'who should come up and put *his* head

---

3   Dion Boucicault, *Selected Plays*, ed. Andrew Parkin (Gerrards Cross: Colin Smythe; Washington DC: Catholic University of America Press, 1987), 272.

over the gate beside me but the Squire's brown mare, small blame to *her*'. The wild and patent improbability of it all gives force and piquancy to the punch line 'That's a lie! For it was your horse shtole me', bull and blarney combined. The charm is in the energy, the inventiveness, and the vividness of the recital to be enjoyed as comedy because of the transparency of the lies and the stage-Irishry of the language. There is an implied deference to correct English allowing audiences to laugh at the *tour de force* of Boucicault's mangled grammar, pronunciation and logic. Boucicault as an actor exploited the subaltern position of Irish English speech while making no claims for the literary quality of his text.

Synge

It was against Boucicault's sort of stage-Irishry that the Irish Literary Theatre was devised in 1897. 'We will show' said Yeats who drafted the manifesto for the would-be theatre, 'that Ireland is not the home of buffoonery and easy sentiment, as it has been represented, but the home of an ancient idealism'.[4] One of the tactics in that campaign of the national theatre movement, and the Literary Revival more generally, was to transvalue the previously mocked Irish English dialect forms into a style to be perceived as poetic. Key to that transvaluation is the language of Synge, not only because of the importance of the special Hiberno-English speech that he gives to his characters but the theory with which he defended that speech in the Preface to *The Playboy of the Western World*.

Against a background of suspicion of his work and the truth of his representation of the Irish peasants, Synge stressed the authenticity of his language: 'In writing *The Playboy of the Western World*, as in my other plays, I have used one or two words only, that I have not heard among the

---

4   Quoted in Lady Gregory, *Our Irish Theatre* (Gerrards Cross: Colin Smythe, 3rd ed., 1972), 20.

country people of Ireland, or spoken in my own nursery before I could read the newspapers'.[5] This pre-supposes a kind of primal pre-literate language before the fall into education, refinement, the world of newsprint. Synge claims that the position of writers working in Ireland at his time was one of privilege because, he says, 'in countries where the imagination of the people, and the language they use, is rich and living, it is possible for a writer to be rich and copious in his words, and at the same time to give the reality which is the root of all poetry, in a comprehensive and natural form'.[6] This is a privilege, however, which will not last much longer. 'In Ireland, *for a few years more*, we have a popular imagination that is fiery and magnificent and tender'.[7] As the Literary Revival generally stressed the Celtic Twilight, the lingering remains of an older deeper culture which Irish writers needed to cherish while they could, so the oral language of the Irish country people for a working playwright like Synge afforded a last contact with that 'reality which is the root of all poetry' before the inevitable advance of modernizing print-culture. 'All art', Synge declared, 'is a collaboration', and the language of his plays represented a collaboration between himself as writer and the country people as speakers.[8] In looking at that collaboration and the literary effects achieved by it, however, I want to focus also on the other collaboration involved, that between the writer and his target audience.

Using Irish English which reproduces syntax and idiom carried over from the Irish language, as Synge so commonly did, gives the defamiliarization which the Russian formalists saw as an essential characteristic of literary language; the unusual constructions, the strange vocabulary draw attention to themselves. But at the same time they naturalize certain aesthetic effects. It is well known, for instance, that Irish has no separate word for 'yes' and 'no'. Instead we have a system of what are known as responsives, ways of answering any question by a full sentence, often an inverted form of the question. Synge exploits this particularly well in the catechism of

5   John Millington Synge, *Collected Works*: IV, *Plays*, Book II, ed. Ann Saddlemyer (London: Oxford University Press, 1968), 53.
6   *Ibid.*
7   *Ibid.*, 54.
8   *Ibid.*, 53.

Christy Mahon in *The Playboy*, when he first appears as a stranger in the country pub, and the local people do not yet know that he has killed his father. They keep trying to guess what he actually did to make him afraid of the police. One of the suggestions is that he was a forger:

> PHILLY.   Did you strike golden guineas out of solder, or shilling coins itself?
> CHRISTY. I did not mister, not sixpence nor a farthing coin.[9]

There is a beautifully balanced symmetry in this, guineas reducing to shillings, sixpences going down to farthings like a Dutch auction. But the cue for this antiphonal structure is provided by the principle of the Irish responsives. And what appears in English an inherent stylization in this principle makes possible a highly patterned theatrical rhythm in the passage over all.

One of the very broadest impressions Synge's stage dialect creates is again derived from its Irish linguistic substratum. There is an extraordinary high level of verbal forms ending in -ing in Synge's language, gerunds, present participles, continuous as against simple forms of the verb. Irish provides reasons for many of these: in its use of gerundial phrases, not 'I sit', but 'I am in my sitting', not 'I have done something' but 'I'm after doing it'; its use of a frequentative, the mode that translates into English as 'do be doing'; and its substitution of participial clauses for conventional subordinate clauses, 'and I going down the road' in place of 'when I was going down the road'. All these are there in Irish; but the frequency with which they appear in Synge is out of proportion to what we might expect in ordinary spoken Irish, much less Irish English. The preference for these forms is Synge's own, the free-flowing, long periods he builds up with them is his style, not a style endemic in the language itself.

One example can be used to illustrate the sort of fluency that Synge creates with this special style. At the beginning of the second act of *The Playboy* Christy is delighted with himself. Instead of being horrified at learning of his crime of patricide, the local people have been thoroughly impressed and he has landed the job of pot-boy in the pub. This is his speech, on his own, the morning after his arrival, relishing his future: 'Well, this'd be a fine place

9   John Millington Synge, *Collected Works: IV, Plays*, Book II, 71.

to be my whole life talking out with swearing Christians in place of my old dogs and cat, and I stalking around, smoking my pipe and drinking my fill, and never a day's work but drawing a cork an odd time, or wiping a glass, or rinsing out a shiny tumbler for a decent man'.[10] This is a quite highly wrought sentence rhetorically, with its balanced clauses – 'smoking my pipe and drinking my fill' – and its triadic conclusion – 'drawing a cork ... wiping a glass ... rinsing ... a tumbler'. But its art is masked by its characteristically Irish English use of paratactic constructions rather than the subordinate clauses which would be normal in standard English: 'and I stalking round', 'and never a day's work'. The normal syntactic apparatus of 'when', 'since', 'because' is suppressed as well as the relative pronouns which are not normally used in Irish: 'which', 'who' and 'that'. With no more sophisticated connectives than 'and' and 'but', Christy may well appear to be thinking aloud, one thought merely unfolding from another, while in fact a very carefully controlled and rhythmically fashioned long sentence is uttered.

In the 'Preface' to *The Playboy* Synge compares the position of Irish writers in his own time to that of the 'happy ages of literature', above all the Elizabethan period. 'It is probable', he says, 'that when the Elizabethan dramatist took his ink-horn and sat down to his work he used many phrases that he had just heard, as he sat at dinner, from his mother or his children'.[11] Again there is the emphasis on the translation of the oral into writing, the literary originating in the non- or pre-literate speech of women and children. But it is no accident that Synge chose the Elizabethan analogy. The other notable feature of the Irish English dialect apart from its substratum of Irish language constructions is its archaic English vocabulary. Words that might have died out of the spoken language in standard English by Synge's time were preserved as fossils in the less modernized dialect in remote parts of Ireland. 'Is my visage astray', asks Christy's father, Old Mahon, when he is being persuaded that he is mad: 'do I look peculiar?'[12] 'Visage' was still current in written English at the beginning of the twentieth century but

10   John Millington Synge, *Collected Works*: IV, *Plays*, Book II, ed. Ann Saddlemyer, 95.
11   *Ibid.*, 53.
12   *Ibid.*, 143.

only as an old-fashioned poeticism. Old Mahon as Irish English speaker can make it sound a convincing part of his idiolect. In the first act Christy is being fought over by Pegeen Mike, the daughter of the pub, and the Widow Quin who is equally interested in the heroic young father-killer, as to where he should lodge. He decides in favour of Pegeen and says politely to the Widow: 'I'm pot-boy in this place, and it's here I'd liefer stay'.[13] The last *OED* instance of this construction, 'I had liefer' = 'I would prefer' is in the eighteenth century, but that does not prevent an Irish English speaker like Christy Mahon having it in his active vocabulary in 1907.

The special quality of Synge's stage dialect is enhanced by these archaic usages. For most audiences and readers of Synge these words would have been associated mainly with classic literary texts, Shakespeare or the Authorized Version of the Bible, foundational works of the canon. They are heard as literary not just because of this association but because, given such associations, to hear them unselfconsciously spoken feels like a restoration of the language, a return to its origins. The literariness of Synge's language derives from the fact that, for those who speak it, it is not literary, not influenced by written forms or an aesthetically privileged style. And so the strangeness of the cross-linguistic effects, the exoticism of the archaic vocabulary, are authenticated by being represented as the normal speech of an Irish English oral community. Such authenticity affords them their own sort of literary authority.

Joyce

Joyce's project, in language as in so much else, was almost exactly antithetical to that of the leaders of the Irish Literary Revival. They sought a newly rich and vivid literary language in the speech of the country people, people who spoke an Irish English as far as possible from print forms and urban

---

13   John Millington Synge, *Collected Works: IV, Plays*, Book II, 91.

modernity. Joyce, committed Dubliner that he was, sought to incorporate all the different idioms of the city into the great carnival of language that is *Ulysses*. He is the master modernist who brought into the play of his book not only parodies of previous literary styles but, for the first time in English, newsspeak, the language of advertising, the various inert discourses of science and technology. In the 'Cyclops' episode, where Bloom clashes with the arch-nationalist Citizen, there is a pastiche of inflated styles constantly undermined by the demotic commentary of the unnamed narrator. The Citizen is based on Michael Cusack, founder of the Gaelic Athletic Association for promoting traditional Irish sports, and this is the subject of one of the arguments between the Citizen and Bloom. Here we get first of all the narrator's colloquial version, followed by the way in which such a debate would have been covered in the nationalist press of the time:

> So off they started about Irish sports and shoneen games the like of lawn tennis and about hurley and putting the stone and racy of the soil and building up a nation once again and all to that. And of course Bloom had to have his say too about if a fellow had a rower's heart violent exercise was bad. I declare to my antimacassar if you took a straw from the bloody floor and if you said to Bloom: *Look at, Bloom. Do you see that straw? That's a straw.* Declare to my aunt he'd talk about it for an hour so he would and talk steady.
>
> A most interesting discussion took place in the ancient hall of *Brian O'Ciarnain's* in *Sraid na Bretaine Bheag*, under the auspices of *Sluagh na h-Eireann*, on the revival of ancient Gaelic sports and the importance of physical culture, as understood in ancient Greece and ancient Rome and ancient Ireland, for the development of the race. The venerable president of the noble order was in the chair and the attendance was of large dimensions.[14]

Joyce here takes off the conventions of the nationalist press of the time in which it was common to pay lip service to Irish as the first national language by Gaelicizing names – here Brian O'Ciarnain's is the pub Barney Kiernan's, Sraid na Bretaine Bheag is Little Britain Street – but the substance of their language is standard fustian English. By contrast with this

14   James Joyce, *Ulysses*, ed. Hans Walter Gabler, with Wolfhard Steppe and Claus Melchior (Harmondsworth: Penguin, 1986 [1922]), 260.

the narrator's voice comes across as genuine Dublin argot, impatient with
the catchphrases of the nationalist movement, such as 'racy of the soil',
one of the slogans of the patriotic *Nation* newspaper, but just as impatient with what he regards as the perversity of Bloom's argument. This is a
very convincing rendering of one kind of Irish speech, with its distinctive
turns of phrase – 'Look at, Bloom', 'he'd talk about it for an hour so he
would', and its occasional Irish word which has passed into Irish English:
'shoneen', from *Seonín*, Little John, a derisory name for an Irishman who
apes English ways. But it has a very different effect from Synge's lyriciz-
ing dialect. The style of the Cyclops narrator is vulgar, slangy, crudely and
vigorously down-to-earth. And as such it acts as bathetic opposite to the
various would-be heroic languages through which it is interspersed. The
narrator is a barroom parasite who speaks as he thinks, a cynical, grubby and
mean-minded voice that reduces down to nonsense any style that aspires
beyond it. Yet the mock-heroic strategy of the whole episode depends on
the fact that the narrator's account, in its authentic colloquialism, comes
across as more real than any of the other languages used.

In a sense what the Cyclops narrator does for that one episode, Molly
Bloom in 'Penelope', does for the whole book. As it opens, we hear Molly in
bed reflecting on the oddity of her husband Leopold's request for breakfast
in bed. It reminds her of an incident we have heard about before in the
novel, when Bloom tried to make up to the devout Mrs Riordan in the
hope of being left money in her will, so that Molly's memories and musings
are more intelligible than they might otherwise be:

> Yes because he never did a thing like that before as ask to get his breakfast in bed
> with a couple of eggs since the City Arms hotel when he used to be pretending to
> be laid up with a sick voice doing his highness to make himself interesting for that
> old faggot Mrs Riordan that he thought he had a great leg of and she never left us a
> farthing all for masses for herself and her soul greatest miser ever was actually afraid to
> lay out 4d for her methylated spirit telling me all her ailments she had too much old
> chat in her about politics and earthquakes and the end of the world let us have a bit
> of fun first God help the world if all the women were her sort down on bathingsuits
> and lownecks of course nobody wanted her to wear them I suppose she was pious
> because no man would look at her twice I hope Ill never be like her a wonder she
> didn't want us to cover our faces but she was a welleducated woman certainly and
> her gabby talk about Mr Riordan here and Mr Riordan there I suppose he was glad

to get shut of her and her dog smelling my fur and always edging to get up under my petticoats especially then still I like that in him polite to old women like that and waiters and beggars too hes not proud out of nothing.[15]

What is most significant about Molly Bloom's soliloquy, from the point of view of this argument, is the relation of the stream of consciousness technique to orality. Stream of consciousness depends on a conventional assumption that what we read is unvoiced thought, the random associative train of ideas and sensations as they flow through the mind. It is to convey such an impression that Joyce here suppresses all punctuation rendering Molly's language as an undifferentiated sequence of words. Yet when spoken aloud, its movement as speech becomes easy to follow, and it takes on an Irish colouring. There is not a great deal in the passage quoted here which is very specifically Irish English in construction or idiom beyond an occasional expression – 'doing his highness', or 'he thought he had a great leg of' = 'he thought he had great influence with'. But Joyce's experiment with Molly's unpunctuated language could be seen as some ultimate extension of the principles underlying Synge's use of dialect. The flow of Synge's stage dialogue depended on the mimicry of oral forms which minimized the organizing markers of educated standard English. Molly's stream of consciousness is a sort of ur-speech going further back towards the origins of meaning than even the pre-literate country people who were Synge's collaborators. In Synge's 'Preface' to *The Playboy* it was from his mother or his children that the Elizabethan male playwright was imagined to have heard the vivid phrases which he wrote down with his inkhorn. Molly's too is an oral and female language setting aside all the conventions of writing which are, by implication, impositions of male literacy. As printed text her language is estranged and becomes a special literary style perceived as such by readers who normally expect apostrophes, commas and full stops as aids to comprehension. As the final anarchic expression of female orality it challenges the authority and authenticity of the many more formal, male dominated discourses of the book.

15   James Joyce, *Ulysses*, ed. Hans Walter Gabler, with Wolfhard Steppe and Claus Melchior, 608.

Doyle

'No writer since Joyce has so raptly conveyed the community of human sounds', wrote a *Sunday Times* reviewer of one of Roddy Doyle's early novels. The comment is typical of the enthusiasm of the British press for Doyle's Dublin working-class fiction from the beginning, and it is significant that he is here aligned with Joyce. Joyce provides the landmark point of comparison for an Irish writer trying to render urban demotic voices. But Doyle's object is a quite different one from Joyce's and in some sense even antithetical to it. In his first novels at least, the *Barrytown Trilogy*, he set his face against the Joycean range of languages, the virtuoso spate of speech and print which is set flowing in *Ulysses*. Doyle's rather is a deliberately depleted Irish English, crude and inarticulate talk, rich only in monotonously repeated obscenities. In place of Joyce's brilliant interplay of oral and print forms, there appears to be only the reproduction of a very basic dialogue liberally bespattered with 'shite's and 'fuck's. And as such the initial reaction to Doyle's work in Ireland was largely dismissive: there was nothing to it, anyone could write like this, it was just an exploitation of the shock-value of the bad language.

Doyle went on to confound his Irish critics by his continued and growing success at home and abroad. *The Van*, his third novel, was shortlisted for the Booker Prize, he won it with *Paddy Clarke Ha Ha Ha*; his later books have cemented his reputation. Two illustrations from the *Barrytown Trilogy* may suggest the nature of the literary language which brought him this sort of acclaim. The *Trilogy* is centered on the Rabbitte family who live in a working-class suburb of North Dublin, a milieu quite unrepresented in literature before Doyle. The first book, *The Commitments* (the basis of Alan Parker's highly successful film and now the West End musical) is about the efforts of Jimmy Rabbitte Jr to create a soul music band; *The Snapper*, the second novel, concerns the pregnancy of Jimmy's sister Sharon, raped by the father of a friend when she was drunk; the third in the series, *The Van*, shows the unemployed Jimmy Rabbitte Sr setting up a fish-and-chip van with a mate.[16]

16   As this essay goes to press, *The Barrytown Trilogy* is being celebrated as the 2015 Dublin: One City, One Book selection.

A well-known passage early in *The Commitments*, when the young Jimmy is evangelizing for soul music as the right style for his group, illustrates the effects Doyle is seeking:

> ... Say it once, say it loud, I'm black an' I'm proud.
> They looked at him.
> – James Brown. Did yis know —never mind. He sang tha'. —An' he made a fuckin' bomb.
> They were stunned by what came next.
> – The Irish are the niggers of Europe, lads.
> They nearly gasped: it was so true.
> – An' Dubliners are the niggers of Ireland. The culchies have fuckin' everythin'. An' the northside Dubliners are the niggers o' Dublin. —Say it loud, I'm black an' I'm proud.
> He grinned. He'd impressed himself again.
> He'd won them. They couldn't say anything.[17]

What Jimmy is putting across here is fundamental to the thrust of the book: as the Irish are marginal within Europe, as post-independence Ireland has tended to be controlled by those with rural backgrounds ('the culchies [i.e. country people] have everythin'') leaving native Dubliners marginalized in their own capital city, so the Dubliners of the socially despised northside are the most marginalized of the lot. Black soul music, the music of another deprived and marginalized group, can be made to speak for them. But look at how the speech of Jimmy is represented here, and the readership for that represented speech which is implied. His language is not only obscene but loud in its political incorrectness. For most of us the word 'nigger' has long been unspeakable because of its history as a term of racist abuse, and it is noticeable that in the film it was changed to the more acceptable 'black'. A part of the comic effect here in fact derives from Jimmy's use of this taboo word, a comedy dependent on the assumption of a politically correct readership who can find it funny in its defiance of decorum.

The speech of Jimmy in its very rendering on the page distances readers from it as speech. Doyle follows Joyce in replacing quotation marks

17   Roddy Doyle, *The Barrytown Trilogy* (London: Vintage, 1998 [1992]), 13–14.

with introductory dashes, but he also uses a notation of longer dashes to convey pauses and ellipses in speech. This is part of what the *Sunday Times* reviewer had in mind when he talked about his conveying 'the community of human sounds'. But he conveys them on paper and to a print readership in a dialogue punctuated with extrinsic narrative statement: 'They nearly gasped: it was so true'. 'He grinned. He'd impressed himself again'. Doyle is rendering a comic drama of the spoken which is only perceptible as drama when mediated through his written fiction.

Another example is taken from *The Van*: Jimmy Rabbitte Sr tries to while away the long days of unemployment by a programme of self-improving reading. He has borrowed from the library *The Count of Monte Cristo* but he is finding it heavy going: 'He picked up the book. Only thirty-nine pages gone and over four hundred to go still and it was shite. He was sure it was good, brilliant – a classic – but he fuckin' hated it. It wasn't hard; that wasn't it. It was just shite; boring, he supposed, but Shite was definitely the word he was looking for'.[18]

We can well imagine the heavy English translation of Dumas' nineteenth-century French with which Jimmy has to struggle here. What the passage does is to allow us – by implication educated readers – the comic joy of liberation from our normal deference before literature – 'it was good, brilliant – a classic'. All of us have probably known at one time or another that sense of dutiful plodding through some book of indisputable prestige, glumly counting up the pages still to get through. We are here temporarily released into a world where that sort of prestige of print is only very dimly felt, and a sharp revolt against it vigorously expressed as 'shite'. It is all the funnier for Jimmy's careful consideration of the *mot juste*, picking between the available terms like the most fastidious of literary critics and deciding that 'Shite was definitely the word he was looking for'. Doyle's style is one that reproduces an oral Irish English as a sort of carnivalesque pleasure for literary readers. The subversion of more correct, proper English actually carries its own sort of authority.

18   Roddy Doyle, *The Barrytown Trilogy*, 371–2.

Heaney

Seamus Heaney was always seen, and saw himself, as a distinctively Irish writer, even though his poetry is quite as significantly influenced by Wordsworth, Hardy and Ted Hughes as it is by Yeats and Patrick Kavanagh. When he was included in a volume of contemporary British poets in the early 1980s he wrote an energetic verse letter in protest.[19] It is not only that politically he places himself as Irish, but the Irish inflections of his writing in English are, in his own view, of defining importance. That makes especially interesting his verse translation of *Beowulf. Beowulf,* as the outstanding epic poem of Old English, stands as the foundation work of the canon of English literature largely constructed in Oxford in the nineteenth century. In fact this translation by Heaney was commissioned for the *Norton Anthology of English Literature.* To take it on was to take on the most ur-English of English poems, to go back to the beginning of the English canon itself. The opening lines of Heaney's translation illustrate how he tackled this as the Irish poet he was:

> So. The Spear-Danes in days gone by
> and the kings who ruled them had courage and greatness.
> We have heard of those princes' heroic campaigns.
> There was Shield Sheafson, scourge of many tribes,
> a wrecker of mead-benches, rampaging among foes.
> This terror of the hall-troops had come far.
> A foundling to start with, he would flourish later on
> as his powers waxed and his worth was proved.
> In the end each clan on the outlying coasts
> beyond the whale-road had to yield to him
> and begin to pay tribute. That was one good king.[20]

Heaney in the Introduction to the translation explains how he encountered *Beowulf* as a student of English in Queen's University Belfast and

---

19   Seamus Heaney, *An Open Letter*, Field Day Pamphlet 2 (Derry: Field Day, 1983).
20   Seamus Heaney, *Beowulf* (London: Faber, 1999), 3.

how its language had come alive for him when he recognized in the Old English vocabulary some of the words familiar to him from the spoken English of his native County Derry, 'thole', to suffer or endure from *þolian*, for example. To find his own modern style for *Beowulf* he had to tune it to a remembered speech which was real for him. He provides a very striking example of this in the poem's very first word. *Beowulf* opens with a one-word exclamation, '*Hwæt*' an expression which most translators render uneasily as 'Lo', 'hark', 'behold', all the sort of archaisms that label the language as translatorese from the start. In Heaney's version he found a solution to this problem in the speech of relatives of his father's, a family called Scullion. 'They had', he says in his Introduction, 'a kind of Native American solemnity of utterance, as if they were announcing verdicts rather than making small talk. And when I came to ask myself how I wanted *Beowulf* to sound in my version, I realized I wanted it to be speakable by one of those relatives'. In the case of the troublesome '*Hwæt*' 'the particle "so" came naturally to the rescue, because in [the Scullions'] idiom "so" operates as an expression that obliterates all previous discourse and narrative, and at the same time functions as an exclamation calling for immediate attention. So, "so" it was'.[21]

In the lines cited, Heaney for the most part uses standard English vocabulary and phrasing in a brilliant recreation of the elaborate alliterative patterns of the Old English. But from time to time we hear a characteristically dialect expression, as in the concluding phrase, 'that was one good king', not 'that was a good king', as the rendering of '*þæt wæs god cyning*!' Heaney does not need to write consistently in something which is identifiably Irish English. Many of his lyrics have in fact an almost purely English diction, belong within a mainstream tradition of English romantic poetry. Yet the *Beowulf* translation may serve to illustrate how his poetic style finds a kind of root authentication in a spoken Irish English, and the success of its high literary mode depends on this sort of underlying orality.

---

21   Seamus Heaney, *Beowulf*, xxvii.

Conclusion

The Irish Literary Revival succeeded in transvaluing Irish English speech. Previously stigmatized as deviant and ignorant blarney, it became instead the hallmark of a popular imagination 'that is fiery and magnificent and tender', as Synge has it in the Preface to *The Playboy*. This belief in the lyrical quality of Irish dialect has taken a remarkable hold in the international literary community since that time. T. S. Eliot, for instance, in canvassing the issues of a poetic drama could see Synge as a special case: 'Synge wrote plays about characters whose originals in life talked poetically, so that he could make them talk poetry and remain real people'.[22] It seems extraordinary that a critic as subtle and sophisticated as Eliot should believe, apparently literally, that Irish peasants 'talked poetically' in real life. Again Irish writers are commonly admired for writing with an extravagance in marked contrast with their more sober and restrained English counterparts. Brendan Behan, in particular, attracted this sort of praise. Kenneth Tynan famously saluted the production of *The Quare Fellow* with the statement: 'It is Ireland's sacred duty to send over, every few years, a playwright to save the English theatre from inarticulate glumness'.[23] Penelope Gilliatt continued in a similar vein about *The Hostage*: 'Language hasn't had an outing like this since *The Quare Fellow*. The English habitually write as if they were alone and cold at ten in the morning: the Irish write in a state of flushed gregariousness at an eternal opening time'.[24] We can perhaps see here a line of descent from the blarneying Irishman with his gift of the gab – the Shaughraun figure – through Synge's poetry-speaking peasants to the licensed high colour of Behan's cons and whores. Although there is a turn away from mockery to admiration, throughout there is an attribution of a different kind of speech to the Irish, a greater fluency, a higher

22 Thomas Stearns Eliot, *Poetry and Drama* (London: Faber, 1951), 289.
23 Quoted by Michael O'Sullivan, *Brendan Behan: a Life* (Dublin: Blackwater Press, 1997), 208.
24 Quoted by Ulick O'Connor, *Brendan Behan* (London: Granada, 1979 [1970]), 199.

colour, a lack of self-consciousness producing its energy and effectiveness as literary language.

This sort of celebration of the oral in Irish English allows us to value its literariness in writing because the oral is taken to renew the very springs of the literary. Heaney's *Beowulf* is all the more poetically effective for its basis in the spoken. But there is a counter-tradition going back to Joyce, in which the colloquial combats the pretensions of written and literary forms. The Dublin voices of *Ulysses*, the voice of the narrator of the 'Cyclops' episode, most radically the unvoiced voice of Molly Bloom's soliloquy, subvert and challenge the range of print discourses with which they are juxtaposed. Yet these also operate as a literary language as they are rendered in print, and play between their origins in speech and their representation to readers. It may be a long way from Molly Bloom's vast unpunctuated stream of words to the broken phrases of Roddy Doyle's Barrytown Dubliners, but both depend on the self-conscious awareness of the formal language rules they flout. The estrangement of literariness depends on norms of language use against which the deviance of the literary can be measured. In the case of Irish English as a literary language these norms are the standard English of formal written discourse. There is no longer an imperial metropolitan centre for such standard English; it is now diffused instead through the globalized world of English which so many of us share. But within such a world, Ireland can still be placed as the site of orality and difference so that the literariness of Irish English as a literary language established at the beginning of the twentieth century by Yeats, Synge and Joyce is still available for a Seamus Heaney or a Roddy Doyle at century's end. Indeed they benefit from the inherited authority which their predecessors succeeded in establishing by their subversion of the authority of print.

BRIGITTE BASTIAT AND FRANK HEALY

Mojo Mickybo by Owen McCafferty: From Written Translation to Stage Interpretation

ABSTRACT

This paper explores the translation of an Irish theatre play into a French context explaining the choice of Owen McCafferty's play, *Mojo Mickybo*, and why the collaboration between two translators from different cultural environments, France and Scotland, was required. Reference will be made to what Lawrence Venuti, in his book *The Translator's Invisibility* (1995), calls 'foreignization' of the text. The translation process, involving a linguistic and geographical displacement, was envisaged as a continuum between the author, the translators, the actors, the director, the set designer, the technicians (sound and lights) and the stage. In order to show the limits and the possibilities of translation we shall address some of the issues raised through this specific translation process and analyse the solutions that were found in order to preserve the strongly oral character of a play characterized by its use of Belfast demotic language/slang.

Owen McCafferty was born in Belfast in 1961 but spent the first ten years of his life in London where his parents had emigrated. After a BA in Philosophy he worked in different trades and started writing plays at the beginning of the 1990s. Over the last twenty years his plays have been performed throughout the world and have won many awards. From February to May 2015, his latest play, *Death of a Comedian*, was staged at the Lyric in Belfast, then at the Abbey in Dublin and finally at the Soho Theatre in London. Previous work includes *Quietly* (2012), *Titanic* (2012), *The Absence of Women* (2010), *Closing Time* (2002), *Shoot the Crow* (1997), *Mojo Mickybo* (1998), *Scenes from the Big Picture* (2003), which won the Meyer-Whitworth, John Whiting and *Evening Standard* Awards. Owen McCafferty does not consider himself as a political writer and a 'Troubles' dramatist, although two of his plays, *Mojo Mickybo* and *Quietly*, have as a backdrop the political crisis and rising violence in Northern Ireland. He has declared on several occasions that he writes 'stories about human beings rather than about politics'.[1]

The decision to translate Owen McCafferty's play *Mojo Mickybo* into French resulted from a series of contacts and collaborations between various French and Irish partners. Through Professors Anna McMullan and David Grant from Queen's University Belfast, the two would-be translators were introduced to the author, who approved the project. We chose to translate this playwright because he had never been translated into French before – although there are translations in Italian, Polish, German and Japanese – and this particular play because the story, although set in sectarian Belfast at the beginning of the 1970s, has a universal appeal. Most of the characters in the play are working-class and our friend Claudie Landy, the director of the 'Théâtre Toujours à l'Horizon' company in La Rochelle, has always been interested in this section of society. One of the translators (Brigitte Bastiat) has been involved in amateur theatre for about fifteen years and she thought the play would be extremely interesting and challenging to direct and perform since the two actors play no fewer than seventeen roles of children and adults, men and women. *Mojo Mickybo* was also chosen because the language used in the play, mainly Belfast slang, was definitely stimulating. That is the reason why the life experience of the other translator (Frank Healy), of Irish descent himself but raised in Glasgow, proved very useful. On the one hand, Glasgow has a history of sectarianism,[2] although not as marked as that of Belfast, and on the other hand, there is a broad similarity between the slangs of these two industrial cities.

In *Mojo Mickybo* (1998), Owen McCafferty shows two small boys of ten who live in different neighbourhoods of Belfast in the early 1970s. The work deals with the construction of identity on several levels: religious (Protestants and Catholics), social and educational (children, parents

1   Interview of Owen McCafferty by Brigitte Bastiat, Queen's University Belfast, 30 April 2009.
2   Thomas Martin Devine, 'The Great Irish Famine and Scottish History', in Martin J. Mitchell, ed., *New Perspectives on the Irish in Scotland* (Edinburgh: John Donald, 2008), 20–30.

and adults), cultural (Ireland and the USA) and gender (masculinities). Fascinated with the movie *Butch Cassidy and the Sundance Kid*, which they know by heart, Mojo and Mickybo form a strong friendship despite their different backgrounds. Mojo is Protestant and comes across as a bit naïve; Mickybo is Catholic, comes from a poorer neighbourhood than Mojo and seems to be much more streetwise. They go to different schools and could never have met anywhere else but on the street since segregated schooling for Catholics and Protestants has always been a feature of life in Northern Ireland. Their meeting and the construction of their friendship question the dysfunctional society they live in and that is on the brink of a terrible crisis. The play functions as a modern myth in that it contributes to the development of a common culture through play, games with superheroes and the cinema. The boys create a world that comes alive through the power of their imagination and where, in their relative innocence, they dream of becoming heroes. However, they are quickly overtaken by the reality of the world of adults, shaped by narratives of sectarian division and exclusion. The violent manner in which the play ends highlights the political imperative which forces the children to choose sides and raises the question of free-dom; the eponymous characters are hopelessly trapped within the webs of prejudice woven by their respective communities. Moreover, by choosing to have all the roles (children and adults, both male and female) played by only two middle-aged male actors, McCafferty pushes back the boundaries of theatrical performance and blurs its realist representational codes, which is one of the reasons why we thought it would be really interesting to bring this very physical type of theatre to France.[3] As they come to play some eight roles each, the two actors have wonderfully challenging parts to perform that make demands on their energy, suppleness and agility.

In a paper given at Queen's University Belfast in April 2011, Carole-Anne Upton discussed the use of swearwords as a marker of identity and community and as a rhythmic strategy for stage writing. She based her analy-sis on a study of the play *Le Labyrinthe* (translation of 'Maze' in French) by

---

3   Oxford Dictionary definition of physical theatre: 'A form of theatre which empha-sizes the use of physical movement, as in dance and mime, for expression'.

Armand Gatti,[4] and in particular on his filmed workshop with people from
Derry in 1981–82, i.e., just after the death of the IRA hunger strikers in the
Long Kesh prison of Belfast (also known as the Maze). A former journalist,
Gatti wanted to use theatre to educate people. His interest in conflicts and
revolutions led him to write a play about three inhumane strikes that took
place in Northern Ireland: the clothes strike (1976), which broke out when
the IRA prisoners were denied their political prisoner status, the hygiene
strike (1978) that was undertaken as a protest against tougher detention
conditions and the hunger strike (1981), which was to be a means to restore
their dignity.[5] Upton realized that the extremely coarse and creative lexicon
used by the Northern-Irish participants to the workshop had completely
disappeared from the French version written by Gatti. She argued that the
French text deliberately toned down the dialogues and watered down the
tense and energetic atmosphere of the workshop composed of Catholics
and Protestants. For her, by omitting this type of language, which is rooted
in an era, a place and a community, Gatti was to some extent 'censoring'
the culture of its inhabitants in his play. Upton further argued that the use
of standardized French to replace slang weakens the message of the play,
which should also be about social, political, linguistic and cultural challenges and differences. Translation specialist David Bellos explains that
'In written prose [...] translators shy away from giving the uncouth truly
uncouth forms of language in the target text'[6] because, according to him,
they do not want to be held responsible for mistakes, slips of the tongue
and attacks on the linguistic norm.[7] It would indeed be interesting to
know whether Gatti was aware of the fact that the Derry people used a lot
of slang and swear words during the workshop in 1981–2 and, if so, why
he chose to ignore it when he wrote Le Labyrinthe. Upton's criticism of

---

4   Armand Gatti, Le Labyrinthe (Pierres Hérétiques, 1983).
5   Armand Gatti archive, La parole errante, <www.archives-gatti.org> accessed 5 May
     2015.
6   David Bellos, Is That a Fish in Your Ear? The Amazing Adventure of Translation
     (London: Penguin Books, [2011] 2012), 200.
7   Ibid., 200–201.

Gatti's translation did influence our approach to the translation of *Mojo Mickybo* as we were more than ever determined to respect the style, tone and slang register of the play.

The specificity of a theatrical text is that it is written to be spoken; it is thus endowed with a strong physicality since, as Henri Meschonnic wrote, 'Oral interpretation cannot be reduced to the mouth only or the sound only, it requires the ear and the entire body as well, through the movements which are inseparably the movements of the language and the movements of the body'.[8] Thus, the translator must pay particular attention to elements that may go unnoticed if the text remains 'unvoiced': prosody, rhythm, intonation, pitch, too many consonants or sibilants. This aspect of the work constituted an interesting challenge in terms of McCafferty's play as these speech elements are integral to the texture and colour of the text. Another difficulty for an actor or an actress may reside in the oral interpretation of perfectly phrased cues that are, however, difficult to 'oralize' without becoming short of breath, either because they are too long or because the acting requires certain body movements that are incompatible with the cues. This is the reason why we worked extensively on the oral and stage interpretation, ensuring we had constant feedback from the artistic team and testing our text by reading it aloud ourselves. We did feel what French theatre director and translator of Chekhov, Antoine Vitez, experienced when he said that 'To translate and to direct are one single activity, it is the art of choice in the hierarchy of signs'.[9]

Translation approaches have evolved over time. Meschonnic wrote that what was once taught in translation courses was '[...] the ideology of the

8   Our translation of 'L'oralité, ce n'est pas la bouche seulement, le son seulement, c'est l'oreille aussi, et tout le corps, par les mouvements qui sont inséparablement les mouvements du langage et les mouvements du corps.' Henri Meschonnic, 'Traduire le théâtre, c'est traduire l'oralité', *Traduire Lagarce* (Besançon: Les Solitaires intempestifs, 2008), 11.

9   Our translation of 'Traduire et mettre en scène est une seule et même activité, c'est l'art du choix dans la hiérarchie des signes', cited by Papazov Boyan, in *Correspondance n°35*, Maison Antoine Vitez, Centre international de la traduction théâtrale (April–August 2006), 2.

language and of the sole transfer from language to language, leading to the cultural effect of the ideology of the natural [...]'.[10] In the 1960s and 1970s the autonomy of translation was limited by the dominance of equivalence, namely the tendency to see the source text as the authoritative text that determines the nature of the target text. However, in the 1980s and 1990s this equivalence approach to the text was challenged and translators began to embrace what was previously treated as shifts or deviations from the source text. During this decade, translation was dominated by functional-ist approaches[11] which see translation as 'a communicative action carried out by an expert in intercultural communication (the translator), playing the role of a text producer and aiming at some communicative purpose'.[12] These approaches generally consider that the function of a text in the target culture determines the method of translation. In our case the purpose of the translation was the performance of a play; thereby the 'oral interpretation', as defined above by Meschennic, constituted the function that led us to choose our approach to McCafferty's text. Nowadays, the word 'passage' tends to replace that of 'translation' for Meschennic who argues that transparency, loyalty and fidelity are not as prevalent as before; the concept of the func-tional authority of the source text has been undermined as the translator now seeks to respect and show linguistic, cultural and historical otherness.[13]

Turning to the various translation strategies we used, we decided to explicitly draw on our respective cultural experiences as a Frenchwoman and a Scot with Irish roots, as well as on our personal amateur practice of theatre and music, to seek to preserve the rhythm and musicality of Owen McCafferty's language in our translation. According to the American theo-rist of translation, Lawrence Venuti, it is impossible for any translation

---

10   Our translation of '[...] l'idéologie de la langue, et du seul transfert de langue à langue, avec pour effet culturel l'idéologie du naturel', Henri Meschonnic, 'Traduire le théâtre, c'est traduire l'oralité', *Traduire Lagarce*, 14.

11   Lawrence Venuti, ed., 'Introduction', *The Translation Studies Reader* (New York: Routledge, 2012 [2000]), 5.

12   Christiane Nord, 'Dealing with purpose in intercultural communication: some methodological considerations', *Revista Alicantina de Estudios Ingleses* 14 (2001), 151.

13   Henri Meschennic, 'Traduire le théâtre, c'est traduire l'oralité', *Traduire Lagarce*, 16.

to render the original text: the translation inevitably produces another text. In his 1995 book *The Translator's Invisibility*, he explains that in the 1980s, German translators in particular started to question 'transparent' translations, often called 'domesticated' translations, *i.e.*, those where the text appears to have been written in the target-language and where the translator remains invisible, their work subordinate to the authority of the source text. According to David Bellos, this is particularly true for English language translations. For example, most translators of English prose use what is called '*tranglish*' (translation in English), a language which erases all dialects or particularities and is standardized and understandable by all English-speakers – but different from the international English used by journalists and scientists.[14] David Bellos goes further by saying that Emile Victor Rieu, the first editor of the 'Penguin Classics' in the 1940s, demanded that books should be translated into a standardized, plain, contemporary British English[15] in which the translator's work was completely invisible. In contrast, some forty years later, the German translators suggested translators should produce texts where the 'foreign' and the 'strange' are accepted and even sought. Venuti defines the terms 'domestication' and 'foreignization' which he applies to different types of translation, stating that 'the terms 'domestication' and 'foreignization' indicate fundamentally ethical attitudes towards a foreign text and culture, ethical effects produced by the choice of a text for a translation and by the strategy devised to translate it [...]'.[16]

For *Mojo Mickybo*, we thus opted for a translation that was sometimes very literal and tended to foreignize the text so as to preserve as much as possible the Belfast English flavour as well as the author's linguistic creativity. The other key priority was to produce a translation that was fluid and easy for the actors, whilst preserving its key features: funny but poetic, coarse but innocent, at the risk of shocking or surprising a French audience less used to such colourful language on stage. First of all, the play seemed to

---

14   David Bellos, *Is That a Fish in Your Ear? The Amazing Adventure of Translation*, 196.

15   *Ibid.*, 305.

16   Lawrence Venuti, *The Translator's Invisibility – A History of Translation* (New York: Routledge, 2002 [1995]), 19.

call for such an approach as its language challenges Standard English and often ignores grammar rules, making it sound almost foreign at times to a non-Irish English speaker. Furthermore, not only is the language a type of English spoken in Northern Ireland, but it is also rooted in the rough, coarse and crude dialect used by the working classes of Belfast. This is where Healy's working-class Glaswegian origins proved most useful. The slang used by McCafferty was familiar to him but what proved particularly important was his grasp of the similar musicality of the English spoken in working-class areas of Belfast and Glasgow. This enabled us to write the play as a musical 'score' where the rhythm and energy of Belfast English could be transposed, at least to a degree, into French.

Nowadays in France there is no such thing as local slang and so the French-speaking Mojo and Mickybo could not have spoken in a local slang. Even if big cities like Lyon, Marseilles or Lille have their own slang, according to Denise François-Geiger,[17] French slang originally comes from relatively homogeneous nomadic groups, such as harvesters, chimney sweepers or more recently, mobsters. However, she dates the development of a common French slang to the beginning of the twentieth century.[18] We could have chosen to make the text sound more modern by using the present lexicon of the Parisian or Marseilles suburbs. However, we decided to use a lexicon that varies, sometimes deliberately timeless, sometimes quite modern, more often rooted in the 1970s.

We chose this solution initially because the play is designed as a narrative, a story that is being remembered by one of the characters who is now in his forties, and the scattering of a more modern slang is a way of almost subconsciously reminding the audience that this is a remembered history, coloured by the sentiments and experience of an older man. In addition, Owen McCafferty himself often uses words rooted in the 1970s which are specifically from Belfast and that allude to celebrities of that era, such as the footballers Pelé and Luigi Riva. We decided not to replace these names

---

17   Denise François-Geiger, 'Panorama des argots contemporains', *Langue Française* 90 (1991).
18   *Ibid.*, 8.

with those of more famous players today such as Messi or Ronaldo because the children in the play use them like magical words: they love to say them, first because they admire the players, but also because their names sound foreign, mysterious and give them strength, just like superheroes do; in the pre-Web 2.0 and multi-sports channel era of 1970, Pelé and Riva seemed about as extraordinary to young boys as Superman. Another example of this is the Belfast word 'weeker' that we chose to translate by 'extra', which equally sounds very 1970s in French. We opted for a slang that can sometimes sound a bit old, but this is a deliberate literary stance. We believe that translators are certainly not authors, but are nevertheless writers and, although influenced by various authors, as writers they have a style of their own. Our text is thus influenced by the French writers Louis-Ferdinand Céline (1894–1961) and Antoine Blondin (1922–91), or the film script writer Michel Audiard (1920–85) in the use of words such as 'taloche' (slap), 'paluche' (mit), 'faffes' (money), 'bibine' or 'gueuze' (gargle) and 'daron' (father) for example. Actually, although this last word is an old slang word that you can find in Céline's work, it has also survived until now, and young people in the suburbs of Paris and elsewhere still use it. In terms of punctuation, like Céline we used dots to translate the dashes of Owen McCafferty. We wanted to connect the work of McCafferty to a French literary tradition which has given its pedigree to slang, because Céline did explode the canons of his time by using street language in his writings, thus inventing a style unheard of in French literature. This choice was also due to the fact that most contemporary French playwrights like Philippe Minyana or Jean-Luc Lagarce favour them too as it allows them to work intensively on the spoken language and its rhythms.

Translating *Mojo Mickybo* entailed keeping mistakes and inventing French expressions to preserve the children's language that McCafferty crafted in the play. For example, when Mickybo says 'they don't like you too', we kept the grammar mistake and translated by 'ils t'aiment pas *aussi*' instead of '*non plus*'. The invented expression 'hollygwaockamoly batman'[19]

---

19   In the 'Batman' movies, the character Robin starts a lot of his sentences with 'holy', as in the expression he uses 'Holy Smokes Batman'.

scripted as one word was translated by 'sacré' for 'holy' (written with two ls in the play) and 'guacamole' for 'gwaockmoly' because they sound the same and refer to Mexican food. The word 'sacréguacamolé batman' sounds both bizarre and amusing in French. A second example is 'Big hairy boot right up the hole an into the lagan' translated by 'un grand coup de botte poilue tout droit dans le trou de balle et hop! dans la rivière lagan'. Again 'a hairy boot' is strange in English and quite typical of children's playground talk because when they find a word funny, they will put it to imaginative use. That is why we kept it in French too. We added 'hop' to try to give it the same rhythm and pace as in the English phrase, which is composed of very short words.

On various occasions we tried to forge our own style and be creative, using 'foreignization'. For instance, we translated the narrator's phrase 'mojo mickybo – as thick as two small thieves', which expresses the complicity of the two boys, by 'comme deux petits larrons enfoirés'. The literal translation in French would be 'deux petits larrons en foire' – 'larrons' meaning 'scoundrels' and 'foire' 'fun fair' – also a well-known expression in French conveying the sense that they get on like two small scoundrels at a fun fair and based on a familiar phrase, 's'entendre comme deux larrons en foire'; however, we changed 'foire' into 'enfoirés', which sounds very similar but actually means 'fuckheads'; we thus coined an expression in French through a pun, to give it more strength and to remain faithful to the slang used by McCafferty. Likewise, we translated 'the man I love header and all as he is' by 'l'homme que j'aime tout taré qu'il est', which sounds odd and foreign in French, because of the long series of words side by side that sounds like a long compound noun.

Transpositions are often necessary, either because a joke does not translate well, because of a pun or a sound, or because of cultural differences. For instance, the name of the ugly character 'Gank the wank', made up of two words that rhyme, was first literally translated as 'Peter le branleur' which also rhymes. Upon reflection, it was found that the French name was harder to use on stage because it had too many syllables; so it was shortened into 'Pete la bite', 'Pete the dick'. Maybe to escape censorship, we have noticed that in the Italian translation of the play by Noemi Abe, under the supervision of Enda Flannelly, as well as in the film that was later adapted by Terry

Loane in 2004, the names of certain characters were changed, 'Gank the wank' becoming simply 'Gank', thus erasing the deliberate childish coarseness of McCafferty's language. Another example of transposition is the typical joke of the 1970s at the beginning of the play: 'How d'ya stop a biafran from drowning? Throw him a polo mint' had to be changed. In France too there were jokes made about Biafra in the 1970s, but French people did not – and still do not – eat polo mints. Therefore, we used a French joke from that era, which can actually translate into English: 'What do you call a grain of rice on the ground? A biafran's puke'. We transposed the expression that Mickybo's father uses to make fun of Australians, 'gooday gooday gooday digger', because a French audience would probably not understand that this was a funny caricature of how Australians speak. Instead, we decided to use stereotypes about Australia that are more familiar to a French audience: 'koala Sydney skippy le kangourou' (koala Sydney Skippy the kangaroo), a reference to the TV show in the 1970s which proved popular in France and is still shown occasionally today. A last example of linguistic creativity and transposition is illustrated by the way in which we translated 'any God's amount of it' when Mickybo asks his dead father if he bled a lot when he was shot: we chose 'comme la Mer Rouge', 'like the Red Sea', which keeps some of the religious connotation but makes it shorter than a literal translation would in French ('toute la quantité que Dieu y a mise') and is more faithful to the rhythm of the original English.

There were other challenges in McCafferty's play, notably his ability to use short words that give speed and rhythm to the text. We found that his use of language could be likened to the way a caricaturist draws, sketching a character or a situation in a few words, as in the phrase 'ice cream in bake gun in mit an – we're sailing back into the wild west'. Twentieth-century French slang is very rich and there was no difficulty in finding equivalents for 'bake' or 'mit' but the translation is longer and does not trip off the tongue or lodge in the memory so easily: 'une glace dans la tronche un pistolet dans la paluche et c'est reparti pour le far west'. It is fair to say that maintaining the musicality of the original play depends on having excellent actors with perfect diction who can speak quickly, swallow the vowels, contract words and still be understandable. We are grateful that this proved the case with the actors Sébastien Boudrot and Damien Henno, who played 'Mojo' and

'Mickybo' in 'Thélème' for the première at the University of Tours as part of the SOFEIR conference organized by Martine Pelletier in March 2012.[20] Again it must be said that we did test our translation orally several times and worked through five drafts before handing out the final – though not definitive – version to the actors and to the director, Claudie Landy.

As Susan Bassnett argues in her book *The Translator as Writer* published in 2006, there is playfulness in the translating process that we experienced first-hand with this play. She adds that the translator is '[…] an insider and yet an outsider simultaneously, standing on the threshold between cultures: the ideal place for a translator, who occupies the liminal space that others step over without a passing thought'.[21] A delicate position indeed, but an exhilarating and compelling one. In the various programmes given to the audience we did not explain the situation of the 'Troubles' in detail despite the fact that French audiences are not familiar with the Northern Irish conflict. In the play, not knowing whether Mojo is Protestant and Mickybo Catholic is important because the playwright uses this ambiguity in order to explain his point that these kids live in a world of their own, and are only secondarily subjected to the absurdity of the sectarian attitudes of adults. After having watched the play in French at the University of La Rochelle in November 2014, some people said that they could not distinguish the Catholics from the Protestants. Even at the end of the play, when Mickybo shouts 'orange bastards' (translated as 'connards d'orangistes') to insult his former friend Mojo, the expression did not make sense to some members of the French audience[22] who did not realize that the term 'orangistes' was associated with Protestant extremists. However, as translators we chose to keep the term 'orangistes' despite its opacity for a French audience, because

---

20   The play was then performed in Royan – Théâtre municipal (December 2012), La Rochelle – Théâtre 'Toujours à l'horizon' (October 2012) and at the University (November 2014), at Limoges University (April 2013), Perpignan University (June 2013), Belfast – QUB (November 2014), Paris – Théâtre de l'Opprimé (December 2014) and at the University of Orléans (December 2015).

21   Susan Bassnett, *The Translator as Writer* (London: Continuum, 2006), 179.

22   Informal discussions with members of the audience after the performance and in class with third-year students.

it rooted the play in a Northern Irish linguistic and cultural context, and also because it did not really matter, the whole point of the play being that the two boys and the two communities were interchangeable, both subjected to the nonsense and cruelty of sectarianism.

Our intention in translating this play was to expose a French audience to a very physical type of theatre associated with a rich, humorous and inventive text. Based on the reactions we have had from members of the audience that we interviewed,[23] we can say that we succeeded because their response was very enthusiastic. They described the play as both entertaining and serious, with deep feelings running through it, giving an original insight into a crisis and a conflict since it is seen through the eyes of children, and as having a universal appeal. They admired the symbolic set, the free-flowing direction and the formidable energy of the two actors who visibly had an exhilarating experience performing all seventeen characters. The approach we adopted did not consider the source text as authoritative but rather our translation was envisaged as a *continuum*, a process we were able and willing to share with the author, the director and the actors. Consequently, we ended up making some changes after the performances, usually with a view to making the 'musical phrases' shorter and sharper, because we feel that in a translation for the theatre, the stage and the oral performance should have authority over the written score. However, others are free to adapt the text to fit a time or a particular audience – be it in any French-speaking country in the world.[24] We hope that our 'score' is sufficiently flexible to allow all sorts of interpretations because we believe that a drama translation is not set in stone but can and should evolve.

23   Informal interviews with about thirty viewers of the performance in La Rochelle, October 2012 and November 2014.
24   Our translation is the only one available in French so far.

BERTRAND CARDIN

Authorities in Crisis and Intertextual Practice: The Example of Colum McCann's *Let the Great World Spin*

ABSTRACT

With its title taken from a poem by Lord Alfred Tennyson and an epigraph that is a quotation from a novel by Aleksander Hemon, Colum McCan's postmodern, and polyphonic novel, *Let the Great World Spin* (2009), provides an opportunity to examine whether authorial authority still exists after Barthes announced 'the death of the author'. The articulation between authority and intertextuality deserves to be studied to make out if these two concepts are compatible or, on the contrary, mutually exclusive, if there is reciprocal dependence, interaction between them, if authority is inversely proportional to the degree of intertextuality, if authority is greater in a text without intertextual 'copresence'. In other words, can we read McCann's novel as evidence that intertextual practice is a sign that authority is in crisis?

Just like the text, the book itself as an object has particular signs that call for response and interpretation. Let us imagine the potential reader's first contact with this novel published in 2009 and written by a certain Colum McCann, a writer he had never heard of before. With the author's name, the reader is informed about a few specific features concerning his identity: the writer is a man of Irish stock. Yet the reader may not perceive the Catholic connotation of the name. Indeed, Colum or Colm comes from Colomba or Colomban, an Irish monk of the sixth century who spread the Good Word on the European mainland. This holy man is characterized by purity and missionary enthusiasm, as the Gaelic etymology of the name testifies, *Colum Cille* meaning 'the dove of the Church'. Colum is particularly venerated by the Catholic Church of Ireland. As for McCann, it is the name of a family from the Province of Ulster who has its own coat of arms on a shield, with a helm topped by a fish, surrounded with oak leaves, under which a small red wolf is usually found, the very name of McCann meaning 'the son of the wolf-cub'. The McCanns were Lords of Clanbrassel, County Armagh. While the first name and surname of the author are evocative of Ireland, the picture or design on the book cover, whatever the edition, depicts New York City and more particularly the Manhattan skyline. Thus, the cover of the book allows the reader to make the connection between Ireland and the United States.

As for the title of the novel, *Let the Great World Spin* metaphorically evokes a content that is difficult to grasp, the main subject being 'the great world', what is more a world that the addressee of the message is supposed to 'let spin'. This title is somewhat enigmatic and probably connotative. Indeed the rhythm of these five monosyllables provides the phrase with a poetic touch which incites the reasonably cultured reader to put forward the hypothesis that this title draws its inspiration from another work and that it may be a quotation. If our reader leafs through the end of the book, the author's note confirms that the title comes from Alfred Lord Tennyson's poem, 'Locksley Hall'.[1]

Then, if the reader turns the first page of the book, he can read an epigraph, a short quotation of two sentences, printed in quotation marks, followed by the name of its author, Aleksandar Hemon, and the title of the book it is taken from, *The Lazarus Project*.[2]

Last, in his discovery of the paratext of *Let the Great World Spin*, the reader who turns a new page notices a dedication to John Berger and Jim Harrison, two writers who are frequently mentioned by McCann in his interviews.

As a result, in the first three pages of the book, no fewer than five authors are explicitly or implicitly conjured up. All of them write in English, whether they are British, Irish or American by birth or adoption. Apart from Tennyson, all of them are still alive but not always well-known writers. By anchoring his novel in the great network of the universal library, Colum McCann apparently does not want the spotlight to be on his own text only, as he, as a writer, does not feel to be in a position of power. As

1   Alfred Lord Tennyson, 'Locksley Hall' (1842), *The Works of Alfred Lord Tennyson* (London: Wordsworth, 2008).
2   Aleksandar Hemon, *The Lazarus Project* (New York: Riverhead Books, 2008).

he places himself into a community of men of letters, he testifies that the value of his text is not only due to himself. McCann is an author but is he in a position of authority, as the extension of the word could imply?

Definitions

The word *auctor* refers to the founder, the originator, the person who starts and establishes, the great or sovereign Author being, according to tradition, none other than God the Creator himself who, at the origin of the world, gives birth and growth. By extension, *auctor* becomes the one who starts and develops a piece of work, acquiring the meaning of the organizing principle, the orchestrator of the text, which is the general sense of the word today. The Latin word *auctoritas* is derived from *auctor*. In its original meaning, authority means being an author. It also refers to the credit or credibility of a writer or a text, and to the power to make decisions and influence other people. The Scriptures, for example, are authoritative because they have this power. Progressively, the word 'authority' has come to refer to the strength of a reference or quotation being used as a model, but it also characterizes someone who is strong and powerful, who enjoys legal ability, official responsibility and moral superiority.

Even if the word 'authority' has taken on new meanings, the notions of strength, power and superiority remain. Yet, are they really suitable for the author? Does the author actually have power and authority? And if he does, is it not by misuse of language? For indeed, what does this power rest on? True, the author is the legal owner of his text; he gives official permission for the text to be published, literally *author*izes it and can vouch for what he wrote. Nevertheless, isn't he first and foremost promoted by what makes him an author, that is his originality, his uniqueness, his *authorship*, in the particular case of McCann, his interest in intertextual practice? By selecting a line to make it the title of his novel, McCann acknowledges that Tennyson's poetry has prestige and authority. As we can see, the intertextual practice appeals to the concept of authority – be it authorial or textual authorities. But isn't the authority of the quoting author put in the shade by that of the quoted author or vice versa? What part does authority play in an obviously intertextual work of literature? The articulation between authority and intertextuality deserves to be studied to make out if these two concepts are compatible or, on the contrary, mutually exclusive; if there is reciprocal dependence, interaction between them, if authority is inversely proportional to the degree of intertextuality, if authority is greater in a text without intertextual 'copresence'.[3] In other words, is intertextual practice a sign that authority is in crisis?

Intertextuality: An offspring of authorities in crisis

It may be useful not to forget that intertextuality established itself in the discourse of literary criticism in a context of crisis. As Antoine Compagnon recalls – it was in 1968 – the author's overthrow which indicated the transition from systematic structuralism to deconstructive post-structuralism was on an equal footing with the anti-establishment rebellion of those days.[4] The concept of intertextuality stems from the death of the author. It results from his questionable authority and it is indeed the author who sparked the controversy over the text in the 1960s. Two theories conflicted on this matter: on the one hand, the defenders of literary history traditionally viewed the author as the ultimate 'explanation' of a work; on the other, a new generation of critics suggested that the interpretation of the *oeuvre* should no longer be sought on the side of the man who had produced it but that the reader should take over as the prime source of power in a text. As a spokesman of this approach, Roland Barthes writes in a key passage that the text liberates an absolutely revolutionary activity that could be called

3   Gérard Genette defines intertextuality as 'copresence between two or several texts' (*Palimpsests: Literature in the Second Degree*, Lincoln: University of Nebraska Press, 1997, 8).
4   Antoine Compagnon, *Literature, Theory and Common Sense* (Princeton: Princeton University Press, 2004), 56.

counter-theological, for refusing to decide on the meaning finally amounts to refusing God.[5] Barthes here alludes to the etymology of the word *auctor*: for him, refusing God is denying the omniscient and all pervading presence and influence of the author in a work of literature. The death of the author gives rise to the birth of the reader, the plurality of the text and the freedom of commenting it, particularly of acknowledging it as a 'tissue of quotations'.[6] Intertextuality is an effect of the death of the author and an offspring of authorities in crisis. Today, with hindsight, common sense incites us to moderate the radical stance of the death of the author and to admit that the creator of the text cannot be completely overlooked. As there is no author without literature, there is no literature without an author. A literary text is indexed by the person who wrote it and registered under his or her name. Any quotation, any reference leads to author figures whose names cannot be cut from the texts they are associated with. The author is not once and for all sentenced to death by literary criticism, but his status is different. The death of the author gives rise to new approaches of the author, but also of authority which now tends to be replaced by authorship.

The authority of the author replaced by the authority of the text (and the vague concept of authorship)

As authority imposes an author with power over his text, authorship considers him as having a regulatory function, without claiming to determine its meaning. The concept of authorship makes it possible to

5   Roland Barthes, 'The Death of the Author' (1968), *The Rustle of Language* (University of California: UC Press, 1989), 66. For Barthes, a figure like an 'author-God' is no longer viable. In place of the author, the modern world presents us with a figure Barthes calls the 'scriptor', whose only power is to combine pre-existing texts in new ways. *Author* and *scriptor* are terms Barthes uses to describe different ways of thinking about the creators of texts. Barthes believes that all writing draws on previous texts, norms, and conventions, and that these are the things to which we must turn to understand a text.

6   *Ibid.*, 65.

maintain the presence of the author without believing in his power and hermeneutic utility. The very status of writing is questioned: what justifies that the author is as he is? What is his position toward his text? Authorship questions the text, refers to its possible conditions and would tend to mean that being an author is nothing else but making one's discourse coherent and assuming responsibility for it. It amounts to making a connection between a text and a name, because authorship supposes the author's uniqueness.

So the question that is raised here is as follows: with five different authors conjured up in the first three pages of *Let the Great World Spin*, is McCann's authorship still valid? Is the only author of the text the man whose name is mentioned on the cover of the book? Or the one who wrote down the title first? In this case, Tennyson would be credited with it. For indeed, by the use of quotations, McCann is not really the person who wrote the text as he is not objectively the only one who wrote it down, even if only his name appears on the book cover. Who is the originator of the message: 'let the great world spin'? Are there as many authors as quotations? It must be admitted that the boundaries of authorship are often blurred.

Although this is the first time one of his books has brought together a quotation-title, an epigraph and a dedication to writers,[7] McCann often signs and authorizes dialogic texts, 'mosaics of quotations'.[8] By a large intertextual practice, because writing also means re-writing, McCann himself acknowledges that he does not write on his own: 'The fact of the matter is that there are many hands tapping the writer's keyboard'[9] and authorship is inconceivable for him without disrupting the authority of his single voice and calling upon other voices. In this respect, the paratext is quite significant as it makes it possible to construct the authority of the text. Indeed

---

7   All books by Colum McCann, except the first, *Fishing the Sloe-Black River*, begin with an epigraph. *Dancer* is the only one which is dedicated to a writer. Apart from *Let the Great World Spin*, no other titles of his novels or books of short stories are quotations.

8   Kelly Oliver, *The Portable Kristeva* (New York: Columbia University Press, 2nd ed., 2002), 85.

9   Colum McCann, *Let the Great World Spin* (New York: Random House, 2009), Author's note, 365.

as authorial authority is questionable insofar as it provides the author with the power to hold *the* meaning of the text; textual authority, on the other hand, seems to be more relevant as it refers to the author's capacity to freely produce his own text without claiming to control its only valid explanation.

The authority of the text: Cause, means and consequence of intertextuality

Harold Bloom contends that any text is a response to a previous one.[10] It implies that a writer has to negotiate with his predecessor's authority. When he quotes a line by Tennyson, McCann enhances the aesthetic prestige of the poem that he conceives as a model of beauty. The authority of the text is the cause of an intertextual practice which rests on a text endowed with consideration. Of course, as it is the title, the name of the author of the original quotation is not immediately mentioned but this absence of signature highlights the authority of the text. And even if the reader does not know the exact source of the quotation, he is nevertheless likely to recognize the intertextual effect. In order to exist, intertextuality needs to be identified as such by the reader. According to Riffaterre, the reader recognizes it when he comes up against the meaning of the text, when he does not manage to grasp what it refers to, but the recognition already contributes to establish meaning.[11] Besides, the author's note which provides the reader with the precise reference to Tennyson's poem at the end of the book makes it possible to check the validity of the intertextual reading. Tennyson's poem is an authority, and by using the authority of another text, McCann turns textual authority into the means of his own intertextual practice.

10   Harold Bloom, *The Anxiety of Influence: A Theory of Poetry* (Oxford: Oxford University Press, 1973).
11   Michael Riffaterre, *Text Production* (New York: Columbia University Press, 1985).

As it is put at the beginning of a piece of writing, the epigraph is also in a position of authority. It establishes a Chinese box structure, a *mise en abyme* since McCann's whole novel is a development of this quotation which is, to some extent, the embryo of the text: 'All the lives we could live, all the people we will never know, never will be, they are everywhere. That is what the world is'. 'All the lives we could live' refers to the heterogeneous destinies of the numerous characters of the novel: a French walker on a cable between the Twin Towers, an Irish priest in the squalor of the Bronx, a Mexican prostitute driven to despair because of her inability to protect her children, mothers of missing soldiers in Vietnam gathered in a luxury apartment of Park Avenue – an odd collection of characters whose voices are mixed to catch and recreate the effervescence of New York City in the 1970s. Polyphonic, the novel is full of a plurality of independent voices with various tones and accents which reveal different social classes and ethnic minorities. In this web of convergences, he depicts the big city as the meeting place of the whole universe, as the word 'world' implies, a word that appears both in the title and the epigraph. New York City is a kaleidoscopic microcosm, a miniature replica of the great world. By the same token, although the diegesis lasts three decades and is essentially anchored in the 1970s, the chronology spans over a greater period of time. Indeed, the simple mention of the Twin Towers of the World Trade Center strikes a particular chord among us, readers of the twenty-first century. The choice of the line 'Let the Great World Spin' is, in this respect, all the more significant as Tennyson's poem, just before this quotation, mentions 'pilots of the purple twilight dropping down with costly bales'. These words which can be considered as premonitory did not fail to draw McCann's attention and proved to be probably decisive in his intertextual choice.

Tennyson as author of *Let the Great World Spin*

Tennyson's art is a jewel of perfection in which the poet gives vent to his melancholy, thoughtful emotion which echoes the great Romantics who came before him. In 'Locksley Hall' particularly, Tennyson shows he can be misled by the mirage of progress offered by the material prosperity of the nineteenth century. Two tendencies are reflected in his verse: one is optimistic and hopeful; the other is clear-sighted and disenchanted. His belief in progress is constantly tinged with skepticism. Against a background of pessimism about the absurdity of life, he celebrates progress in a disillusioned voice and tackles all that drives the human being to despair, considering that he often proves to be in a situation with no other solution but violence in all forms, including war. These remarks do not fail to take on another meaning in the light of the events which led to the destruction of the Twin Towers, a catastrophe filmed live under the eyes of millions of dumbfounded viewers who, like the poet in his days, wondered if they were the victims of an illusion and could have taken up his words as their own: 'Eye, to which all order festers, all things here are out of joint'. These echoes justify the presence of the poet who expresses himself in *Let the Great World Spin* and somewhat becomes the author of the novel, like a ghost who suddenly comes back to life, as Harold Bloom contends.[12] *Let the Great World Spin* contains undeveloped potential texts, but also revives other texts that remained within the realms of possibility.

The novel is divided into four books and each book is composed of chapters, each of which is given a title. The titles of three chapters are quotations taken from 'Locksley Hall': the last part of the first book takes over and develops the title of the novel, 'Let the great world spin for ever down'; the second book ends with a section whose title 'the ringing grooves of change' completes this line, the initial quotation of the poem being: 'Forward, forward let us range,/Let the great world spin for ever down the ringing grooves of change'. The final section, in the fourth book, is entitled 'Roaring Seaward, And I Go', which are the last words of the poem.

These inter-titles, these quotations which are evenly distributed in the whole novel, confirm Bloom's theory and lead the reader to think that Tennyson could be considered as the author of the novel because he *could* write such a text today. Novel writing would then be contemplated as the reactivation of a possible text which had been abandoned in the past of

<hr/>

12   Harold Bloom *The Anxiety of Influence: A Theory of Poetry*.

creation. The haunting, recurrent echoes of Tennyson's voice make him the virtual novelist, in any case, one of the authors invited by McCann to take part in the dialogue. Right from the cover of the book, there is ambiguity as the literal text conceals another text from which it borrows its title, a title which refers both to the diegesis of the novel and to the work within the work. The polyphonic characteristic of the text raises the problematic dimension of the very definition of authorship. The cover of the book mentions only one name but this name assumes a somewhat collective writing. In addition to the ghostly shadow of the poet in the novel which, to some extent, makes Tennyson the author of *Let the Great World Spin*, what is more surprising is the opposite movement in this intertextual practice: indeed Colum McCann can also be envisaged as the author of 'Locksley Hall'...

McCann as author of 'Locksley Hall'

Besides the poetic quotations in the novel, astonishing allusions to some scenes of the novel can be picked up in the poem. Thus, not only does the poem have an influence on the novel and seem to contain the seeds of it, but the reading of the poem in the light of the novel allows us to detect new elements in 'Locksley Hall'. For example, Philippe Petit, the man who walked on a cable between the towers of the World Trade Center one summer morning in 1974, could probably repeat Tennyson's words:

> Comrades, leave me here a little, while as yet't is early morn:
> Leave me here, and when you want me, sound upon the bugle-horn?

In his motivation to achieve this exploit 400 metres above the ground, wouldn't he say, along with the poet:

> There methinks would be enjoyment more than in this march of mind,
> In the steamship, in the railway, in the thoughts that shake mankind.
> There the passions cramp'd no longer shall have scope and breathing space.

The novel provides an explanation which allows the reader to interpret the poem otherwise. The intertextual game makes it possible not only to update the older text, but also to establish interaction between present and past literary works. Likewise, many lines perfectly suit some characters of the novel who could take them up as their own to narrate their experiences, whether it is Jaslyn, Adelita, Corrie, Ciaran, Joshua or Claire. The following lines could very well be uttered by the tearful mother mourning for her son who died in Vietnam:

> Where is comfort? (…) Comfort? Comfort scorn'd of devils!
> That a sorrow's crown of sorrow is remembering happier things
> Drug thy memories, lest thou learn it, lest thy heart be put to proof,
> In the dead unhappy night, and when the rain is on the roof.

The intertextual practice is amazingly productive, because not only does the first text direct the reading of the second, but the first one can also be read in the light of the second. The traditional notion of influence founded on the metaphor of a flow, on a chronological linear conception of history is here denied: the intertextual connections are considered apart from any chronological link. Instead of being under somebody's influence, the writer absorbs and transforms the previous text. In this case, Tennyson's poem transforms McCann's novel which modifies it in return. As a result, the meanings of the texts are to be found in the interdependent connections they establish with one another. Outside chronological linearity, texts are the active, productive elements of a large system which refer to one another and can be understood only through one another. They are a common good from which anyone can draw. As any text is likely to be taken up, it cannot be limited to what its author actually wrote, but it keeps on being written by the authors who quote and rewrite it. Thus, 'Locksley Hall' is not only Tennyson's work, but the uncompleted amount of its intertextual journey made by adding its past and future variants together. Among these variants, McCann's novel re-works it and gives it a new meaning. And the meaning is to be searched for first in the dialogic connection between them. It circulates from one text to another. It is no longer what the author of the first text meant, as it is not what the author of the second text means. The meaning results from interaction between both. Interaction establishes some discontinuity which is characteristic of intertextuality. In reaction against the authority of linearity, *Let the Great World Spin*, which can be described as kaleidoscopic or postmodern, on the one hand, makes up a whole and provides continuity but, on the other, fragments and interrupts the text it quotes. Any intertextual connection both respects the quoted text by using it again and, at the same time, gives it a rough handling, as it breaks it up by introducing discontinuity. Therefore, in essence, intertextuality may be considered as a crisis which is, by definition, some form of discontinuity introduced in a process which had so far been continuous. Playing with the dialectic of continuity and discontinuity, McCann's novel partakes of repetition and alteration, of authority and transgression. It negotiates with the authority of texts and establishes polyphonic dialogues. This plurality shows his will to disrupt monolithic unicity and makes *Let the Great World Spin* – as any postmodern, intertextual work – a protesting, anti-establishment novel.

Hemon *authorized* by McCann

In his essay *Paratexts: Thresholds of Interpretation*, Gérard Genette remarks that when the title of a book is a quotation, the supporting epigraph is imperative to give some justification.[13] *For Whom the Bell Tolls* by Ernest Hemingway, for example, starts with a few lines by John Donne from which the novel borrows its title. Here, though, the title is not justified by the epigraph but by inter-titles. Besides, McCann chose to put at the beginning of his book a short extract from a novel by one Aleksandar Hemon, published in 2008, that is to say a few months before *Let the Great World Spin* which, though it was written by another hand, echoes the title. As we said earlier, the repetition of the term *world* is a parallel that makes sense. What's more, the identity of the quoted author is as important as

---

13   Gérard Genette, *Paratexts: Thresholds of Interpretation* (Cambridge: Cambridge University Press, 1997), 160.

the quotation itself: the writer mentioned is supposed to vouch for the text it precedes. And yet, here, on the contrary, McCann himself, the author of the novel, surprisingly, seems to be the one who vouches for the short piece of writing that is put at the beginning of his book because, unlike Tennyson, Aleksandar Hemon is not a well-known writer.

Hemon was born in Sarajevo and stayed in Chicago for a few months in 1992. As he was living in the States, Sarajevo was besieged and he could no longer go back home. Three years later, Hemon published his first book in English. *The Lazarus Project* is his third novel. It narrates the journey of Vladimir, a Bosnian exile in the US who wants to write the story of Lazarus, a young jewish Ukrainian killed in Chicago in shady circumstances by a police officer one century earlier, in 1908. With a friend of his, a photographer, Vladimir crosses Ukraine and various Eastern European countries to finally reach Bosnia, so haunted by images from the war and the madness of the world that Tennyson's line 'Let the Great World Spin' would be a perfectly suitable title for Hemon's novel. *The Lazarus Project* has a lot in common with *Let the Great World Spin*: both of them are postmodern novels teeming with ideas, alternating fiction with illustrated facts, reflections on the past and the present, on life and the world, on the native land and the country of adoption. For indeed, Hemon and McCann are two divided writers whose identities are questioned by their dislocation. They are neither rooted nor uprooted, neither sedentary nor nomadic but exiles. This is why McCann is familiar with Irish as well as American culture. He looks at his adopted culture through the lenses of his native culture and vice versa, and devotes himself to maintaining the gap between both. This dual membership establishes a dialogue which is mirrored in his literary work by intertextual practice. According to McCann, being nationalist, sectarian and proud of oneself is as ridiculous as for an author to declare himself or herself as the only holder of authority. This is why he is so attached to this phenomenon of cross-fertilization[14] among literary texts.

The Lazarus Project is a book that McCann read and appreciated, hence his choice to quote a sentence from the novel at the beginning of his

14   Neil Corcoran, *After Yeats and Joyce. Reading Modern Irish Literature* (Oxford: Oxford University Press, 1997), preface, ix.

own text. Writing and reading are intertwined. The writer is first a reader and his taste for a text which so simply and sincerely expresses the interest he shares in others, in their lives, in the world, justifies his choice to insert a quotation of this novel in his own. But whereas Tennyson's poem is considered as a founding text, Hemon's quotation is valued differently here, in spite of the authority conferred upon it by its specific position. Although the quoted author's reputation is not really established, his text is given authority insofar as its extract provides the epigraph to the novel. As McCann, in his interviews, mentions the names of authors to make them known because he considers that they are not estimated at their true value, he chooses to cite *The Lazarus Project* in order to show the importance he attaches to the text and reinforce its authority. If he is endowed with any power, the author can suggest perspectives and increase the authority of someone else's text. Once a text is the subject of intertextual practice, it is given authority. When it is quoted in an epigraph, this authority is all the stronger. Authority becomes a consequence of intertextuality. By quoting a text with lesser prestige, McCann lends credit to Hemon's text and *author*izes its author. Thus, in the paratext of *Let the Great World Spin*, the title exemplifies that intertextual practice can be founded by authority, whereas the epigraph proves that authority can also be founded by intertextual practice.

McCann *author*ized by Berger and Harrison

Let the Great World Spin is dedicated to two authors, John Berger and Jim Harrison. In view of these writers' respective dates of birth, 1926 and 1937, the dedication, written by an author who was himself born in 1965, that is to say one generation later, can be read as a tribute from a son to his father. Indeed, when he mentions Berger as his 'master'[15] McCann recognizes him

---

15   'Mon maître, John Berger' (<www.lexpress.fr/outils/imprimer.asp?id=823679&k=15>).

as a mentor and model, a symbolic father. Gérard Genette sees a connection between father and son in the paratextual references to writers of the previous generation: 'The young writers (...) give themselves the consecration and unction of a prestigious filiation'.[16] The paratext displays an affiliation, which establishes a tradition of men of letters, from the nineteenth-century ancestor to the novel writer and his fellow author quoted in the epigraph, via some symbolic fathers whom they regard as their masters. McCann discloses a close relationship with these writers through the medium of his dedication.[17] Though it is not specified if this relationship is a purely artistic connection between writer and reader or a tie between men who personally know and appreciate one another, the dedication nevertheless keeps its function as moral, intellectual and aesthetic support. As McCann emphasizes in different interviews, he admires Berger and Harrison – and admiration, according to Neil Corcoran, is a response to a predecessor's work[18] – for their attention to the world, for their acute vision of the real, for their courage too. Indeed these writers fight with the weapons of fiction; they are committed, resistant to the established order, to the authorities' speeches and ideologies: they are protesters. They lend their support to the

16   Gérard Genette, *Paratexts: Thresholds of Interpretation*, 160.
17   It must be borne in mind that the name of John Berger is repeatedly mentioned in the paratexts of McCann's books. For example, at the start of *Zoli*, there appears an epigraph taken from Berger's book, *And our Faces, my Heart, brief as Photos*. Besides, McCann frequently refers to the English writer in his interviews: 'I read books because people like John Berger create stories that call the world into silence' ('Conversation with Sasha Hemon', <www.colummccann.com/interviews/hemon. htm>). He quotes him as well: Berger's sentence – 'Never again will a story be told as if it were the only one' – is cited in McCann's interviews with Robert Birnbaum (John Cusatis, *Colum McCann*, Columbia: The University of South Carolina Press, 2011, 20) or with Joseph Lennon (Susan Cahill & Eoin Flannery, eds, *This Side of Brightness: Essays on the Fiction of Colum McCann*, Oxford: Peter Lang, 2012, 170). This citation so often punctuates his discourse that McCann sometimes forgets to mention the source. Nevertheless he must know that it is taken from Berger's novel *G.* (London: Bloomsbury, 1972, 133).
18   Neil Corcoran, *After Yeats and Joyce. Reading Modern Irish Literature*. preface, viii.

common people, to the outcasts, to those who are overlooked by society
and share with them 'the same respect for the Earth, the same sense of
precariousness, the same concern when you look at the sky' (Berger) without ever lapsing into maudlin realism or moralizing pathos. These writers
are 'reporters who open their eyes and ears',[19] just like McCann himself
who really seems to be their worthy heir. Finding his place in this literary
tradition, McCann promotes his own text and presents it as the fruit of
a work that aims to be like Berger and Harrison's productions. In theory,
these two writers beforehand authorized McCann to mention them in
his dedication. Somehow or other, they are responsible for the novel that
pays tribute to them and show their support and contribution to it. To
some extent, they also vouch for the book that they most probably read
and could have written themselves. The relationship between writers and
readers is both reflexive and symmetric. Because he is an interpreter, any
reader is, to some extent, the author of the text. Even if he is not a writer,
even if the novel is not dedicated to him, he is nevertheless invested with
an authority, because he can indefinitely interpret the text. Promoted the
producer of the text, he is equally the producer of the *meaning* of the text
and, thus, its author somehow. The difference between writing and reading is then abolished and gives the reader an authority that the author was
formerly credited with.

Conclusion

The motif of connection or connectedness starts with the illustration of
the cover of *Let the Great World Spin* which, from below, depicts a tiny
silhouette walking on a cable between the World Trade Center twin towers.

19   André Clavel considers John Berger as 'un reporter qui sait voir et écouter'.
      (André Clavel, 'John Berger, l'Anglais volant', *L'Express* (1 February 2009) <www.
      lexpress.fr/culture/livre/john-berger-l-anglais-volant_815592.html>.

It is prolonged by the paratextual components of the novel. The latter are places of connection, of *mise en abyme*: as the title is connected with the text it introduces, but also the one it quotes, the epigraph is connected with the title and the text, as the dedication shows a connection between authors. These relationships confirm that McCann does not give his name to one text alone but to a connection between texts. His name becomes the pivot on which the practice of literature revolves, a means of intertextuality which incorporates his work in a particular connection with other texts. This source of fruitful exchanges revitalizes the notion of authorship, which is no longer envisaged as a distinctive mark but as the connecting mirror effect between them. As we said before, intertextuality is subsequent to a crisis of authority, as its birth immediately follows the death of the author. And yet, intertextuality is all the more connected with the crisis of authority as it shatters the authority of *the* text. In this case, would the authority of the intertext be conceivable? As the authority of the author is replaced by the authority of the reader, the authority of the text could also be replaced here by the plural, shared authority of the intertext. The word, however, does not seem to be appropriate any more: indeed authority, in this case, is scattered in a multiplicity of texts called upon in an unceasing movement to such an extent, that it finally dissolves and no longer makes any sense. Intertextuality *is* crisis: it introduces discontinuity in a continuous process. And yet, as any crisis, it does not remain boxed in but suggests revival and resumption. Intertextuality is free, rebellious and intractable. It oversteps any notion of hierarchy, of authority as it oversteps any spatiotemporal limit, since the national borders do not make sense any more, since the present and the past interact and make the literary work immortal. As Genette contends in *Palimpsests*, intertextuality constantly re-launches old works in a new circuit of meaning,[20] confirming the idea developed by Borges for whom literature is inexhaustible insofar as one book already is.[21] This book does not only have to be re-read, but also re-written.

20   Gérard Genette, *Palimpsests*, 453.
21   Jorge Luis Borges, *The Total Library: Non-Fiction 1922–1986* (London: Penguin, 2007) 244.

In a utopian vision, all publications are but one, endless big book and all authors are one. If it is so, the principle of contemporary writing ties up with the question raised by Foucault who himself borrowed the expression from Beckett: 'What matter who's speaking? Somebody said: what matter who's speaking?'[22]

22   Michel Foucault, 'What is an author?', *Power. The Essential Works of Foucault 1954–1984, volume 3* (New York: The New Press, 2001), 293.

AUDREY ROBITAILLIÉ

'Come Away, Stolen Child': Colum McCann's and Keith Donohue's New Readings of the Yeatsian Motif

ABSTRACT

This essay looks at the way Colum McCann and Keith Donohue take up the stolen child motif in their works, respectively the short story 'Stolen Child' from the collection *Fishing the Sloe-Black River* (1994) and the novel *The Stolen Child* (2006). Both use intertextuality with W. B. Yeats's oeuvre to parodically rewrite the motif, in Linda Hutcheon's understanding of the term 'parody'. The contemporary writers thus set themselves in the footsteps of the canonical Irish author, while at the same time asserting their difference, in an approach that reflects their personal situations and highlights their interests in issues of exile and identity.

'Come Away, O human child!/To the waters and the wild'. These lines from William Butler Yeats's poem 'The Stolen Child' from his first collection *The Wanderings of Oisin and Other Poems* (1889) have set the canon for Irish writing about fairy abductions and changelings ever since.[1] The Nobel Literature Prize winner found his inspiration for this poem in Irish folklore, where fairies, *sí* in Irish, often abduct people and take them to the Otherworld, sometimes leaving in their place a wizened creature called a changeling. In the natural setting of his own County Sligo, Yeats in this poem tells of fairies luring a boy away to their realm, far from the reality

---

1   William Butler Yeats, 'The Stolen Child', *The Wanderings of Oisin and Other Poems* (London: Kegan Paul, Trench & Co., 1889), 58–60, later revised and included in *Crossways* as part of his *Collected Poems* (New York: MacMillan, 1933). The poem was written in 1886 and published the same year in a magazine, later re-published as part of the collection *Poems and Ballads of Yound Ireland* in 1888 (W. B. Yeats, *Poems and Ballads of Young Ireland*, Dublin: Gill & Son, 1903 [1888], 12–13).

of a sorrowful world. These lines evidence Yeats's desire to escape the harsh reality of life, as he himself wrote: 'I have noticed some things about my poetry I did not know before, [...] that it is almost all a flight into fairyland from the real world and a summons to that flight. The chorus of 'The Stolen Child' sums it up [...]'.[2] In Yeats's poetry, the realm of the *sí* stands for the power of the imagination, in opposition to the modern Victorian way of life that surrounded him.[3] The Irish fairies of his poems who appear amidst a green and mystical Sligo scenery thus contrast with the materialistic, urban, rationalistic England where the poet lived.[4]

Two contemporary writers, Dublin-born Colum McCann and the American author Keith Donohue, have since written their own versions of the changeling story. McCann published a short story, 'Stolen Child', in his first collection, *Fishing the Sloe-Black River* (1994), while Donohue's first novel, *The Stolen Child*, came out in 2006. The titles of these works are obvious intertextual references to Yeats's poem and this essay sets out to analyse how they challenge Yeats's canonical use of the motif in an attempt to (re)define their own Irishness. Measuring themselves against Yeats is a way for them to claim their heritage, acknowledging Yeats's authority while subverting it and therefore distancing themselves from it. These writers' parodic approaches also mirror the ambiguity of their own personal situations. This study will thus first focus on how the authors engage with the folk and literary traditions on changelings, with references to Irish folklore and to Yeats's poem, then discuss how each writer is reusing and subverting these motifs and to what ends.

2   William Butler Yeats in a letter to Katharine Tynan on 14 March 1888, in Roger McHugh, ed., *W. B. Yeats, Letters to Katharine Tynan* (Dublin: Clonmore and Reynolds, 1953), 47.

3   Michael O'Neill, 'Early Yeats: "The Essences of Things"', in Edward Larrissy, ed., *W. B. Yeats, Visions and Revisions* (Dublin: Irish Academic Press, 2010), 39.

4   Mary Helen Thuente, *W. B. Yeats and Irish Folklore* (Totowa: Barnes and Noble, 1981 [1980]), 5.

Irish folklore and Yeats: Engaging with tradition

McCann's short story may initially seem unrelated to folklore, despite its
title. It deals with an Irish expatriate, Padraic, who works as a counsellor in
a blind children's home in Brooklyn. He is to give away one of the girls at
her wedding with a Vietnam veteran much older than she is. He has become
attached to her and is rather reluctant to see her married, repeating that this
is 'no day for a wedding.'[5] The urban setting of New York City contrasts
with Yeats's wild Sligo countryside. McCann writes of police sirens blaring
and of the sun, 'coming up like a stabwound, leaving smudges of dirty light
on the New York City skyline'[6] while Yeats portrayed his homeland 'where
the wandering water gushes/From the hills above Glen-car,/In pools among
the rushes/That scarce could bathe a star.'[7] Yet, the text is interspersed with
references to Irish folklore and to Yeats's poem. McCann describes Ireland
as a 'wild country where trees ran on one another's backs until they reached
either ocean.'[8] This echoes Yeats's 'to the waters and the wild', playing on the
same lexical fields of wilderness and water. In a similar fashion, McCann
writes: 'Padraic had come far across an incomprehensible ocean, from a
place called Leitrim.'[9] This is reminiscent of the story of the otherworldly
princess Niamh who took Oisín beyond the sea, to the Land of the Young,
Tír na nÓg. This well-known episode of the Irish Fenian Cycle of tales has
precisely been poetically rewritten by Yeats in his *Wanderings of Oisin*. But
McCann also directly refers to Yeats's 'The Stolen Child', quoting in italics lines from the poem. While Padraic is napping after his nightshift, 'he
hears the poem that he sometimes quoted her when they walked in the
park. *For the world's more full of weeping than you can understand.* [...] He
remembers strolling in the park with the echoing mythology of Ireland.

5   Colum McCann, 'Stolen Child', *Fishing the Sloe-Black River* (London: Phoenix,
     1995 [1994]), 95, 97, 101.
6   *Ibid.*, 95.
7   W. B. Yeats, 'The Stolen Child', *The Wanderings of Oisin and Other Poems*, 58–60.
8   Colum McCann, 'Stolen Child', 99.
9   *Ibid.*, 97–8.

Come away, stolen child.[10] The deliberate intertextuality between the two works, separated by almost a hundred years, is highlighted by these italics, although McCann does not quote Yeats explicitly. Julia Kristeva defines intertextuality as the 'textual interaction which takes place inside a single text'.[11] In his short story, through these italics, McCann interacts with Yeats's poem, shedding new light on the original text as well as using it for his own creative purposes.

The young black bride's name is Dana, and Padraic explains to her who Dana was in Irish mythology: 'He told her about Dana, the Irish goddess who was believed to have come from North Africa in ancient times. Dana was in charge of a tribe of druids, the Tuatha de Dannan [sic], who landed on a fair May morning and conquered the country by ousting the Firbolgs, the men with the paunchy stomachs. She had magic that could control the sea, the mist, the sun, and the very sounds and shapes of the morning'.[12] Dana was indeed the goddess of the Tuatha Dé Danann, the mythical tribe of gods of Ireland, later called the *sí* according to common interpretations.[13] The free indirect speech used in this extract and especially in the last sentence quoted shows Padraic romancing the story of the Tuatha Dé Danann. It reveals how, in Padraic's mind, Ireland is associated to the natural world. This is again exemplified later on: 'Padraic talked to her of somewhere different, some place where her namesake had been long ago. Dana imagined thick forests, boats made from the hides of cows, valleys where drizzling rain settled heavily on long grass'.[14] The tight link between Padraic's homeland and nature explains why a connection is made in the

10   Colum McCann, 'Stolen Child', 102. [McCann's italics].
11   Julia Kristeva, 'Problèmes de la structuration du texte', in Philippe Sollers, ed., *Théorie d'ensemble* (Paris: Seuil, 1968), 312: 'cette interaction textuelle qui se produit à l'intérieur d'un seul texte'.
12   Colum McCann, 'Stolen Child', 99.
13   John Carey, *A Single Ray of the Sun, Religious Speculation in Early Ireland* (Andover: Irish Studies Publications, 1999), 12–13; Dáithí Ó hÓgáin, *Myth, Legend and Romance: an Encyclopaedia of Irish Folk Tradition* (New York: Prentice Hall Press, 1991), 185.
14   Colum McCann, 'Stolen Child', 100.

short story with Yeats's poem, where the landscape is omnipresent, from the 'rocky island' of Sleuth Wood, to the moonlight on the stream and the waterfall of Glencar. The choice of the main protagonist's name, as well as the quotations from Yeats's most famous poem, highlight McCann's deliberate intertextuality with the canonical author of Irish literature and with Irish folk tradition, as does the connection between Ireland and the natural world. The young Irish writer follows in the footsteps of Yeats, using similar themes and tropes for his short story.

Keith Donohue's novel is also set mostly in America but the references to Irish folklore are more obvious and more numerous than in McCann's text. This may be due to the genre chosen: Donohue wrote a novel, while McCann opted for a short story. The whole novel in fact revolves around the changeling tradition: the main character, a seven year-old boy called Henry Day, is abducted by a troop of wild children living in the woods, who call themselves 'changelings'. One of them takes his appearance and assumes Henry's life, becomes Henry Day, grows older, marries and has a child, while the real Henry turns into Aniday the changeling. The author indicated that their names were deliberately chosen to be similar and yet different, to mark the idea that they are each other's alter ego in the novel.[15]

Donohue takes up the traditional changeling story, but removes the otherworldly dimension, making the wild children more real. Whereas the fairies of the folk-tales belonged to the Otherworld, thus shrouding them in the mists of mystery, Donohue decides to make his changelings part of the real world, living on the fringes of society. His changelings live in the woods and take turns in exchanging their existence with a human child to come back to human life. They can live as changelings for hundreds of years, waiting for 'the change' to happen, echoing the Irish tradition that sometimes the changeling left in place of the stolen child was an old fairy. A folk story from West Kerry tells of a boy who has been with the 'good

---

15   Keith Donohue, interviewed by the author, 'Away with the Fairies, The Motif of Fairy Abduction and of the Changeling, From Irish Mythology to the Irish Diaspora' (PhD thesis, Queen's University Belfast & Université de Caen Basse-Normandie, 2015), Appendix 2.2.

people' for six years, while 'an old fairy two hundred years old from the county Donegal' is sitting at home in his stead.[16]

There are many more parallels with the Irish tradition in the novel. For instance, the new Henry is an excellent musician and singer, able to 'sing like a bird' and play like a 'natural', whose teacher does not believe he is a beginner.[17] Fairies were said to be very fond of music and changelings in particular are excellent musicians, as depicted in numerous folk-tales in which a fairy substitute starts playing the bagpipes or the fiddle. The changeling 'play[s] the like of such music [the tailor] never heard' in a tale from Carlow,[18] and in a story from Donegal, the neighbour hears 'the nicest music ever he heard' when the creature plays the fiddle.[19] Henry plays neither the bagpipes nor the violin, but he is a gifted pianist and tries his hand at the organ.[20] In the novel, Henry in fact says: 'Playing music is the one vivid memory from the other life'.[21] This evokes both the fairies' love of music in general and the changeling nature of Henry.

The main character who is stolen in this novel is a boy, Henry, and this too is reminiscent of the folk narratives, in which male infants were more likely to be taken away by the fairies than girls.[22] Henry also calls the changelings the 'devils in the woods',[23] thereby reminding the reader of the way the fairies were perceived in recent centuries as malevolent or

---

16   Jeremiah Curtin, coll. and Seamus Ó Duilearga, ed. 'Fairy-Tales from West Kerry', *Béaloideas* 13.1/2 (June–December 1943), 260.

17   Keith Donohue, *The Stolen Child* (London: Vintage, 2007 [2006]), 40.

18   Pádraig Ó Tuathail, 'Tales of the Fairies' in 'Folk-Tales from Carlow and West Wicklow', *Béaloideas* 7.1 (June 1937), 82.

19   National Folklore Collection 348: 200–1, 'Daoine Beaga'.

20   Keith Donohue, *The Stolen Child*, 226, 53–9.

21   *Ibid.*, 243.

22   Séamas Mac Philib, 'The Changeling, Irish versions of a migratory legend in their international context', *Béaloideas* 59 (1991), *The Fairy Hill is On Fire! Proceedings of the Symposium on Supernatural in Irish and Scottish Migratory Legends, Dublin 7–8 October 1988*, 131; Susan Schoon Eberly, 'Fairies and the Folklore of Disability: Hybrids and the Solitary Fairy', in Peter Narváez, ed., *The Good People: New Fairylore Essays* (Lexington: University Press of Kentucky, 1997), 235, 240.

23   Keith Donohue, *The Stolen Child*, 176.

mischievous if not treated properly. But Henry's phrase is equally reminiscent of fairies understood as fallen angels, who would have ended up in
hell after being expelled from Heaven for supporting Lucifer's rebellion,
had not God closed the gates of Hell before they reached it. They thus had
remained on earth, according to Irish beliefs.[24]

Links to Ireland in general are numerous. It can be guessed for example
that Henry's mother is Irish: 'I knew your mother; she loved to nestle you
on her lap as she read to you old Irish tales and called you her "little man"'.[25]
Two of the changelings were also from Irish emigrant families before being
stolen.[26] Proof of this is that they have retained Irish names: Smaolach is
a variant dialect form of *smólach*, meaning 'thrush', while Luchóg means
'mouse'. Both names interestingly refer to animals living in the woods. They
also speak Irish on rare occasions:

> '*Ní mar a síltear a bítear* [sic],' he said.
> 'Smaolach, if I live to be a thousand years, I'll never understand your old language.
> Speak English to me'.[27]

The Irish phrase is significant: it means 'things are not always as they seem'.
For those who can understand them, the words refer to the misleading
appearance of the changelings.

The narrative is sprinkled with intertextual references to Yeats's works
as well, such as the voice Henry hears when he is being abducted: 'A hoarse
voice whispered something that sounded like 'Come away' or 'Henry Day'.[28]
Similarly, when one of the changelings, Igel, is about to perform the change
and steal a boy's life in the real world, he says 'Come away, human child'.[29]
When the changelings accidentally meet a woman on the road, though they
are supposed to remain unseen and unheard from humans, they invent 'a

---

24 Angela Bourke, *The Burning of Bridget Cleary, a true story* (London: Pimlico, 1999),
    27–8.
25 Keith Donohue, *The Stolen Child*, 185.
26 *Ibid.*, 140.
27 *Ibid.*, 237.
28 *Ibid.*, 12.
29 *Ibid.*, 155.

narrative of the waters and the wild' to make up for their absence and avoid being punished by the leader.[30] As in McCann's narrative, Donohue's intertextual references to Yeats are implicit and not quoted as such. Neither is the poet mentioned in the acknowledgements to *The Stolen Child*. As with McCann, the use of the natural world imagery as in the poem is devised to further the continuity with Yeats's heritage. The links with Irish folk tradition, stronger than in the short story, reinforce the idea that Donohue is treading in the footsteps of the canonical Irish writer.

Subverting tradition

These references in both writers' works to Yeats can be seen as a way for them to acknowledge his literary authority. Yet, the main question lurking in the readers' minds is indeed: who is the 'Stolen Child' in these stories? The absence of a definite article in McCann's title, unlike Yeats's, suggests that the 'Stolen Child' may not be one particular person. Thus Dana could be Padraic's stolen child since he is giving her away rather unwillingly at her wedding, even suggesting: 'There's always time to change your mind, you know'.[31] Reminiscent of the fact that young brides were the adults most likely to be taken away by the fairies in Irish folklore, this interpretation of Dana as the child stolen by the Vietnam veteran is endorsed by Bertrand Cardin who sees it as a parody of Yeats's poem, following Linda Hutcheon's postmodernist definition of parody.[32] She defines parody as a paradoxical approach which 'both incorporates and challenges that which

---

30   Keith Donohue, *The Stolen Child*, 34.
31   Colum McCann, 'Stolen Child', 106.
32   Bertrand Cardin, 'Entre conformisme et résistance: le procédé parodique dans les nouvelles de Colum McCann', *Conformismes et Résistances: Actes du Congrès de la SOFEIR* (Lille: Université Charles de Gaulle, 2009), 78. <http://cecille.recherche. univ-lille3.fr/IMG/pdf/Conformismes_et_resistances-3.pdf>.

it parodies'.[33] McCann takes up the stolen child figure but transposes it into a totally different setting, the urban cityscape of New York, in which an old veteran takes away a young bride. The Irish writer subverts Yeats' model by changing the parameters of the age-old narrative. This subversion, added to the references reinforcing Yeats's authority, contributes to a parodic reading of the original poem.

The other blind children in the Brooklyn home can also be seen as stolen children, kept away from the world. The narrator calls them 'those forgotten blind children, the snot rags of society'.[34] The home occasionally sounds more like a prison: when Padraic leaves after his 'graveyard shift', 'a clutch of blind children have their heads stuck out the bars of the lower windows'. The idea that they are locked away is emphasized by them not being allowed to attend Dana's wedding, though the best-behaved of them eventually do. They are referred to as 'birds with broken wings, unable to get off the ground'.[35] This again underlines the freedom they lack, trapped in the home. In the same way, Will, the Vietnam veteran Dana is about to marry, is a stolen child in that his youth and innocence were taken away from him by the war. This idea is evoked through his mother's words to him in a letter suggesting that he is 'washed in the blood of the Lamb', meaning he is blessed and will be safe, but Will and the reader rather understand it as an echo of the innocent lamb sacrificed in the bloodshed of the Vietnam war. The irony of the mother's words is highlighted by a letter Will wrote to her, on his way back from the war, 'in an airplane full of cripples and body bags', hinting at the idea that 'Lamb' should have been replaced by 'Vietnam' since they happen to rhyme.[36]

But it is most of all Padraic who seems to be the actual stolen child in the story, especially since it is narrated in the third person from his point of view, with a homodiegetic narrator in an internal focalization, to use

---

33   Linda Hutcheon, *A Poetics of Postmodernism, History, Theory, Fiction* (New York: Routledge, 1988), 11.

34   Colum McCann, 'Stolen Child', 96.

35   *Ibid.*, 96.

36   *Ibid.*, 103–4.

Gérard Genette's terms.[37] This comes in opposition to Yeats's poem where the fairies are the focus of the narration. Padraic is the one who does not belong. This is epitomized by the language difference: Padraic's pronunciation reveals he is a foreigner to America. Indeed, 'when Dana first heard him talk, she thought he must have swallowed a very tiny insect or bird that made his voice the way it was.'[38] And she later tries to figure out which creature could be stuck in his throat: a cricket, a thrush or a praying mantis are the three options that she hesitates between, evoking at once the benevolence of Carlo Collodi's character in *Pinocchio*, the liveliness of the natural world and a more worrying figure. His accent reveals his otherness, the fact that he is out of place in America, like the changeling in the human world.

Like Yeats's human child, leaving the real world of kettles boiling and calves lowing on an Irish farm, McCann's character wants to leave the harsh reality of the children's home in New York. Padraic tells his wife Orla that he 'hate[s] it there now'.[39] She thus suggests: 'I graduate in six months. We can leave then. Go back to Ireland. Or you can get that job in Oregon'.[40] In the same way that the child is fleeing from the sorrow of the world in Yeats's poem, Padraic wants to move away from the sadness of the children's home and of giving away Dana, in whom he had high hopes, a sadness he has also seen in the Vietnam veteran's eyes: 'There was a ferocious sadness in the veteran's eyes that made everyone in the carriage turn the other way while he spun along, clanging the tin can back and forth in gloves that had no fingers'.[41] This sense of escapism and longing for another place is hinted at with the reference to Philip Larkin's poetry collection *High Windows*, which Padraic's wife has been reading.[42] The image of the window is liminal, since windows are situated in-between the inside and the outside. Gillian Beer has stated that 'all the materials set into a window frame [...] seal the

37   Gérard Genette, *Figures III* (Paris: Seuil, 1972), 206, 251–9.
38   Colum McCann, 'Stolen Child', 97–8.
39   *Ibid.*, 101.
40   *Ibid.*, 103.
41   *Ibid.*, 104–5.
42   *Ibid.*, 97.

passage between outer and inner, inner and outer'.[43] The liminality of the window imagery evoked through Larkin's book is echoed by that of the stolen child, who is liminal as well, since he crosses boundaries between the real world and the Otherworld, pertaining after his abduction both to the fairies and to the humans. Padraic, who has been crossing borders and seas, can therefore be seen as a liminal character in that sense, and may therefore be a stolen child.

Padraic is in fact the stolen child of Ireland, exiled away in an American Otherworld. The idea that the protagonist wants to escape back to Ireland is suggested by the quotations from Yeats's poem. Whereas the original line is 'Come away, O human child!', McCann has Padraic say, mistakenly, 'Come away, stolen child'.[44] When Yeats portrays the fairies abducting the child to the Otherworld, McCann on the contrary implies that the stolen child is taken back to the real world, since his sentence is the opposite to Yeats's. Ireland is indeed the world Padraic wants to go back to, the 'normal' world:

> Padraic laughs and tugs at his shoelaces. 'Some day for a wedding, huh?'
> 'Ah, it's not too bad as far as I can see.' [...] 'At least the sun is shining. We got married in the pissings of rain, remember?'
> 'Yeah, but we were normal and that was Ireland.'
> 'Since when was Ireland normal?'[45]

This implies that America is abnormal, extra-ordinary, therefore a kind of Otherworld. Eóin Flannery has seen this subversion of the Yeatsian Otherworld motif as a critique of the canonical model.[46] By introducing the idea of exile, McCann indeed gives another dimension to the concept of the changeling. He is thus re-using Yeats's motif of fairy abduction illustrating a sense of longing for some other world, but he is also reversing it,

43 Gillian Beer, 'Windows: Looking in, Looking out, Breaking through', in Subha Mukherji, ed., *Thinking on Thresholds, the poetics of transitive spaces* (London: Anthem Press, 2011), 4.
44 Colum McCann, 'Stolen Child', 102.
45 *Ibid.*, 101–2.
46 Eóin Flannery, *Colum McCann and the Aesthetics of Redemption* (Dublin: Irish Academic Press, 2011), 37.

since Ireland is where Padraic wants to be, and not what he wants to leave behind. With Yeats, the stolen child was going away from the real world to the Otherworld, while Padraic wants to move away from the Otherworld to go back to the real world, Ireland. By reusing Yeats's canonical figure of the stolen child in an unexpected way, among the blind children of Brooklyn, in the New York subway, amidst Vietnam veterans, McCann is subverting Yeats's authority on this theme. Despite their common Irishness, the contemporary writer wants to show his distance and difference from the literary canon through this subversion of possibly the most well-known of Yeats's poems. Yet, like Yeats who was denouncing the materialism of Victorian England by contrasting it with his mystical Sligo, McCann moves away from an urbanized America to go back to an idyllic Ireland, thereby creating a dialogue between tradition and modernity. He introduces a multiplicity of readings of the character of the stolen child, and subverting the original poem, and yet aligns himself with the literary tradition, therefore parodying Yeats, demonstrating both his deference and his irreverence towards the authoritative figure.

While Colum McCann uses the Yeatsian motif of the changeling to investigate exile and emigration, Keith Donohue focuses on the broader issue of 'identity and belonging',[47] by depicting two characters going through an identity crisis. Although his title is *The Stolen Child*, his novel is about two characters who have exchanged their lives and are haunted by their past and by each other. Aniday speaks of Henry in this way: 'That man had what had been intended for me. The robber of my name, stealer of my story, thief of my life: Henry Day'.[48] Both are longing to know who they are. Aniday wants to know who he was before being stolen; he spies on Henry Day and loiters around his old house, thus accidentally meeting his father at the beginning of his life in the woods. Henry Day yearns to know who he was in his first human life, before being stolen and changing

---

47   Keith Donohue in 'BookBrowse.com Interview', *Keith Donohue's Official Website*,
      2013. <http://keithdonohue.com/library/view/bookbrowse.com_interview/
      accessed 23 May 2013>.
48   Keith Donohue, *The Stolen Child*, 273.

back into Henry Day. This leads him to attend a hypnosis session where he gets confirmation that he was the son of German emigrants to the United States. He then picks Germany as his honeymoon destination, hoping to learn more about his past while over there. Henry's German connection is a veiled allusion to German folk-tales, where the changeling stories may have originated.[49]

Both characters are engaged in 'solv[ing] the riddle of [their] identit[ies]' as Aniday has it in the narrative.[50] Indeed, the recurring question Henry is asked in the novel is 'Do you know who you are, Henry Day?' a question actually valid for both characters.[51] The story is narrated using internal focalization, alternatively from Henry's and Aniday's point of view. Donohue explained: 'I've read books with more than one narrator, and the technique seemed right for this novel about the divided self [...] The other difficulty was trying to write in two different first person voices that are essentially the same person – the original Henry Day and the person trying to become Henry Day – but with enough of a difference to be discrete.'[52] When Henry is the first-person narrator, he always refers to his belongings as 'Henry's', marking that he is not the real Henry.[53] It is only at the end that he learns to accept his past and who he is, stating 'I am no longer the boy I was once upon a time, and he [Aniday] has become someone else, someone new. He is gone and now I am Henry Day'.[54] The double focus of the narration thus illustrates the issues at stake in the book.

49   The first mention ever of a changeling occurs in German sources as *wihselinc* (modern German: *Wechselbalg*) in the eleventh century and a strong changeling tradition is recorded in Germanic areas, leading to think that this could have been the area of origin of the changeling lore (Jean-Michel Doulet, *Quand les démons enlevaient les enfants, les changelins: étude d'une figure mythique*. Paris, Presses de l'Université de Paris-Sorbonne, 2002, 35–6).

50   Keith Donohue, *The Stolen Child*, 100.

51   *Ibid.*, 183.

52   Keith Donohue in 'BookBrowse.com Interview'.

53   Keith Donohue, *The Stolen Child*, 192.

54   *Ibid.*, 310.

It is also significant that Henry should have entitled the symphony he has composed 'The Stolen Child'.[55] His inspiration came from his own story: 'a work about a child trapped in his silence, how the sounds could never get out of his own imagination, living in two worlds, the internal life locked to all communication with outside reality'.[56] In the same way that music was very important for the fairies in the old tales, this symphony is the means for Henry and Aniday to be reconciled, with each other as well as each to his own story and future. In the folk-tales, music was seen as the link between humans and fairies. Barbara Hillers has indeed remarked that 'music functions almost as a marker of fairy-otherness; their pursuit of music earmarks the fairies, just like their deathlessness, or their ability to shape-shift [...]' She goes even as far as saying that music is a shorthand symbol for the Otherworld.[57] The symphony becomes the symbol of Henry's and Aniday's otherworldly connection.

Donohue's novel is centred on the folk motif of the changelings, making them the main protagonists of his narrative. The American author uses various references to the changeling tradition, from Irish folklore and allusions to German folk-tales to Yeats's poem. Donohue does not focus exclusively on Yeats, although he has admitted that it is Yeats's poem which inspired him to write the novel.[58] He uses Yeats's well-known motif of fairy abduction, but his novel is not about escapism, it is about the characters' quest for identity. Donohue has acknowledged that subversion was how he chose to approach the changeling motif: 'All very funny, contemporary and subversive, which is how I decided to approach the changeling legend'.[59] He indeed subverts Yeats's ideal of a magical, mesmerizing fairyland. If, according to Stephen Camelio, 'Yeats's use of mythology and folklore in his

55   Keith Donohue, *The Stolen Child*, 308.
56   *Ibid.*, 295.
57   Barbara Hillers, 'Music from the Otherworld, Modern Gaelic Legends about Fairy Music', *Proceedings of the Harvard Celtic Colloquium* 14 (1994), 59, 68.
58   Keith Donohue in 'BookBrowse.com Interview'.
59   *Ibid.*

poems is an ode to traditional Ireland',[60] Donohue is turning the Yeatsian world of the *sí* into a miserable life on the fringes of human society. By using a first-person narration, he also strays from the Yeatsian path, further subverting the iconic poem.

Understanding parody

Both writers parody Yeats's poem by placing themselves in the tradition of the canonical writer, using themes and references to his 'The Stolen Child' for their first published work, as well as subverting this model in their narrative fictions, adding new dimensions to the motif of the changeling in so doing.

Colum McCann weaves the fabric of such a motif with new meanings of exile and emigration. He is himself an Irish expatriate, living in New York City, and has actually obtained dual citizenship. He has recognized that the United States was his own *Tír na nÓg* when he was a child.[61] As reflected by Colm Tóibín, who has stated that 'Irish fiction is full of dislocation and displacement',[62] McCann has admitted that exile is one of his main themes. He said: 'I have written about exile since my earliest collection, *Fishing the Sloe-Black River*, when I was in my twenties. It has – though I wasn't always entirely aware of it – been my obsession for two decades'.[63] This is visible in his 2009 novel, *Let the Great World Spin*, when

60 Stephen Camelio, 'Colum McCann: International Mongrel' (MA dissertation, Queen's University Belfast, 1999), 11.
61 John Cusatis, *Understanding Colum McCann* (Columbia, SC: The University of South Carolina Press, 2011), 15.
62 Colm Tóibín, Introduction to the *Penguin Book of Irish Fiction* (London: Penguin, 1999), xxxiii, quoted by John Cusatis, *Understanding Colum McCann*, 36.
63 Colum McCann in '*Zoli* Interview, Q&A with Michael Hayes', *Colum McCann's Official Website*: <http://colummccann.com/interviews/zoli-interview-qa-with-michael-hayes/> accessed 22 May 2013.

he writes 'we bring home with us when we leave. Sometimes it becomes more acute for the fact of having left'.[64] The same idea is expressed in an article for the *Irish Times*: 'Odd word, home. It seems to exist in only one place, but we cart it with us wherever we go'.[65] His previous novels *Zoli*, about a gipsy woman travelling Europe in search of a home, and *Dancer*, about artist Rudolf Nureyev exiled in Paris from the USSR, were also variations on the same theme of exile. This motif is consistent with the geography of McCann's life: despite residing in New York, his origins are in Ireland. He himself said in an interview: 'New York is the city of exiles – everyone comes from somewhere else. Ireland has been for years a country of exiles – everyone wanting to be somewhere else'.[66] The liminal aspect of McCann's life, perfectly mirrored by his dual nationality, in fact reflects that of his characters, and particularly Padraic here. The writer once said, in an interview no longer available on his website, 'I sometimes feel like a man of two countries'.[67] Hence the appeal of the changeling and stolen child motifs, liminal figures *par excellence*.

It is McCann's liminality and his belonging to two places at once which become significant when he refers to the works of Yeats in his own writings. This has been referred to by the Australian poet Vincent Buckley as the notion of 'source-country'.[68] Ireland is the source-country for the author and he is therefore using Ireland's canonical literary figure and symbols to claim his Irish identity and heritage. Eóin Flannery has described McCann's approach as a 'process of cultural negotiation, wherein national identities are not forsaken or diluted; respective pasts are not abandoned

64   Colum McCann, *Let the Great World Spin* (London: Bloomsbury, 2009), 59.
65   Colum McCann, 'Irish Identity is a work of art, not political expediency', *Irish Times* (16 March 2013).
66   Colum McCann, '*This Side of Brightness* Interview', *Colum McCann's Official Website*: <http://colummccann.com/interviews/this-side-of-brightness-interview/> accessed 22 May 2013.
67   Colum McCann, '*Everything in This Country Must* Interview'. *Colum McCann's Official Website*: <http://www.colummccann.com/interviews/everything.php> no longer available online.
68   Vincent Buckley, 'Imagination's Home', *Quadrant* 140 (March 1979), 24–5.

but re-imagined in contemporary moments of encountering the "other"'[69] McCann's 'Stolen Child' is indeed an example of his wish to embrace his mixed Irish and American heritage in his writing. Again, in Flannery's words, 'McCann shows us the productive interaction of the archaic local with the alien international'.[70] McCann is thus taking on not only Irish folklore and mythology, but also Yeats, because the latter has become a symbol of Irishness. The young Irish-American writer blends this marker of identity with others, such as the New York setting, in an attempt to define his own heritage. It can thus be argued that this short-story is part of McCann's explorations of what it is like to be an emigrant and what an exile's relation to the homeland is.

In the light of Linda Hutcheon's words on parody, McCann's irreverence towards Yeats's model, contrasting the magical Ireland of the poem and the harsh Brooklyn setting of his narrative, can be seen as an acknowledgement of Yeats's authority as well as a claim to his Irish roots. Indeed, Hutcheon describes parody 'as repetition with critical distance that allows ironic signalling of difference at the very heart of similarity [...] this parody paradoxically enacts both change and cultural continuity'.[71] The intertextual process allows the writer to both challenge the literary authority and, at the same time, show the continuity between them. Bertrand Cardin has described parody as a way to give back to a forgotten text its aesthetic dimension, a way to give homage to it without admitting it.[72] In this case, because Yeats's poem is so well-known, McCann's acknowledgement of Yeats's canonical status becomes less a confession between the lines than a claim to their common Irishness. To subvert one's (literary) authority, one needs to acknowledge it. McCann is following in the footsteps of the canonical Irish writer to better signal his own originality. The rewriting

69   Eóin Flannery, *Colum McCann and the Aesthetics of Redemption*, 47.

70   *Ibid.*, 40.

71   Linda Hutcheon, *A Poetics of Postmodernism, History, Theory, Fiction*, 26.

72   Bertrand Cardin, 'Entre conformisme et résistance: le procédé parodique dans les nouvelles de Colum McCann', 80: 'La parodie redonne un caractère esthétique à un texte ou un terme oublié [...] et fonctionne comme un hommage qui ne veut s'avouer comme tel'.

of the changeling figure into characters undergoing an identity crisis is in itself a challenge to the authority of the folk and literary motifs.

Donohue's personal situation too seems to have affected his rewriting of the changeling figure. His characters are liminal, half-human, half-fairy, old and young at the same time, halfway between two worlds. The American writer has recognized that his familial situation when he was a child certainly influenced the writing of his first novel: 'My dad used to call me, the middle child of seven, "the youngest of the oldest, and the oldest of the youngest". Being dead smack in the middle of a large Irish-American family, it is no wonder that I have felt like a changeling myself now and again'.[73] The liminality of his characters could in fact be mirroring Keith Donohue's situation as an Irish-American. It is significant that the protagonist of the novel, Henry, was a German-American boy in his first life, before the change. His hyphenated condition, as part American but part from somewhere else, reflects Donohue's. The quest for identity of his protagonists could indeed be seen as his own. Similarly to McCann, the liminality of the characters and of the author is embodied within the work by the intertextuality established between the contemporary writer's text and Yeats's poem. Some of the words in the novel are Donohue's but some are another's. This ambiguity puts into relief the issues brought about through the motif of the changeling. Donohue himself said in an interview: 'I wasn't even aware of my Irish roots until going off to college'.[74] So he is using the 'source-country' as inspiration for his explorations on identity. Using Irish elements for his first novel is a way for Donohue to explore and claim his Irish ancestry, at the same time subverting the motifs to distance himself from them and emphasize his otherness, parodically marking his difference from Yeats with deference.

The two writers thus re-use the motif of fairy abduction and of the changeling in a deliberate reference to Yeats in order to position themselves

73   Keith Donohue, 'An Autobiographical Note from Keith Donohue', *Amazon*, 2012.
      <www.amazon.fr/Stolen-Child-Keith-Donohue/dp/0099490595/ref=sr_1_1?ie=
      UTF8&qid=1331205700&sr=8-1> accessed 8 March 2012.
74   Keith Donohue in 'BookBrowse.com Interview'.

as part of his tradition and therefore indicate their own Irishness. While Colum McCann, like Yeats, focuses on the feelings of longing for another world but ignores the changeling tradition *per se*, preferring that of fairy abduction, Keith Donohue chooses to have the changelings as the centre of his novel to bring up the theme of identity. The authors appropriate Yeats's canonical motif, by relating it to themes that are significant for them such as exile and identity. This can be seen as an attempt to claim their own heritage.

But while they acknowledge the canonical symbol of Irishness represented by Yeats and his poem, they distance themselves from it, giving both folklore and classical Irish literature a more modern take. They set their changeling stories in completely different contexts from Yeats's, emphasizing the urban in opposition to the Yeatsian stress on nature. The form of writing they choose distances them from his literary authority, which is then in crisis. Whereas they set their work in the vein of Yeats's and thus mark their belonging to the Irish literary tradition, they also subvert Yeats's take on folklore as a form of emancipation from this authoritative figure. Their works are both traditional and original, showing at the same time their Irishness and their otherness. Parody creates here a partial crisis for the literary authority represented by Yeats. The ambiguity of their parodic retellings of the stolen child story in fact reflects their own personal situations, in between two countries, as well as mirroring the changeling motif itself. Both works evidence the fact that folk motifs such as fairy abduction and the changeling have survived within the Irish diasporic communities because of inherent themes such as liminality, already present decades ago in the folk narratives. These figures have been reused and their meanings broadened to express significant issues relating to the diaspora, thereby suggesting how relevant folklore can still be today.

Audrey's work is kindly supported by Le Conseil Régional de Basse-Normandie.

MEHDI GHASSEMI

Authorial and Perceptual Crises in John Banville's *Shroud*

ABSTRACT

In *Shroud*, John Banville stages his narrator-protagonist as a literary theorist very reminiscent of Paul de Man. Drawing on de Man's own deconstructionist theories regarding the question of referentiality and the problem of (self-) representation, Axel Vander's self-conscious narrative becomes increasingly obsessed with the nature of his own perceptions and representations. The narrative, in turn, becomes a solipsistic account that stretches and eventually splits Vander's sense of self between a spectral and corporeal existence. In other words, the very attempt at finding authenticity leads him to further alienation from the real. The aim of this paper is to explore the way in which *Shroud* presents not only a crisis of authenticity, but also an authorial (as well as authoritative) crisis in which Vander's very sense of self is undermined.

John Banville returns to his familiar theme of the relationship between fiction and reality in *Shroud*,[1] another example of what Linda Hutcheon calls 'historiographic metafiction'.[2] Banville models his protagonist, Axel Vander, on Paul de Man, the deconstructionist literary theorist, whose early writings for a pro-Nazi newspaper were posthumously uncovered, marring de Man's reputation as a prominent literary thinker. The second novel of Banville's latest trilogy – the others being *Eclipse* and *Ancient Light*[3] – *Shroud* is a first-person account and takes the form of an autobiographical

---

1   John Banville, *Shroud* (London: Picador, 2002).
2   Linda Hutcheon, 'Historiographic metafiction: parody and intertextuality of history', in Patrick O'Donnel and Robert Con Davis, eds, *Intertextuality and Contemporary American Fiction* (Baltimore: Johns Hopkins University Press, 1989).
3   John Banville, *Ancient Light* (London: Viking, 2012).

confession while simultaneously drawing on de Man's own deconstructionist theories regarding the question of referentiality and the problem of (self-)representation mediated by language.[4] Partly mirroring de Man's life, it depicts a dying academic struggling with a troubled past and present physical pain. Axel's career as a renowned literary theorist is highly reminiscent of Paul de Man's on several counts. Like de Man, he moves to the United States to pursue a career in literary studies with a strong focus on Romantic poetry. He nearly loses his reputation because of revelations of a dark past; at the beginning of the novel he receives a letter from an Irish student named Cass Cleave threatening to unveil his pro-Nazi collaborationist past. Further into the novel, however, we realize that he fears the revelation of yet another 'darker' secret: he is not Axel Vander. In fact, he 'purloined' his friend's identity while escaping across a war-stricken Europe and the 'real' Axel died before the narrator fled from Nazi Germany to avoid persecution because he was Jewish.

This chapter firstly reads *Shroud* in relation to Paul de Man's 'history' as well as his theory of representation. Secondly, it studies the way in which the narrative moves away from de Man's idea and increasingly turns into a narcissistic universe that solipsistically over-evaluates Vander's own psychic reality. Finally, it traces the consequences of such introspection for the narrator's subjectivity and argues that what seems at first to be a crisis of authenticity for Axel is, in fact, a crisis of authorial (as well as authoritative) perceptions in which Vander's very sense of self as well as his grip over reality are undermined.

4   Elke D'hoker has previously used de Man's essay to read Banville's *The Untouchable* in which she sees a 'surprising convergence' between Banville's narrative's 'metaphoric diction' and de Man's essay. Although my essay initially follows a similar argument concerning *Shroud*, it will diverge substantially. See Elke D'hoker, *Visions of Alterity: Representations in the Works of Banville* (Amsterdam: Costerus, 2004), 203.

Autobiography

The first-person narrator of the novel claims that the aim of his narrative is to 'explain myself, to myself, and to you' (5)[5] and refers to the text as 'this record' (396) or 'this confession' (261) suggesting it is to be read as a form of confessional autobiography. Indeed, any autobiographical discourse draws on memory and Banville has always been fascinated by the nature of memory and the way the past becomes inscribed in human consciousness. In his first major work of fiction, *Birchwood*, the narrator says: 'We imagine that we remember things as they were, while in fact all we carry into the future are fragments which reconstruct a wholly illusory past.'[6] In this sense, autobiography cannot simply be a truthful account of a life-history since it draws primarily on bits and scraps of memory one keeps of oneself. To put it in Freudio-Lacanian terms, what the subject depicts in his autobiography is the way he perceives his sense of self or ego which, according to Lacan, is based primarily on a series of imaginary identifications.[7]

By using an autobiographical discourse in a fictional novel, Banville seems, once again, anxious to complicate the distinction between reality and fiction. By basing a fictional character on the life of a real historical figure, *i.e.*, Paul de Man, he seems to agree with de Man himself who blurs the supposed distinction between autobiography and fiction. De Man claims that contrary to the conventional assumption that 'life *produces* the autobiography as an act produces consequences' it is 'the autobiographical

---

5   All references to *Shroud* will henceforth be indicated in bracketed page numbers.
6   John Banville, *Birchwood* (London: Minerva, 1992), 12.
7   Lacan locates the ego in what he calls the imaginary order. He argues that the ego, or one's sense of self, originates during the mirror stage where the child identifies his image in a mirror. He/She then derives his sense of 'I' from this image. Jacques Lacan, 'The Mirror stage as formative of the *I* function as revealed in psychoanalytic experience', Bruce Fink (trans.), *Ecrits* (New York: W. W. Norton & Company, 2006), 75–81.

project' itself that produces and determines the life it is aiming to portray.[8]
De Man's idea that the life narrated by an autobiographical persona is not
necessarily the life that was led by the author is grounded in the recognition that narration is constantly undermined 'by the technical demands
of self-portraiture and thus determined, in all its aspects, by the resources
of [the] medium'.[9] Autobiography for de Man is not a genre or a mode,
but a figure of reading or of understanding that occurs, to some degree, in
all texts. If this is the case, then autobiography as such does not exist and
what remains is a body of textual representations whose authenticity one is
never able to 'authentically' ascertain. Aware of the resulting undecidability Axel equates story with history (91) and calls history 'a hotchpotch of
anecdotes, neither true nor false' (49), reaffirming its undecidable validity.

Autobiography and masking

Axel remarks towards the end of the novel that, all along, he has 'manufactured a voice' and a 'reputation' which are not authentically his (329). He
finds himself in the position of an actor in the ancient world: 'I think of an
actor in the ancient world [...] The crowd knows him but cannot remember his name [...] He has his mask [...] The white clay from which it was
fashioned has turned to the shade and texture of bone [...] it fits smoothly
upon the contours of his face. Increasingly, indeed, he thinks the mask is
more like his face than his face is [...] Man and mask are one' (286–7).
Having lived by the name 'Axel Vander' for so long, the narrator finds it
difficult, if not impossible, to unearth his 'true' face underneath the mask
of 'Axel Vander'. He is unable to conceive of himself independently from
the name 'Axel'. Like the ancient actor, he has become his mask. Although

8   Paul de Man, *The Rhetoric of Romanticism* (New York: Columbia University Press,
     1984), 69.
9   *Ibid.*

his identity as Axel is a 'manufactured' one, this seems to be all that he can hold onto. He has become 'Axel Vander'.

De Man understands prosopopeia as the defining trope of autobiographical discourse. He sees it as 'the fiction of an apostrophe to an absent, deceased or voiceless entity, which posits the possibility of the latter's reply and confers upon it the power of speech'.[10] According to de Man, prosopopeia is a figure of speech which means 'face making', for to have a voice metonymically implies having a mouth, and to have a mouth implies having a face. Fabricating a mask, thus, becomes an inevitable process of self-representation. In addition, as soon as one engages in representing his 'self', he is caught in what de Man calls the 'figural field' of language which inescapably posits him in figuration – the process of both providing and creating a figure.[11] To put it differently, since the means by which one attempts to fashion an autobiography is language as a field of metaphoricity, one can never escape the constructive aspect of the medium. Thus, one is required to read autobiography as a process of self-construction carried out by the autobiographical mask/voice.

This is a view constantly entertained by Banville in various narratives and *Shroud* is no exception. Axel mentions having written a book entitled *The Alias as Salient Fact: The Nominative Case in the Quest for Identity* (100) which he discusses later when he muses on his identity as being/not being Axel Vander: 'If, as I believe, as I insist, there is no essential, singular self, what is it exactly I am supposed to have escaped by pretending to be Axel Vander? Mere being, that insupportable medley of effects, desires, fears, tics, twitches? To be someone else is to be one thing and one thing only' (286). If, like history, identity is textual and if one's sense of self is a mere story one tells or hears about oneself, then there is no original self to be uncovered from beneath the fictional mask. If real being includes an incoherent 'medley of effects', then being 'someone else' seems a more convenient alternative since it involves being 'one thing only' rather than a myriad of

10   Paul de Man, *The Rhetoric of Romanticism*, 76.
11   Paul de Man, *Allegories of reading: figural language in Rousseau, Nietzsche, Rilke, and Proust* (New York: Columbia University Press, 1979), 270.

incoherent things. That is the 'salient fact' of Axel's identity. Indeed, the readers will keep referring to the narrator as Axel because he does not provide his name before he became Axel.

Autobiography and defacement

Insofar as the narrator has no original identity behind the mask of *Axel*, his self-conscious writing of his life-story destabilizes his reality as well as his sense of self. Far from rendering his sense of self more meaningful, his autobiographical discourse proves all the more complicated, resulting in the occasional unknotting of his reality as well as a series of incoherent selves. He claims that 'my prentice falsehoods [...] had come back to undo me' (12) and he speaks of his 'gradual process of thinning and fading' (381). He also complains that the 'margins of [his] world were disappearing' (18) and refers to moments when he feels not to be 'wholly present ... not so much a person as a contingency, misplaced and adrift in time' (68–9). He notices others' 'faceless shadows standing before them in the glass' (341) and during a dream-like epiphany he perceives 'a bloated, faceless thing' (351) approaching him from above threatening voicelessly to attack. The disintegration of his coherent self is also accompanied by his physical deterioration; aging, rotting, and smelling like 'something that had died under a bush' (301).

One intriguing motif with regards to self-representation in *Shroud* – one that can be seen as the origin of the narrative's title – is the Shroud of Turin which is referred to as 'the first self-portrait' (156).[12] After a talk Axel delivers at a literary conference in Turin, Kristina Kovacs, a former mistress of Axel's youth, half-ironically expresses her surprise at the fact that Axel did not mention the Shroud in his discussion regarding 'effacement' (156).

12   The Shroud of Turin is an old cloth featuring the image of a man who has apparently suffered crucifixion. The image is believed by many Christians to be that of Jesus-Christ upon his crucifixion/resurrection.

Here, the discussion of the Shroud can be read at two levels. On the first reading, it conjures up the idea of shrouding, that is to say, covering, concealing, or obscuring. Indeed, Axel confesses to his 'shrouded past' (338) hidden behind a 'borrowed [...] purloined, reputation' (64). He claims to have 'manufactured a reputation' (329) 'made up wholly of poses' (329). One could assume that he takes to writing this confession to achieve his 'true' self behind the 'façade' and 'imposture' of a false name (285). Here, the idea is that there is some form of truthful coherent self which has been shrouded or masked, which, by means of a self-revelatory confessional narrative could be unearthed.

However, on a second reading of the Shroud in relation to Axel's narrative, a different interpretation may emerge. As Cass insists on visiting the Shroud, Axel ironically tries to convince her that it is 'a fake' (307). Indeed, the authenticity of this 'self-portrait' of Christ remains disputed as it might be a mere painting 'fabricated' in the Middle Ages, and not at the time of Christ's death/resurrection. Even if we accept that the image on the Shroud is 'real' and not painted, there is no evidence that it 'truly' belongs to Christ and not to someone else. As they do not get to see the 'real' Shroud, Cass and Axel are told about 'a reproduction of the Shroud' (311) being exhibited somewhere in Turin echoing a duplication of yet another duplication of the real thing – in this case Christ's face. Things become even more ambiguous for those who do not believe Christ ever existed ... Ultimately we have a representation of a representation without a coherently conceivable referent – a signifier, that is to say, without signified. The thing itself, Christ's face, is only present to us through a representation whose authenticity is far from being fully ascertained.

Similarly, Banville's narrator steals the identity of a person called Axel Vander so that the narrator is not 'really' Axel Vander. Ironically, towards the end of the novel it is suggested that the 'real' Axel Vander was himself a fake, having forged an untruthful personal history. He was not 'really' who he claimed to be either and it is hinted that he was a Jew, like the nameless narrator and like Christ himself (404). So if Axel Vander is not Axel Vander – *i.e.* the narrator – and if the real Vander was not who he claimed to be then what does the name Axel Vander 'really' and 'truthfully' refer to? Just like the Shroud of Turin, it is a signifier whose signified remains elusive. The narrator is undergoing what de Man calls 'defacement'.[13] According to de Man, inasmuch as autobiography as *prosopopeia* confers a mask, it also 'defaces', that is to say, it 'deals with the giving and taking away of faces, with face and deface, *figure*, figuration and disfiguration'.[14] Autobiography disfigures the figure of *prosopopeia* and defaces the face it confers, disfiguring the very mask it aims to restore. So long as language is the means of telling and giving meaning to a life, autobiography is caught up in the figurative dimension of language which simultaneously undoes this very meaning. In other words, it *defaces*. Since all language perpetually fails in its aim to bring sense and coherence to a life, autobiography can never be autobiographical because it constantly 'fail[s] to produce a face incapable of disfigurement'.[15] So at best, autobiography is really no more than a representation of biography rather than the thing itself. De Man's idea of 'a linguistic predicament' is that insofar as language is imposed on the arbitrary production of texts by readers who take them actually to refer to something, language cannot possibly posit its own meaning.[16] Indeed, autobiography can represent the voice and name of the subject but the result is a distorted representation of one's self and/or mind. To put it in de Man's words, it 'veils a defacement of the mind of which it is itself the cause'.[17]

Self-conscious of his 'effacement' the narrator claims: 'I pause in uncertainty, losing my way in this welter of personal, impersonal, impersonating, pronouns' (285). The result of self-representation for Axel is a myriad of faces and selves and, instead of one stable identity, he has ended up with several unstable ones. Consequently and paradoxically, unable to tell a coherent self-story, he almost abandons writing an autobiography and, instead, calls for Cass Cleave to write his biography, hoping to arrive at a

---

13   The narrator in *Shroud* refers to 'Shelley's defacement' (121) which is a combination of
      the titles of two of de Man's articles namely 'Shelley Disfigured' and 'Autobiography
      as Defacement'.
14   Paul de Man, *The Rhetoric of Romanticism*, 76.
15   Martin McQuillan, *Paul de Man* (London: Routledge, 2001), 74.
16   *Ibid*.
17   Paul de Man, *The Rhetoric of Romanticism*, 81.

better representation of himself (156). At the same time, he claims the aim of his narrative is an attempt 'to explain myself' (5) and 'to redeem something of myself [...] some small, precious thing that I can buy back' (6). Axel nonetheless insists on the existence of the self. He is unable to 'rid [him] self of the conviction of an enduring core of selfhood amid the welter of the world, a kernel immune to any gale that might pluck the leaves from the almond tree and make the sustaining branches swing and shake' (27). He is convinced that amid the confusion he will be able to retrieve a core, an essence, resistant to the world's chaos. The metaphor he utilizes is very telling: the almond tree contains leaves and almond shells. While the leaves are seasonally removed by the wind, the almond seeds remain 'immune' to the wind thanks to the hard shell protecting them. Like the almond tree, he acknowledges that part of his self is akin to the leaves in that it constantly changes, dies and is reborn. However, there also exists, for him, a kernel which contains the innermost essence of his selfhood. In other words, he believes that despite the textual nature of all selves, he is able to retrieve some essence of selfhood hidden somewhere under a protective shell and, that the means to do so is to write his confession. This seems in contrast to de Man's idea of the impossibility of self-representation in autobiography. The reason for this defiance is arguably Axel's extreme narcissism. In turn, he cannot accept that there is no true, singular self. Consequently, his narrative moves away from de Man, the very figure the novel's protagonist is based on, and aims at finding authentic identity. In what follows, it will be argued that in defying the inexistence of a coherently representable self, Axel's narrative universe falls prey to an even further crisis, that is crisis of a unified perceptual field as such, thereby forcing Axel to tread in uncanny territory.

Crisis of self-perception: From dualism to bifurcation

Axel is subjected to a 'heightened sense of self-awareness' (333) which occasionally disrupts his very perception of himself: 'what made me flinch, surely, was an over-consciousness of self' (41). This is evident in Axel's

troubled relation with his reflection. Gazing at the mirror he has 'the sensation then, as so often, of shifting slightly aside from myself, as if I were
going out of focus and separating into two' (68). Elsewhere, 'in the smoked-
glass doors of the departure hall', the mirror functions as a locus where the
narrator and his reflection 'must meet in mutual annihilation' (28). The
mirror never reflects a singular being, but either splits or obliterates his
sense of self. At some occasions, the mirroring surface generates a weird
reflection: 'Wet still from the bath, I dripped on the floor, in the darkly
gleaming surface of which I could see yet another, dim reflection of myself,
in end-on perspective this time, like that bronzen portrait of the dead Christ
by what's-his-name, first the feet and then the shins, the knees, and dangling
genitals, and belly and big chest, and topping it all the aura of wild hair and
the featureless face looking down' (38). He perceives his reflection from an
'end-on perspective', from bottom to top, resulting in a statue-like figure.
Then he likens the figure to a 'bronzen portrait' of Christ reminiscent of
Mantegna's famous statue. While Christ's portraits generally depict Christ's
face with somewhat detailed features, Axel's reflection/portrait is 'featureless'. Although a portrait is precisely supposed to produce one's detailed
image, Axel's is featureless. Nonetheless, the aura of light generally present
around Christ's face is retained in Axel's portrait, though it is made not of
light, but produced by the reflection of his disheveled hair. Axel ends up
with a featureless face surrounded by a fake aura. The mirror-surface generates not so much a reflection of the real, but problematizes the narrator's
relation with his body by distorting his face, marring his self-identification.
At the same time, by juxtaposing the religious reference to the 'dangling
genitals' as well as the mock aura, the mirror introduces an excess, something
more than the bodily reflection. Axel goes on: 'I have begun to feel that I
am falling off myself, that my suety old flesh is melting off my skeleton and
soon will all be gone. I shall not mind; I shall be glad; I shall rise up then,
bared of inessentials, all gleaming bone and sinew smooth as candle wax,
new, unknown, my real self at last' (8). In contrast to the depiction of the
body as a troublesome extension, the *I* is emphatically reiterated several
times, rendering the dualism all the more explicit.

Insofar as the body is always localized in a single point of time and
space the bodily dimension is partly what singularizes an existence. As

Lacan demonstrates in his early work, the mirror functions as the foundation for self-consciousness. Self-recognition is constituted during what he calls 'the mirror stage' during which the *I* is 'precipitated in a primordial form'.[18] The perception of the body in an external reflexive surface serves as the basis for the constitution of the ego. The 'specular image' generated by the mirror, according to Lacan, renders the perception of one's body whole. This sense of unity structures self-experience and simultaneously perpetuates an eternal search for unity. Lacan demonstrates that identification with the specular image is in fact a defense against an otherwise chaotic and fragmented body. The crucial point that he stresses, however, is that the foundation of self-recognition is based on an image generated outside of the self. That is to say, identification is paradoxically based on a fundamental otherness: one can only acquire a self as long as one accepts an other to be him/herself. One has to take to be one's self that which does not immediately emanate from one's immediate being within, but, rather that which is generated on a surface without. This moment of imaginary identification, says Lacan, is characterized by a rivalry between the subject and the other because 'it is in the rival that the subject grasps himself as ego'. The mirror, thus, both produces a self and simultaneously splits it, both gives one a self and simultaneously introduces an otherness at the heart of it. The subject is able to overcome this alterity by (mis-)recognizing the other as oneself. This (mis-)recognition is facilitated by the signifier. With regard to Axel's narrative, this otherness is predominantly present in their relation with their specular self. He is stuck in a world tinted by the constant presence of the imaginary other – what Axel calls 'shadowy otherself' (28) – precisely because identification does not take place. What is more, Axel, as we have seen, comes across an excess which defines his relationship with his corporeality.

Axel's intense and narcissistic preoccupation with finding his self within coincides with an extreme solipsism that derails his imaginary identifications. This eventually dualizes his sense of self, resulting in the

---

18   Jacques Lacan, 'The Mirror stage as formative of the I function as revealed in psychoanalytic experience', 76.

bifurcation of the narrating *persona*: 'I could hear myself breathing in the mouthpiece, as if I were standing behind my own shoulder' (38). Elsewhere he perceives himself to be 'cloven in two' (13); he claims 'I had the sensation [...] of shifting slightly aside from myself, as if I were going out of focus and separating into two' (68) and that '[t]here sleeps in me another self' (106). He is by a spectral image of himself. In a word, he is haunted by that which he is so insistently obsessed with, namely, himself. The result is horrifying for Axel in that far from arriving at a kernel of true self, he encounters an extra, an uncanny supplement.

Duality: Spectral selves

Banville has always been interested in the twin motif in fiction. Both Gabriel Godkin and Gabriel Swan in *Birchwood* and *Mefisto*[19] yearn to find their missing twin since their incomplete self is played out in the fact that they see themselves whole only if they succeed in finding their missing siblings. In the Art Trilogy (*The Book of Evidence*, *Ghosts*, and *Athena*), the twin motif turns into the double motif. According to Elke D'hoker, in *The Book of Evidence*,[20] the figuration of the double primarily stems from the narrator's contradictory images of himself. The double, says D'hoker, polarizes his sense of self between 'a consistent pattern of superior versus inferior self-images', between the 'inner self' as opposed to the 'outer self'.[21] Caught in between this duality, says D'hoker, the narrator's 'real self' is in constant oscillation, resulting in the alienation of his 'true' identity.[22]

---

19   John Banville, *Mefisto* (London: Minerva, 1993).

20   John Banville, *The Book of Evidence* (New York: Vintage Books, 1989).

21   Elke D'hoker, *Visions of Alterity: Representations in the Works of Banville*, 176–7.

22   *Ibid.*, 178. D'hoker views the double's function as the deconstruction of the binary of true and false self. Furthermore, while in *Mefisto*, the Felix figure is the narrator's 'split-off evil self', in the case of *The Book of Evidence*, the Bunter figure eludes such a clear-cut differentiation (*Ibid.*, 138).

One of the most recurrent variations of the double in the trilogy *Eclipse*, *Shroud*, and *Ancient Light* is autoscopic vision. The latter is the experience during which the subject sees one's other self suddenly separate from oneself.[23] The self as such splits into both subject – the seer – and object – the seen. It is a fully fledged illustration of the crisis of self-perception as a unified being. Axel recounts an incident of having been beaten by a couple of thugs: 'Curiously, I recall the incident from outside, as if I had not been part of it, but a witness, rather, a bad Samaritan hanging back in the bushes. I see myself there, walking purposefully along a path with high laurel hedges on either side' (290). This autoscopic incident mirrors what Alexander Cleave experiences on stage in *Eclipse*. In the latter novel, the most distinctive instance of autoscopia occurs when Alex is on stage and 'suddenly everything shifted on to another plane and I was at once there and not there. It was like the state that survivors of heart attacks describe, I seemed to be onstage and at the same time looking down on myself from somewhere up in the flies.'[24] It is a weird moment at which he is irreparably divided into the actor and the spectator, in the *here* of acting and at once in the *there* of being in reality. Although what Axel experiences in *Shroud* does not take place while he is on an actual theatrical stage like Cleave in *Eclipse*, the way the experience is narrated by Axel, situates it within the theatrical. Key in Axel's description is 'witness' which defines Alex's relationship with the incident as a spectator *witnessing* scene.[25] Indeed, the word *scene* itself is reiterated on numerous occasions in Axel's depiction of his memories (19, 37, 46). More importantly, in so far as Axel's identity is stolen, (theatrical) acting and role-playing has been an inherent part of his life since he fled Europe and settled in America as Axel Vander. Ironically, role-play, in a sense, is more paramount in Axel's case than in the case of the actor-narrator of *Eclipse*.

23   D'hoker identifies several 'autoscopic instances' in the art trilogy and rightly claims that it is 'a familiar feature in all of Banville's novels' (*Ibid.*, 177) and demonstrates a clear-cut instance of the narrators' split (178).
24   John Banville, *Eclipse* (London: Picador, 2000), 89.
25   John Banville, *Shroud*, 290.

During the autoscopic incident both narrators' *Is* are separated from their acting body. This moment of self-separation creates in them an irremediable crack splitting them into a duality, which they are forever unable to stitch back into oneness.[26] Traditionally, Samuel Weber claims, 'the body [is] considered to be a self-contained vessel and as the vehicle of a no less self-contained soul.'[27] Nonetheless, in the theatrical mode 'the body no longer serves to demarcate the internal self-containment of the subject.'[28] The theatrical act, says Weber, is always 'an appeal to the other' qua audience. This constant appeal to the other creates an 'opening' towards the other that undermines the self-containment of the self as well as that of place. To put it differently, it cracks open the supposedly enclosed space of the individual self. Through its address to the other who is in another place and another time, the actor's act is no longer self-contained. As a result, 'the "individual" body is revealed to be a highly divisible container whose function [...] remains essentially indifferent to that which it contains.'[29] Secondly, Weber demonstrates that 'the ambivalent dynamics of repetition' on stage 'undercut[s]' and 'hollow[s] out' self-containment.[30] Through her entry into an 'alien body and soul' the individual undergoes a transformation during which she 'is no longer simply here, but here and there at once'. The simultaneous and paradoxical being 'here' and 'there'

---

26   Theatricality is a central motif in all of Banville's fiction. This is evident, for instance, in that the narrators constantly demonstrate their confusion in using the verb *to act*. Their *acts* in reality are often transformed into *acts* for an audience, thereby contaminating their every gesture, rendering it theatrical.

27   Weber traces the idea of the 'embodied individual' to early Modernity. According to Weber, specifically, 'since the Reformation', the body has functioned as 'the privileged site of the autonomous subject', Samuel Weber, *Theatricality as Medium* (Fordham: University Press. 2004), 317. The idea of the autonomous individual is intricately linked to the conception of the 'individual body', says Weber, in that the body 'serves to demarcate the internal self-containment of a subject' (Samuel Weber, *Theatricality as Medium*, 317).

28   *Ibid.*

29   *Ibid.*, 318.

30   *Ibid.*, 9.

'splits the oneness' of the self-contained individual 'by rendering (and rending) it repeatable.'[31]

As Weber emphasizes, what results from this division should not be mistaken for 'plurality'. That is to say, the individual is not divided between two self-contained 'selves' but should be seen as in constant oscillation between a duality. The result is 'the fracturing of the individual as such.'[32] It is not that the individual has now two selves, or masks, between which he is able to alternate. Rather, it is indicative of a fundamental rupturing of the self that destabilizes its coherence and self-identity. The narrator then is caught in a peculiar mode of 'self-abandonment' in which he does not 'merely cease to exist' but 'persist[s]' as a 'dividual', 'divided between life and death, spectator and actor, strange and familiar, entering an alien body and soul on the one hand, while on the other, remaining sufficiently detached to see [himself] taking leave of [his self].' Weber calls this an 'impossible situation' which 'splits the site itself, rendering it something like a ghost of itself, lacking an authentic place and a proper body.'[33]

The experience of the double brought about by autoscopia in *Shroud* has two consequences in Banville's aesthetics of the double in his later work. Firstly, the double does not so much demonstrate the evil persecuting other in the traditional sense of the *doppelganger*. Neither is the double related in the narrator's dealing with contrasting images of the self as D'hoker identifies in Banville's earlier work.[34] Rather, the autoscopic double in *Eclipse* is a literal duplication of the self as such, resulting in the undecidability of the location of the narrator's true self. It resonates most with what Derrida calls 'duplicity without an original.'[35] Secondly, the duality leads to the speaking 'I' becoming spectral. Axel's immediate sense of self as such is transformed into a ghost. His self is stretched between two ends, creating an opening at the core of his self-perception. The predicament posed by the double for

---

31   Samuel Weber, *Theatricality as Medium*, 41.
32   *Ibid.*
33   *Ibid.*, 42.
34   Elke D'hoker, *Visions of Alterity: Representations in the Works of Banville*, 176–7.
35   Jacques Derrida, *The postcard: from Socrates to Freud and beyond*, Alan Bass (trans.), (Chicago: The University of Chicago Press, 1987), 270.

Axel undermines his narcissistic search for his true self. That is to say, the double brings about the impossibility of accepting that the self is singular and that it can never be doubled. The fantasized double is an illusion that translates his inability of accepting to reconcile himself with his singularity. His interiority, in turn, is no longer housed inside, but oscillates between his body and a spectral shadow, a supplement.

Conclusion

Though he is fixated on finding the frame that can enable him to see reality as it is, Axel's narration always deranges that frame. His epistemological search in finding the true core of selfhood leads him to uncanny perceptions in which the real becomes unreal and his familiar self becomes foreign. Alongside *Eclipse*, *Shroud* is what Derrida calls 'the virtual space of spectrality' which distinguishes literature from the discourse of the traditional 'scholar'. In contrast to the latter, Banville's work is arguably an example of how 'theatrical fiction' and 'literature' is not concerned with 'the sharp distinction' between 'the real and the unreal, the actual and the inactual, the living and the non-living, being and non-being', but with the undecidable, indeterminate, and the ephemeral spectral.[36] In this sense, the authority of the narrators is undermined at the level of personal experience, that is, their most immediate and intimate interiority. The crisis *Shroud* represents is the crisis of subjectivity itself. It is an example of the way in which Banville's fiction aims at problematizing narrative subjectivity by presenting layered, divided narrators bereft of individual character.

36   Jacques Derrida, *Spectres of Marx: the state of the debt, the work of mourning, and the new international*, Peggy Kamuf (trans.), (London: Routledge, 1994), 11.

VIRGINIE GIREL-PIETKA

Looking for Oneself in Denis Johnston's Plays: Authorities in Crisis and Self-Authorship

ABSTRACT

Denis Johnston's plays all stage characters challenging authority, disowning the collective images put forward by the communities they belong to, and undoing canonical stage characters. As he wrote from the first decade of the Irish Free State up until the aftermath of World War II, Johnston was concerned about authority, laws, national policies and traditions as both conditions and threats to individual freedom and self-expression. The purpose of this chapter is to show that challenging authority is a way for his characters to shape their identity. It focuses on two plays which stage wars or rebellions, denouncing as nonsense some stifling attempts at creating collective identities, and granting the characters to create meaning for themselves. Self-authorship is presented as a way out of the crisis of identity which is triggered by authorities in crisis. Johnston's work also asserts the authority of the art of theatre to stage man's predicament.

Denis Johnston's plays all stage characters challenging authority, disowning the collective images put forward by the communities they belong to, and undoing canonical stage characters. As he wrote from the first decade of the Irish Free State up until the aftermath of World War II, Johnston was concerned about authority, laws, national policies and traditions as both conditions for and threats to individual freedom and self-expression. When the authority of various political powers is unsettled, people lose their bearings. Conventional ways of representing men and clear-cut relationships between them are to be questioned. The dramatist turned his back on the realistic trend which pervaded the Irish stage from the 1920s to the 40s, and explored theatrical means to stage man's inner doubts and fears, his never-ending quest for identity, his constant efforts to create and assert himself as an individual. This chapter will show that challenging authority is a way for Johnston's characters to shape their identity. The focus will be on two plays which stage wars or rebellions, denouncing as nonsense stifling attempts at creating collective identities, and granting the characters to right to create meaning for themselves. Johnston thus re-defined theatrical creation as a way of resisting conventions at a time when the Irish national stage was given to clichés. To the dramatist, self-authorship is a way out of the crisis of identity which is triggered by authorities in crisis. His work also asserts the authority of the art of theatre to stage man's predicament. That is why it should be granted more authority today.

The word 'authorities' may refer to the people in charge of enforcing the law in a country, like the State or the police, as well as to specific sets of rules, like the laws themselves. Authorities are supposed to keep society in order so they are in a crisis when their subjects are led to question or overthrow them, either because they are too weak and can no longer be taken seriously, or when they overstep their power and impose normative and actually crippling rules on individuals. In literature or any other art, such a crisis may also occur when canonical patterns are challenged. Soon after the Second World War, Irish dramatist Denis Johnston gave a radio talk on 'the present state of Irish letters' in which he deplored the narrow scope of Irish drama which was still portraying the 'peasant quality' at a time when the worldwide chaos should have inspired new inquiries into human nature. To him, Ireland's neutrality in the conflict had provided the Irish with a 'detached viewpoint' on the World War which made the country a privileged site to produce a new literature that would explore international human troubles rather than what he called 'the domestic problems of 1906'.[1] He had personally started questioning the authority of Irish drama in providing 'a mirror' either 'to the nation'[2] or 'to human nature'[3] some twenty years earlier. He kept on challenging it both in form and theme, staging characters who, just like their creator, are led to overthrow the ready-made images imposed on them so as to become their own authors. In the process, however, they emphasize the potential authority of theatre to stage man's predicament. The dramatist's personal experience as one of

---

1   Denis Johnston, *Collection of manuscripts kept at the University of Ulster* (Coleraine, 1947), B2.

2   Christopher Murray, *Twentieth-Century Irish Drama: A Mirror up to Nation* (Syracuse: University Press, 2000).

3   William Shakespeare, *Hamlet* (1603) (Oxford: Oxford University Press, 1987), 248.

the first war reporters to enter Buchenwald at the end of the war urged him on even more to look for new ways to do so. This chapter focuses on two plays which show that the characters' longing for self-expression and their individual quest for meaning, whether it be successful or not, were parts of an attempt to make the Irish stage authoritative again. We will first see how Johnston stages the limits of mimetic drama in *A Fourth for Bridge*, a one-act play written in 1947 and set during the Second World War.[4] This will lead to the poetics of the absurd, which is at work in that play, as a medium suited to such a topic. But because the dramatist claimed to be on an 'endless search for the best way of saying what [he] ha[d] to say',[5] he also explored other ways to make drama meaningful as we will see by focusing on *The Golden Cuckoo*,[6] a play in which the protagonist's theatrical behaviour allows him to outgrow his absurd condition.

Of costumes and men

In *A Fourth for Bridge*, Johnston stages soldiers from the various countries involved in the Second World War. The play is set on a military aircraft during the war but the soldiers do not know which countries they are flying over so it is never clear who is in command. A German officer first tries to identify another soldier thanks to his uniform:

GERMAN.   Excuse, please. What does this costume represent?
HUSSAR.   Oh, just bits and pieces, old boy. 4th Hussars, actually.
GERMAN.   Ach – the cavalry! It is the recognized costume of the English Hussars? Yes?
HUSSAR.   Well, I wouldn't know, actually. We're not fussy.[7]

4   Denis Johnston, *The Dramatic Works of Denis Johnston, Vol. 2* (Gerrards Cross: Colin Smythe, 1979), 163–93.
5   *Ibid.*, 9.
6   *Ibid.*, 195–276.
7   *Ibid.*, 172.

The German officer's English is a bit hesitant so he refers to the uniform as a 'costume', which turns it into a theatrical prop. In mimetic drama, that is to say when the action on the stage is said to imitate human action, a costume is supposed to convey information about a character, like his social background or his job. Here the soldier could not care less about what his uniform stands for. To him, it is nothing but a miscellaneous collection of items which does not make sense: 'just bits and pieces'. As the uniform is deprived of any specific meaning, mimesis does not work anymore. It is even openly shown as a trap later on when the soldiers disagree about the place they should head for. The pilot does not care about the others' plans as long as he believes that he is the only man able to pilot. That's why the others decide to pull the wool over his eyes thanks to the Air Force Type's uniform:

YANK:	Say, bud, you can fly the kite!
AIR FORCE TYPE *(horrified)*:	Me?
YANK:	You're in the Air Force, aren't you?
AIR FORCE TYPE:	Don't be silly. I'm an administrative type.
YANK:	Aw, who cares whether you can fly it or not? We'll put a bluff on this guy.[8]

The pilot is taken in by the deluding prop but the spectators cannot be. Thus the uniforms come to blur the characters' identities instead of revealing them. Similarly, the weapons that the soldiers carry cannot settle the struggle for power as they turn from hand to hand and become ineffective. The balance of power, or rather of powerlessness, is thus struck thanks to ineffective theatrical props that bring about a truce. Once everyone has been rendered harmless the characters move on to talk freely about their personal sense of not belonging in their respective nations:

ITALIAN *(suddenly)*:	[…] Mussolini makes me sick.
HUSSAR:	Good for you, old man. And you can throw in our far-flung Empire.
ITALIAN *(delighted)*:	You mean it?

8   Denis Johnston, *The Dramatic Works of Denis Johnston*, Vol. 2, 180.

HUSSAR:	Definitely. The farther it's flung the better.
AIR FORCE TYPE:	Bloody nuisance, if you ask me.
HUSSAR:	Glad you agree. Of course, I'm a conservative myself, so don't quote me.
AIR FORCE TYPE:	Of course not. You can speak freely. *(To the German)* How about Hitler, old boy? What's the form there?
GERMAN:	I will tell you what I think. I think Hitler is a crazy lunatic. That is what I think. *(Outbreak of pleased and surprised agreement.)*
ITALIAN:	But not as crazy as Mussolini. *(They argue together, giving exaggerated parodies of Fascist salute)*[9]

All of them are bored with their countries and ashamed of the people at their heads who have abused their authority so that their subjects no longer acknowledge it. Even England is not referred to as one of the allied forces but through its Empire, that is to say as another oppressor. When the hussar disowns the Empire, he adds that, being a Conservative, he should not, which makes it clear that the part he plays in society is at odds with his personal feelings. So when the Air Force Type comforts him that they can speak freely on that plane, he means that they are free from the national authorities they are expected to abide by. The German and Italian officers parody the well-known theatrical salutes of Hitler and Mussolini to suggest that those leaders actually stage their power but are about as devoid of meaning as the soldiers' uniforms. In fact the soldiers disown the official collective stance of their respective nations which they feel estranged from. Notwithstanding their various origins, they are all individuals longing for freedom of speech. The aircraft provides them with a utopian neutral space where they can stand up to national authorities. But the play then questions the possibility for such utopian escape in times of war.

9   Denis Johnston, *The Dramatic Works of Denis Johnston, Vol. 2*, 187–8.

Back to Nonsense

The soldiers' resistance fails to reach any positive outcome. Because they have wasted some time arguing, they are finally forced to make an emergency landing for lack of kerosene. They do not know where they are so they fear for their lives and finally have to disown the personal opinions they have just expressed:

> GERMAN: My friends, this is very serious. For a time I think we have forgotten ourselves. Now we're back to the war and to sanity. [...] In our quarreling we have all forgotten that we are enemies. But that is all over now. We must cease from quarreling and be at war once more.[10]

By neutralizing their national identities they have 'forgotten [them] selves', that is to say forgotten their official parts as each other's ally or enemy. The final reversal is presented as a return 'to sanity' although the German's lines sound insane. His contradictory sentences indeed reveal the nonsense of such labels: while quarreling they have forgotten to be enemies and now they should stop quarreling to be at war. In fact, the only way for them to get off that plane without being considered traitors is to agree on a pact of silence which stifles their personal views. They actually end up seeking protection under their respective national masks, adopting again the official discourses they have questioned:

GERMAN:	Heil Hitler! *(He jumps out)* [...]
YANK:	My country 'tis of thee! *(He jumps)*
ITALIAN:	Avanti. Vincere. Duce!
HUSSAR *(stopping him)*:	That's enough. *(The Italian jumps. To the Air Force Type)* Say something for England.
AIR FORCE TYPE:	Taxi! *(He jumps)*
HUSSAR:	Where did you say it was, old man?
RUSSIAN PILOT *(stuttering furiously)*:	It's P-p-p-p-p

---

10   Denis Johnston, *The Dramatic Works of Denis Johnston*, Vol. 2, 192.

HUSSAR: Don't tell me. I can guess. *(He shoves the pilot out, and turns and sits down with a burst of maniacal laughter. That is the end of this play.)*[11]

Although it negates individual opinions, allegiance to authority is paradoxically a question of life or death. Because of the war, the individuals are denied any personal authority or self-determination. The German and Italian soldiers repeat in earnest the fascist salutes they were making fun of. The other characters find it harder to reconcile themselves with their respective countries. The American's lyrical quote from a famous patriotic song celebrating the 'land of liberty' may be an ironical comment on the paradoxical necessity to forgo individual freedom and join the war against totalitarian regimes. As for the Royal Air Force type, his most unofficial reference to England – 'taxi!' – shows that his country no longer means anything to him. Even in so extreme a situation, there seems to be nothing to say about England, a burlesque debunking of the imperial power on the part of the Irish dramatist. But this collapse of values and landmarks is symptomatic of post-WW2 literature, in which man has to cope with 'the feeling of the absurd', as defined by Albert Camus in *The Myth of Sisyphus*, that is to say the feeling that he is definitely estranged from his environment as he no longer has 'any memory of a lost motherland nor hope for a promised land'.[12] Such a feeling is conveyed by characters who are torn between their aspiration to do something and their failure to fulfill their expectations. In *A Fourth for Bridge*, three characters are first looking for a fourth partner to play a game of bridge and forget about the war. Then all the characters argue about the place they should escape to. When they realize that they are not enemies at heart, they may reach a compromise. But the pilot's anger in the end, and his inability to utter the name of the place where they are finally landing, suggest that the various courses he has been forced to take have actually cancelled the trip: they have come back to where they started from, the Italian island of

---

11   Denis Johnston, *The Dramatic Works of Denis Johnston, Vol. 2*, 193.
12   Albert Camus, *Le Mythe de Sisyphe* (1942) (Paris: Gallimard, 1997), 20. My translation.

Pantelleria. The full-circle journey becomes a figure of nonsense, which explains the desperate laughter that concludes the play. This is an anti-denouement that contradicts Aristotelian drama insofar as the plot does not unfold to reach a final stage in which conflicts have been resolved and tension alleviated. It rather explores the poetics of the absurd which 'strives to express its sense of the senselessness of the human condition and the inadequacy of the rational approach by the open abandonment of rational devices and discursive thought'.[13] Writing just after the discovery of the concentration camps may account for the dramatist's need of such poetics to deride conventional drama's plan to portray man as an understandable and predictable creature, able to work his way to a logical ending. Although the characters in that play cannot escape national authorities, the dramatist stages the limits of mimetic drama and very efficiently outgrows them.

Such criticism characterizes all of Johnston's plays. Nevertheless he was not quite satisfied with the poetics of the absurd either, which he considered too bleak an outlook on man's destiny. In a lecture on his own work that he gave in the 1950s, he declared himself 'out of sympathy with contemporary trends such as the Theatre of the Absurd [...] which regards any didactic purpose as merely silly'.[14] This may explain why, along with *A Fourth for Bridge*, he also wrote plays staging forms of rebellion which the protagonist fights to the end so as to avoid sinking into a nonsensical world. Though faced with a general collapse of meaning, the Johnstonian hero never surrenders and never allows empty mainstream discourses to stifle his own voice, as we will see with *The Golden Cuckoo*. The play was first written and created at the Gate Theatre in 1939, but then revised and published together with *A Fourth for Bridge* in the same volume in 1954.

---

13   Martin Esslin, *The Theatre of the Absurd* (1961) (London: Methuen, 2001), 24.
14   Denis Johnston, Collection of manuscripts kept at Trinity College, Dublin, 51/23.

Theatre as a medium to create meaning

In *The Golden Cuckoo*, an old man has been hired by a newspaper to write an obituary. Having done his job, he expects to be paid for it. But it turns out that the man this obituary deals with is actually still alive. So the old man's paper cannot be published or remunerated. Feeling that he has been swindled, the old man sets out to demand justice. He is called Dotheright, although he is not aware of this at first as his name has been distorted and everyone calls him Duthery. A lawyer's clerk advises him to keep his self-control and avoid any row for fear he might never get another job. A taxi driver, who claims to have taken part in the 1916 Rising, protests that if everybody behaved so safely, there would have been no Rising in Dublin. So the old man is faced with the same alternative as Irish nationalists: should he work for justice to be done in a constitutional way or in a revolutionary way? He is ready to try both: 'We will begin with the constitutional. If it fails we will think again'.[15] The newspaper's boss refuses to pay his wages but offers to re-employ him in other jobs as compensation. Clear-sighted Dotheright will not be bribed and points out the nonsense of the situation: 'You mean that in consideration of your paper refusing to pay me what it owes me already, I am to continue to work for it'.[16] Although his counsel keeps telling him that he should 'have some sense' and not behave like a madman, the old man leaves the place still intent on getting his fair wages. He considers filing a lawsuit but is turned away because he cannot afford to pay the fees in advance, which embitters him even more as he feels justice favors the rich and has therefore become unfair.

On his way back he walks past the local post office where a ceremony is about to take place. The wife of an American senator has come over to inaugurate a plaque commemorating one of her ancestors who was the leader of a peasant rebellion against serfdom in England. Her tribute asserts the authority of historical rebels who laid the foundations of democracy:

15   Denis Johnston, *The Dramatic Works of Denis Johnston, Vol. 2*, 223.
16   *Ibid.*

'Where would we be today without our Rebels? Would we be living in a free land where the rule of laws guarantees the rights and liberties of even the humblest?'[17] Of course, her speech strikes Dotheright as not only legitimizing rebellion but also making it a responsibility for people to stand up for their rights. He realizes that those words of praise are devoid of meaning at present and takes it upon himself to make them meaningful again. He joins Mrs Tyler on the stage from which she is talking and calls for a new rebellion. The scene turns into a parody of 1916, with Dotheright announcing a new Democracy in which the people would be granted their natural authority again and treated fairly. Claiming the legacy of the Irish rebels, he breaks into the local post office to occupy it. Of course the scene is deflated because the village shop does not look like the GPO and Dotheright is not as famous as Patrick Pearse. The burlesque situation is further emphasized when the journalists cut the broadcast and *Parsifal* is played on the radio just as Dotheright pulls off the awning of the shop to wave it as a flag. Despite this burlesque debunking of the Grail hero, a parallel is drawn between the old man and Perceval, the chosen one whose epic quest for secret meaning is to be successful. Perceval is no Irish hero like Cuchulain, who in Yeats's words 'stalked through the Post Office' in 1916 as Pearse had 'summoned him to his side'.[18] Thus Dotheright is set in an international context of crisis and quest for meaning at the very moment when he claims his Irish legacy. Such an international outlook is precisely what Irish drama lacked at the time, Johnston thought, although Irish history should enable the country to set an example to the world:

> Now is it too much to ask that our own writers [...] should [...] turn their free intelligence [...] from the problems of the noble peasant to the question of human survival? We have always been political heretics, and having fought the cause of small nationalities during the Imperialism of the 19th century – and having won our point, thank God – is it too much now to hope that Ireland can once again fly in the face of world tendencies and produce the International man?[19]

17   Denis Johnston, *The Dramatic Works of Denis Johnston*, Vol. 2, 240.
18   William Butler Yeats, 'The Statues' (1938), *The Collected Poems of W. B. Yeats* (London: Wordsworth, 2000), 282.
19   Denis Johnston, *Collection of manuscripts kept at the University of Ulster*, B2.

To the dramatist, the 'International man' should be 'the man who knows where he comes from and is not ashamed of the fact, but does not allow that knowledge to influence his judgment as to what is best for the human race'.[20] That may account for the fact that he summoned the Grail hero to the side of his modern Irish rebel. Moreover Dotheright uses the material at hand to stage a theatrical rebellion, thus paying tribute to Irish rebels such as Pearse, who are remembered for their histrionic behaviour and eloquent speeches which have become landmarks in Irish history. He also reminds us what efficient use may be made of theatrical props when a dramatist decides to endow them with meaning, as in the early days of the Irish national theatre when the stage was to arouse in the audience a national sense of belonging.

Despite the fact that the ceremony aimed at celebrating rebels, Dotheright is arrested by the police, which suggests that even 1916 has been hijacked as a symbol of the nation: the Rising has become part of the official discourse and is no longer allowed to be the expression of a resistance to authority. The lawyer's clerk, the taxi driver and the members of the press fear that they might also be held responsible for the troubles. So they all testify that Dotheright is a madman, thus exemplifying once more the hypocrisy the old man rebelled against. The latter is therefore sent to the madhouse, and the play seems to reach a modern tragic ending in which the character feels like an outcast: 'I am betrayed. Oh Heaven – betrayed! [...] *(He grows very calm as he gazes upwards.)* Is there nobody up there?'[21] He tried his best to prove that the democratic values society stands on were still valid. But he finally feels estranged from a place where nonsense is granted authority while a fight for meaning is discarded as madness. The play therefore verges on the absurd, as another character very aptly sums it up: 'Every decent thing you do only turns round and kicks you in the pants'.[22] Because the world he lives in no longer provides

---

20 Denis Johnston, *Collection of manuscripts kept at the University of Ulster*, B2.
21 Denis Johnston, *The Dramatic Works of Denis Johnston, Vol. 2*, 263.
22 *Ibid.*

him with any authoritative landmark, Dotheright no longer believes in a responsible Creator or Supreme authority that man may abide by.

Yet, he is finally given a chance to overcome on his own that nonsensical world. He is finally released from the madhouse but once granted his freedom, he freely decides to go back there and forsake such company as provided by society: 'I am going back where I belong. I prefer the company there [...] they all fully recognize my official position'.[23] This is a happy ending of his own making as he finally feels rehabilitated: 'Justice is of little importance when you know that you have been right', he concludes, giving full meaning to his name.[24] What is more, the taxi driver gives him the medal of honour that he was awarded on account of his supposed involvement in the 1916 Rising: 'It's better for him to have it. I'll tell you no lie [...]. I never occupied a Post Office'.[25] The play also ends with a miracle. Although everyone made fun of Dotheright's desperate attempt to breed a cock in the hope that it would lay some eggs, the animal finally lays one. The medal and the miraculous egg show that the old man has definitely won his bet to create some new meaning for the people, animals, and objects he is to live among. In the process, he also reasserts the authority of the stage to create meaning out of unexpected, unrealistic or seemingly meaningless material, which allows Johnston to question once more the authority of mimetic drama.

The title page of *The Golden Cuckoo* describes it as 'an irrational comedy', implying that it should be possible for a play to depart from rationality and still provide man with new ways of realizing what is going wrong around him and how he could try to improve his condition. At a time when old landmarks no longer make sense, it is up to every one of us to look for new authoritative ones, and that is what set Denis Johnston on his constantly renewed search for an authoritative stage. He thus proved to be an 'international' dramatist, paying tribute to his histrionic legacy but turning his 'free intelligence [...] from the problems of the noble peasant

---

23   Denis Johnston, *The Dramatic Works of Denis Johnston*, Vol. 2, 273.
24   *Ibid.*, 274.
25   *Ibid.*, 272.

to the question of human survival' and to the authority of art in promoting it. The two plays under study appeared on the British and American stages and televisions in the 1940s and 1950s. One may wonder, however, why *A Fourth for Bridge* has never been produced in Ireland and *The Golden Cuckoo* was only given a short run at the Dublin Gate Theatre (1939) and a short revival at the Dublin Gaiety Theatre (1956). Now that we are faced again with a crisis that shakes the foundations of our society, that some people are rising to question totalitarian regimes, and that Ireland prepares to commemorate her 1916 rebels, let us hope Irish theatres will rediscover one of their own most authoritative offspring.

CHANTAL DESSAINT

'Suffer the little children...': Éilís Ní Dhuibhne's Strategies of Subversion

ABSTRACT

In the late 1990s and early 2000s, a series of television programs broadcast on both RTE and BBC television denounced cases of systemic abuse suffered by Irish children mainly between the 1930s and 1970s in Roman Catholic-run institutions and in the state childcare system like the Reformatory and Industrial Schools, generating a deep and lasting crisis of confidence. This essay argues that the Irish short story writer and novelist Éilís Ní Dhuibhne found in her work ways to express this deep trauma, confirming that fiction can often make up for the blanks left in historiography. The three works chosen in this study, *The Dancers Dancing* and two short stories, highlight the various strategies, mainly indirect and subversive, Ní Dhuibhne resorts to in order to challenge the authority of Church and State.

In the late 1990s and early 2000s, a series of television programs broadcast on both RTE and BBC television denounced cases of systemic abuse suffered by Irish children mainly between the 1930s and 1970s in Roman Catholic-run institutions and in the state childcare system like the Reformatory and Industrial Schools. This is the case of a documentary film series entitled *States of Fear*[1] in 1999, of *Primetime: Cardinal Secrets*[2] in 2002, or of O'Gorman's *Suing the Pope*[3] in 2003. These broadcasts, whose titles clearly challenge figures of authority, exposed the climate of secrecy and denial in the face of controversial accusations and the collusion between Church and State in what John Cooney terms an 'era of "kid glove" treatment

---

1   *States of Fear* is a documentary series produced by Mary Raftery. It was broadcast on RTÉ between April and May 1999.
2   *Primetime: Cardinal Secrets* was also broadcast on RTÉ in 2002.
3   *Suing the Pope* was broadcast on the BBC.

of the Catholic Church by gardai [...] who for decades did not think it
their job to interrogate churchmen accused of abusing innocent children'.[4]
Similarly, government inspectors turned a blind eye to the chronic beatings, rapes and humiliation suffered by children in Irish Catholic schools
and orphanages as the nine-year long Commission to Inquire into Child
Abuse released in 2009 revealed.

Even if the media widely contributed to exposing those scandals and
provided victims with the opportunity to voice their sufferings, the fact
remains that the trauma lies deep in the Irish psyche and may need other
forms of utterance than verbal testimony. It is often in literature that the
unsaid and unsayable find their true means of expression, because fiction
can often make up for the blanks left in historiography. This essay will
argue that this is the case with Irish short story writer and novelist Éilís Ní
Dhuibhne, born in Dublin in 1954, who has been described as a literary
ethnologist.[5] She is particularly well known for work that often combines
modern narratives and folk tales, thus providing a reverberating perspective
on the present and the past. As Caitriona Moloney underlines, her 'respect
for history, as well as her awareness of its omissions, allows her to create
fiction that re-imagines women's often silent historical record'.[6] Indeed,
the writer's attention has often been drawn to the plight of women and
children as voiceless victims of abuse. In a 2001 written correspondence
with Jacqueline Fulmer, she declared: 'I am in fact quite critical of the
Catholic Church, of its attitude to women, of its cruelty to Irish children

4   John Cooney, 'Collusion of Church and State Led to Huge Loss of Faith',
     Irish Independent (27 November 2009), <www.independent.ie/irish-news/
     collusion-of-church-and-state-led-to-huge-loss-of-faith>.
5   'I've recently been described as a literary ethnologist, partly, I think, thanks to my
     background in folklore ethnology. [...] I read wildly in the field of ethnology generally
     and collected plenty of ethnographical lore – especially during my years as a collector
     on the Urban Folklore Project, 1979–80, and during my year studying folklore in the
     university of Copenhagen, 1978–9. I'm interested in the detail of life: how people
     inter-relate'. Christine St Peter, 'Negotiating the Boundaries, an Interview with Éilís
     Ní Dhuibhne', *Canadian Journal of Irish Studies* 32.1. (2006), 70.
6   Caitriona Moloney, 'Exile in Ní Dhuibhne's Short Fiction', in Rebecca Pelan, ed.,
     Éilís Ní Dhuibhne, Perspectives (Galway: Arlen House, 2009), 107.

in its orphanages and schools in the past. My feeling is however that the whole of Irish society colluded with all of this ghastly misbehaviour, that the society had the church it wanted. It was at certain stages a deeply sadistic, cruel society, of which the Catholic Church was a part.'[7] The word 'colluded' clearly indicates that, for the writer, Church and society are both to be held responsible for the repression of the individual, and are part of 'the social and cultural web that enmeshed everybody', to quote from one of the author's short stories.[8] This collusion was mainly the result of the nationalist ideology propounded by de Valera's conservative government with its emphasis on 'the special position' of the Catholic Church as stated in the 1937 Constitution of Ireland. The constitution 'attempted to incorporate Catholic social principles into the everyday life of the people [and] seemed to indicate that it was the government's intention to turn its part of Ireland into a homogeneous Catholic state'.[9] The term 'homogeneous' points to the process of standardization operated on both a political and religious level with all its pernicious side-effects. The three works chosen in this study, a novel and two short stories, will highlight how Ní Dhuibhne uses fiction in order to expose the detrimental consequences of this agenda. As we shall see, the strategies she resorts to in order to challenge the authority of Church and State are mainly indirect and subversive strategies that range from irony, the use of a colloquial language, to tropic transfer.

Her novel *The Dancers Dancing*[10] is a bildungsroman that deals with the linguistic stay of an adolescent girl who, like hordes of teenagers before and since, was sent to the Gaeltacht in 1972 in order to improve her practice of Irish. The rehabilitation of the Irish language was indeed a fundamental

7   Jacqueline Fulmer, *Folk Women and Indirection in Morrison, Ní Dhuibhne, Hurston, and Lavin* (Aldershot: Ashgate, 2007), 179.

8   Éilís Ní Dhuibhne, 'The Moon Shines Clear, the Horseman's Here', in David Marcus, ed., *Phoenix Irish Short Stories 2003* (London: Phoenix, 2003), 135.

9   David George Boyce, *Nationalism in Ireland* (London and New York: Routledge, 1991), 352.

10   Éilís Ní Dhuibhne, *The Dancers Dancing* (Belfast: The Blackstaff Press, 1999).

part of de Valera's vision of Irish nationhood[11] and though a champion of
the language herself,[12] Ní Dhuibhne exposes in an ironical way at the very
beginning of the novel how Irish was used by the State to mould its citizens or subjects at a very early stage: 'Orla has a special linguistic mission
in life, and it is not the mission of every good citizen, which is, according
to the teachers in her school, to speak Irish. It is rather to stamp out every
trace of local English dialect from her surroundings, rather as Church and
State in Ireland have recently been aiming to eliminate sex from the Irish
way of life' (12).

The parallel established between language and sex suggests that the
policy implemented by State and Church partakes of an indoctrination
aiming more at fashioning teenagers into chaste Catholic citizens[13] speaking
a standardized version of Irish than at developing their proficiency in the
language or helping them discover its beauty and variety. Indeed there is no
place for diversity in this linguistic program: although Orla is able to speak
the Donegal Irish spoken at home by her father, she refrains from doing
so in public, knowing that anything deviating from the 'shoddy, modern,
inaccurate Dublin Irish' (34) would make a laughing stock of her. Orla is
thus faced with a sort of insoluble double bind and is torn between two
figures of authority and two loyalties: on the one hand, she has to fulfil the
mission imposed by State and Church by speaking this 'inaccurate Dublin
Irish' and on the other hand, she feels that by doing so she is betraying her
loyalty to her father's Donegal roots. She is all the more tempted to comply

11   At the 1937 Fianna Fáil Árd Fheis he declared: 'The only way to hold our nation [...]
     is by securing our language as the language of the Irish people' (Michele Dowling,
     '"The Ireland that I would have" De Valera and the creation of an Irish national image',
     20th-century Contemporary History, De Valera and Fianna Fáil, *History Ireland*
     5. 2. (1997), 37–42, <www.historyireland.com/20th-century-contemporary-history>.
12   She has written several novels for children and plays in Irish, as well as an article
     entitled 'Why Would Anyone Write in Irish?', in Ciaran Mac Murchaidh, ed., *'Who
     Needs Irish?': Reflections on the Importance of the Irish Language Today* (Dublin:
     Veritas Publications, 2004), 70–82.
13   The notion of chastity is indeed inseparable from de Valera's vision of a pious rural
     nation with 'comely maidens dancing at the cross roads' as mentioned in what came
     to be called his 'dream speech' delivered on St Patrick's Day 1943.

with the State and Church agenda, however, as she is part of an educational system that is sexually prejudiced: 'Knowing too much is a burden Orla has been given to carry because she is a girl. Girls read and learn and in consequence know too much. [...] Now on top of everything else she knows languages: tongues – or at least myriad dialects' (34).

Since girls are not supposed to be too intelligent and to show off their knowledge, Orla chooses not to speak those 'myriad languages'. But then, she is faced with a conundrum that she is at a loss to solve when she hears the baffling message of a religious figure of authority: 'Comprehension of myriad tongues is one of the gifts of the Holy Ghost [...]. Some understand many tongues and some speak many tongues. You would think, Orla thought, when she heard the gaunt, thief-eyed Bishop McQuaid citing those words, that the same people must do both. But no' (34). The expression 'gaunt, thief-eyed Bishop McQuaid' is of course very significant. At the time (in 1972), Orla could not have been aware that this supposedly reliable religious figure was covering up paedophile clerics whose molestations he chose not to refer to the police, thus allowing hundreds of other children to suffer sexual abuse. But on a very instinctive level, as the term 'thief-eyed' shows, she is able to sense contradictions in adult figures of authority, which prompts her to adopt a safer behaviour rather than rely on their words. Ní Dhuibhne's denunciation of institutional hypocrisy is all the more subtle as the situation is seen from the point of view of a young teenager who does not have enough maturity or hindsight to analyse the situation properly. Ní Dhuibhne thus exposes in an indirect way the detrimental effect of an educational agenda that ends up puzzling gifted schoolgirls like Orla, and incites them to conform, to join the dull and meek lot rather than stand out and show their skills.[14]

In such an educational surrounding, open-mindedness is certainly not a virtue that children in general are expected to develop; this is symbolized by

14   Her classmates have perfectly assimilated this linguistic standardization and reject any non-conformist behaviour. Orla remembers how a very intelligent, mature and confident girl named Mary Darcy came back from Connemara 'with an accent fit to catch a whale' and how 'other children laughed in her face', obliging her 'to cave in and revert to the language of her peers' (34).

the windows of the Irish college in Donegal which are so high that nobody can see the outside world: 'These windows, the windows of every national school in Ireland, have been designed expressly to prevent children looking out of them' (20). It is even more significant that the religious statues of the Virgin and the Sacred Heart contained in the classroom should have been placed carelessly on windowsills 'as if someone had taken them and plonked them down anywhere at all' (19). The statue of the Sacred Heart is even 'turned back to front, looking out of the window instead of into the room' (20), as if the classroom windows served as shop windows for religion, and the school was just a branch of the Church destined to promote a message more concerned with decorum (or decoration) than with faith.

However, those adolescents on holiday in the Gaeltacht will be provided with an opportunity to get round the moral and intellectual conformism imposed by Church and State. As the novel ironically shows, two elements in particular enable them to challenge and subvert this educational program: nature and dancing. Nature provides them with the opportunity to get into contact with their own wildness as is emphasized at the beginning of the novel with the epigraph, a four-stanza poem by Hopkins entitled 'Inversnaid' which focuses on a 'darksome burn' and epitomizes the notion of wildness and liberation:

> What would the world be, once bereft
> Of wet and wildness? Let them be left,
> O let them be left, wildness and wet;
> Long live the weeds and the wilderness yet.[15]

The burn plays a central role in the novel: five chapters respectively entitled 'The Burn scene 1', 'The Burn scene 2' etc. punctuate the narrative and underline Orla's personal initiation into womanhood. Indeed, it is after the fifth contact with the water of the burn that she has her first period and is at the same time confronted with the discovery of tiny skulls which will turn out to be the remains of babies killed by an ancestor convicted

---

15   Gerard, Manley Hopkins, *Poems of Gerard Manley Hopkins* (New York: Oxford University Press, 1960).

of infanticide. The fifth scene also marks for her a significant act of transgression: while walking along the burn she allows herself to pronounce the
word 'fuck' as well as all the taboo words she knows (201). By doing so she
challenges moral and educational constraints but also religious and gender
ones since 'the very worst words, concerning the devil and sex, were left for
the exclusive use of extremely angry or extremely uncivilised men' (201).

The notion of transgression is in fact metaphorically announced at
the very beginning of the novel: in the first chapter of the novel entitled
'The map', the narrative voice describes an airplane view of the scenery
where the river is presented as 'endlessly beginning and endlessly ending'
(2); the little adolescent figures seen from above are said to be 'on their
little journeys, back and forth and up and down and in and out, until they
move out of the picture altogether, over the edge, into the infinity of after
the story' (2). This expression 'over the edge' clearly underlines how the
natural setting inseparable from this linguistic stay provides the teenagers
with the opportunity to transgress the constricting social and moral norms
imposed on them during their stay and to challenge the figures of authority
that enforce those norms: when Headmaster Joe announces in a threatening voice that no teenager is to play in the burn and accuses Orla of having
washed her clothes there (208–9), she is relieved to learn that he is not
aware of the numerous walks she and her friends have taken along the river.

The second element that allows the teenagers to renegotiate the discursive construct that imprisons them is the act of dancing. As Christine
St Peter beautifully demonstrates in her article entitled 'Burn, Road, Dance',
this constraint is part of a social discourse that aims at moulding the teenagers' very bodies: '[...] the individual body is also, and importantly, part of
a larger social weave. The promise of the *bildungsroman* and its sub-genres
[...] comes up against the social discipline that requires that everybody be
tailored into the social fabric'.[16] Irish dancing is indeed part of the program
and its complicated pattern – it is compared to 'having to do a Euclid theo-
rem with your legs' (48) – can first appear as yet another form of constraint.

16   Christine St Peter, 'Burn, Road, Dance', in Rebecca Pelan, ed., *Éilís Ní Dhuibhne,
      Perspectives* (Galway: Arlen House, 2009), 43.

But once they have mastered the required discipline, they reach a kind of trance, so that the very dance that is supposed to imprison their teenaged bodies and inscribe them in a prescribed geometric pattern paradoxically becomes a territory of liberation and expansion. This liberating pattern is described as an epiphany: 'The Irish college dances […], every step in time to the music, every movement perfect. It's Carrickmacross lace, it's the river running, it's the salmon leaping, it's the ploughman ploughing, it's the spinner spinning, the boatman sailing, the fellow fishing, the fire flaming. It's the dancers dancing' (235–6). By stressing the powerful link between the dance and 'the river running', as well as with ancestral activities like spinning and fishing, this passage reconnects the teenagers with the past and proposes a renegotiation of the social fabric that is no longer an entrapping net. The dance becomes a place where everything is deterritorialized, as is suggested by the boisterous rhythm of the sentence and by the merging of the different activities. The social network thus recreated by the syntax appears as a liberating one because it is definitely linked with the rhythm of nature ('it's the river running, it's the salmon leaping'). So *The Dancers Dancing* is more than just a *bildungsroman* about adolescent girls: it also proposes a subversive message where the linguistic and cultural program contrived by Church and State in order to tailor those teenagers into good Catholic citizens turns out to be their very means of liberation and provides them with the opportunity to challenge the figures of authority that endorse it.

With 'Sex in the Context of Ireland',[17] it is the physical and moral abuse endured by children in orphanages in the 1920s which is denounced by Bella, a prostitute who works in the district of Mountjoy Square. If the style of this short story is completely different from the previous novel, as the first-person narrator's colloquial and cheeky style is transcribed phonetically, the issue raised is nonetheless poignant due in particular to all the silences that punctuate Bella's narrative. Bella and her sister and brother were raised at the Good Shepherd Convent which she renames 'the Good

17   Eilis Ni Dhuibhne, 'Sex in the Context of Ireland', *The Pale Gold of Alaska* (Belfast: The Blackstaff Press, 2000), 109–33.

shagging Shepherds' as she personally suffered sexual abuse from a nun. With a blasphemous kind of humour, she tells about the first time the nun led her into the coalhouse:

> Once [Sister Assumpta] gave me a cut of bread and sugar after finding me crying in the middle of the night and trying to scale the ten-foot wall [...] after Mother Christopher of the Holy Angels had been havin a go at my holy backside with her holy mother and father of a bamboo cane. [...] Instead of going to the hall, where they usually did the beatings [...] she turned and went into the coalhouse. [...]
> She had me feeling [her breasts] in no time at all.
> Janey Mack! Well ye probably know yerself what big boobs feel like. Bird's Jelly Deluxe.
> Meanwhile she was into my drawers.
> It wasn't as bad as the hidins. [...]
> I don't fancy Bird's Jelly Deluxe to this day. But she was clean – apart for the coal acourse. (114–16)

The means chosen here to denounce the physical abuse is a blasphemous humour where religion is clearly laughed at (with the terms 'my holy backside with her holy mother and father of a bamboo cane'); but behind this humour, what makes Bella's testimony moving is the more subtle emotion that can be perceived behind the unsaid and the unsayable. Indeed, we cannot help being moved by Bella's way of diverting emotional issues and transferring them onto details (like the reference to the jelly or the nun's cleanliness) rather than on the true trauma she experienced at that moment. Besides, the term 'hiding' and its double meaning (both the act of beating someone and the act of concealing) exposes the hypocrisy of the Catholic Church as well as the collusion of the local people who did hear the cries of the beaten children but did nothing to denounce their ill-treatment: 'Women and men on their way to Mass or the Novena up in Gardiner Street. They woula heard the screams of [my brother]. [...] Nobody paid a blind bit of heed. I do think [...] that the people of Dublin like that sound, the sound of poor childer bein beaten to death' (113). This is also why Bella's speech is full of silence. When she mentions her brother's and sister's death – her brother was beaten to death at the age of six – she merely says: 'I never told anyone what I knew about me brother [...] He didn't know to keep his mouth shut. That was a rule of theirs when they were at ye, you were supposed to keep quiet. [...] Me sister died of natural causes. That is to say hunger. Aided and abetted by other things but I'll say no more' (112–13). Highlighting the silence and self-censorship behind Bella's speech is a way for Éilís Ní Dhuibhne to involve the readers' participation by making them imagine the missing parts in the prostitute's story. Besides, the fact that Bella's speech should be transcribed phonetically obliges the readers to *listen* to Bella's speech rather than to read it: 'I can hear ye sayin now, talk proper, talk so we don't halfta strain our delicate ears to listen and to understand what it is ye're sayin. Well I won't and if yez can't understand it's your loss' (111).[18]

This emphasis on silence, orality and on sound metaphors also aims at subverting the power of the *written* word imposed by Church and State, and this is why Ní Dhuibhne deliberately chooses to feature a cheeky, outspoken prostitute as a spokeswoman in this short story. As in *The Dancers Dancing*, Éilís Ní Dhuibhne draws our attention onto the power of language and the way it can be perverted for political and ideological reasons. When referring to the general 'hibernization' of the nation and the return to gaelicized names that was the hallmark of de Valera's government, Bella makes it clear that this linguistic purge necessarily bodes ill for her and her friends since the return to a 'pure' language goes hand in hand with the return to a 'pure' nation where prostitutes like her are certainly not welcomed:

> 'Ireland is free. The Dublin Metropolitan Police is now the Gawrda Sheehauna.'
> 'Them Irish names is always bad news.'
> 'Especially for the like of us Irish means crawthumping.'[19] (120–1)

18   The importance of hearing is also emphasized by Bella's choice of a musical metaphor when she evokes the way children were ill-treated: 'All I'll say about it is this. The sound. The blow of wood or leather on children's skin. That was the music of the good shepherd' (112).

19   Éilís Ní Dhuibhne's denunciation of this perversion of language is not devoid of a certain self-derisive tone, as is shown by Bella's comment on names starting with a 'Ni-something', a name frequently found among the visitors of the Legion of Mary: 'A lot of them had names in Irish. Weird. Nee this Nee that. Long noses thin mouths big hair spotty skin. That's what Nee means if you want my opinion' (128). A similar ironical comment was already present in *The Dancers Dancing*: 'People have clownish

Far from seeing the Irish language as a return to something more congenial
and authentic, Bella and the other prostitutes feel threatened by it. Bella
even considers finding refuge in England because this country seems safer
to her as it does not define itself as a 'Free State'. The passage clearly underlines the Orwellian absurdity of a language policy ruled by a nationalist
ideology where words like 'free' end up signifying the opposite of their
original meaning:

> 'I'm going to England'
> 'To England?' [...]
> 'It's not a Free State, is it?'
> 'No.' [Mrs Catskin] shook her head. (133)

Bella and her friends are aware that what is at stake is the desire not
only to purify the language but also to purify the mores of the Irish nation.
Mrs Catskins, Bella's procuress, declares: 'It's the Free Staters [...] Them
and the Legion of Mary! [...] They're religious' [...] 'Religion is a dangerous thing' (133). Indeed, the emerging nationalism of that period tended
to see prostitution as the legacy of colonialism and this political movement found in Catholic conservatism, particularly with the help of the
Legion of Mary founded and led by Frank Duff, an ally to carry out a
program of moral reform. The Legion of Mary received the co-operation
of Dublin Police Commissioner, General William Richard English Murphy,
a collusion that led to the closing down of brothels in Monto, the Dublin
red light district, in 1925, as is corroborated by Bella's testimony:[20] 'Only
a few weeks later, one Saturday night, [Frank Murphy] had the whole
place cordoned off be the police and raided. After a hundred years.

---

names. [...] Bally this and Ballyslapdashinmuckerishthat. Irish restores to them dignity
and elegance. So [Orla] thinks, happily abandoning her own name in English, Orla
Crilly, and calling herself Órla Nic Giolla Chrollaigh' [...] 'She thinks [her name]
looks difficult, and important' (31).

20   Following a police raid on 12 March 1925, the campaign ended with 120 arrests and
the closure of the brothels. The financial viability of the district had already been
seriously undermined by the withdrawal of soldiers from the city following the
Anglo-Irish Treaty in 1921 and the establishment of the Irish Free State in 1922.

Five hundred years' (132). It is not only prostitution that the legion and the police are seeking to eradicate but also centuries of city life in an attempt to rewrite Ireland's social and moral history. Indeed Frank Murphy, a fanatical visitor of The Legion of Mary (his name being an ironical mixture of Frank Duff and Willam Murphy), professes not only to wipe prostitution out of the country but also to 'eliminate all sexual activity in Ireland'. He wants Ireland to be 'the purest, holiest, most chaste nation in the world' (131). As a subversive counterstrategy to oppose this dangerous policy that aims to repress the sexuality of a whole people, the prostitute's individual and colloquial voice is thus made to stand out. Her testimony appears as an appropriate medium to counterbalance the dangerously nationalist and life-denying discourse spread by so-called figures of authority like Frank Murphy: Bella clearly exposes the hypocritical attitude of a man who obviously relishes hearing the prostitutes' stories and whom she describes as a 'soft-spoken oul pervert [...] barefaced liar and hypocrite' (132).

If Bella is critical of this ideological coalition and openly expresses her opinion in a cheeky, outspoken way in spite of self-censored passages, it is not always the case with all of Éilís Ní Dhuibhne's heroines. Another short story entitled 'The Catechism Examination' published in 1988[21] shows how a mature female narrator remains unable to articulate her trauma years after witnessing the cruel behaviour of a school mistress to a schoolgirl. Here, the author no longer resorts to irony, humour and derision as in the first two works. Her strategy rather relies on the unsaid and the use of metaphors in order to expose in an even more oblique way the brutality of the collusion of Church and State when applied to school life.

The short story relies on a central metaphor present in the incipit where the narrator is reminded by the blurred image of a hedge on a foggy

---

21   Eilis Ni Dhuibhne, 'The Catechism Examination', *Blood and Water* (Dublin: Attic Press. 1988), 91–100. Also published in *Midwife to the Fairies* (Dublin: Attic Press, 2003), 44–51. In her interview with Christine St Peter, Ní Dhuibhne underlines the fact that this short story was published before the media gave a large coverage to child physical abuse: 'There has been a great deal of exposure of this recently, but when I wrote "The Catechism Examination" one heard nothing about it' (Christine St Peter, 'Negotiating the Boundaries', 72).

day of a lesson she attended when she was a schoolgirl. During a lesson two days before the catechism examination, the school mistress behaved in a particularly cruel manner to a girl named Mary Doyle. Miss O'Byrne had spent the three previous months hammering the two hundred and thirty questions on the syllabus into the children's brains. But Mary Doyle, who was mentally retarded,[22] failed to remember the correct answers. The school mistress punished her, slapping her fingers twenty-three times with a ruler, until Mary collapsed on the ground. When Father Harpur came on the examination day, he only asked the pupils to recite the Lord's Prayer, and with a mild tone made them promise to say it every day for the rest of their lives. The priest reminded them that Jesus Christ said 'Suffer the little children to come unto him', a sentence that can be interpreted in an ironical way, knowing the ordeal Mary has gone through. This sentence denounces in a subversive way how religion and school collude to abuse all those children who do not conform to the intellectual standard required by institutions. The priest's words also contain paedophiliac overtones, as is suggested by the narrator who, although she tells her mother that the priest was nice, instinctively mistrusts him and adds: 'But I do not like the priest. I do not like him at all' (99). As Ní Dhuibhne points out in an interview, even if the priest did not actually beat the girl, he is a Pontius Pilate-like figure who is aware of 'the horrendously crazy, frenetic activity coming up with the First Communion' and who silently condones the school mistress's cruelty: '[He] keeps his hands clean. [...] He just comes in at the end and smiles, and doesn't get involved in any way. But he must know what's going on. He turns a blind eye'.[23]

The examination episode is mentioned no more, and is followed by a short final paragraph stating that the pupils got their afternoon off and that the narrator and her mother went to a Spring Show, a visit that she remembers with delight. This epiphanic note, however, seems to be in

22 That girl may simply have suffered from dyslexia, a disorder that was not diagnosed at the time, as Ní Dhuibhne mentions in an interview: Caitriona Moloney and Helen Thompson, 'Éilís Ní Dhuibhne', in *Irish Women Writers Speak out: Voices from the Field* (Syracuse, NY: Syracuse University Press, 2003), 114.

23 *Ibid.*, 113.

contradiction with the painful incident that has just taken place and that is hardly commented upon by the narrator. The last sentence only mentions that 'it was a calm April day. Dull and poignant with the promise of summer. Like today' (100). In fact, here again, it is up to the reader to provide the narrator's missing thoughts. As Anne Fogarty underlines in her preface to *Midwife to the Fairies* in reference to that short story: '[Éilís Ní Dhuibhne's] fictions urge us to read between the lines, to become alert to gaps and omissions and to supply the broken links between seemingly unconnected events. Many of [her] stories hinge, for example, on unspoken realizations, as in the instance of the oblique memories in "The Catechism Examination", which recall the cruel treatment by her teacher and peers of a young girl, considered to be slow and different'.[24]

The obliqueness of the story is centered on the reference to the dull and foggy day and to the hedge mentioned both at the beginning and at the end of the short story, framing it as it were. The fog is indeed here to symbolize the blurring of landmarks, the confusion entailed in the narrator's mind by the school mistress's vicious behaviour. The catechism lesson marked for her a turning point when her trust in religious and school institutions was definitely shaken, even if she does not acknowledge it openly. Her very first sentence 'SOMETHING ABOUT the way the garden hedge looks today gives me a feeling I would have difficulty in describing' suggests that the clue is to be found in that very hedge. The hedge is described in the following paragraph as a quiet, neat line, separating the garden from the road (91), just as the lines drawn by the wall and the sea are said to be 'just lines, grey and dark and black'. This insistence on demarcation lines and limits constitutes in fact the key symbolism of the short story, and it is indeed in terms of limits that the narrator speaks of her school mistress just before mentioning the horrible lesson: 'I don't like Miss O'Byrne, but I have always trusted her not to go too far. She is an adult, she knows the limits' (95). On that particular day, Miss O'Byrne however transgressed the limits of severity, showing herself needlessly cruel, and that is why the narrator as a girl can no longer look up to adults as figures of authority. It is

---

24   Anne Fogarty, Preface to *Midwife to the Fairies* (Dublin: Attic Press, 2003), x.

to be noticed however, that the narrator's feelings of loss and disillusion as well as the implicit criticism they contain are not articulated. They are not even consciously realized by the girl, as is suggested by the reference to the 'strange' feeling which she 'would have difficulty in describing, although [she] recognizes it very well'. All the things that have not been articulated are thus indirectly expressed through the image of the hedge on a foggy day.[25] Another short story entitled 'The Blind' and published twenty-four years later in *The Shelter of Neighbours* also contains an implicit denunciation of the unhealthy attitude of a priest to two schoolgirls enrolled to collect money for St Lucia's School for the Blind. The priest sits the narrator's friend on his lap while repeatedly fetching sweets in his 'deep, dark soutane pocket' to give to the girls (264). Nothing more explicit is mentioned and it is up to the reader to fill in the gaps left by the narrative.[26]

As we can see, metaphors clearly play a key role in Éilís Ní Dhuibhne's way of writing because they provide a language substitute, a tropic transfer of meaning and constitute a receptacle where meaning is deferred. As such, they play an important part in her strategies of indirection because they are an appropriate means to circumvent the insidious ideological manipulation of language operated by Church and State. In an interview with Jacqueline Fulmer, the author explains why they constitute in her eyes a privileged mode of expression: 'Metaphor or symbol can distance writer and reader from an idea while simultaneously deepening its impact and meaning. [They] carry resonance like music. They speak to us in a language we understand in our hearts and imaginations but may not find possible to translate'.[27]

The image of the hedge is all the more powerful as it contains a metatextual message: it invites the reader to go beyond the limits of the text in

25 The term 'hedging' is also used by linguists like Robin Lakoff. It refers to a technique that consists in weakening the act of language and disguising it through strategies of indirection. Robin Lakoff, *Language and Woman's Place* (New York: Harper and Row, 1975), 53–6.

26 Éilís Ní Dhuibhne, *The Shelter of Neighbours* (Belfast: Blackstaff Press, 2012), 264.

27 Jacqueline Fulmer, *Folk Women and Indirection in Morrison, Ní Dhuibhne, Hurston, and Lavin* (Aldershot: Ashgate, 2007), 180–1.

order to find the implicit message, just as the river in *The Dancers Dancing* went over the edge of the story. In this respect, the author's way of writing can be seen as an illustration of Virginia Woolf's definition of the feminine sentence, which she describes as being 'of a more elastic fibre than the old, capable of stretching to the extreme, of suspending the frailest particles, of enveloping the vaguest shapes, [a sentence more concerned with] the atmosphere of the table rather than [with] the table; [with] the silence rather than [with] the sound'.[28] Éilís Ní Dhuibhne's way of writing is all the more feminine as it rehabilitates both the power of orality and of metaphors. Indeed, just like orality, metaphors contribute to reassert the authenticity of the female *voice*, since they re-establish a spontaneous link with speech, as Béatrice Didier underlines in *L'Écriture-femme*: 'Writing will no longer appear to women as a form of betrayal of speech if they know how to create a writing that conjures up the flow of speech with its jolts, its ruptures and its cries. The image in feminine writing spontaneously renews the link with oral tradition and enables the written text to remain spoken or sung'.[29]

By choosing to concentrate on three female characters, Orla, Bella, and the female narrator in 'The Catechism Examination', Éilís Ní Dhuibhne manages to rehabilitate the female voice and to assert the necessity for women to resist the insidious indoctrination operated by Church and State, particularly in matters of language and sexuality as we saw with *The Dancers Dancing* and 'Sex in the Context of Ireland'. However, if her pungent irony holds up to ridicule religious and political figures of authority, she is also careful not to fall into the trap of a systematic accusation of those figures. Her writings show that the blame is also to be laid on all those who chose

---

28   Virginia Woolf, 'Review of *Revolving Lights* by Dorothy Richardson', in Deborah Cameron, ed., *The Feminist Critique of Language* (London; New York: Routledge, 1990), 72–3.

29   'Écrire n'apparaîtra plus à la femme comme une sorte de trahison par rapport à la parole si elle sait créer une écriture telle que le flux de la parole s'y retrouve, avec ses soubresauts, ses ruptures et ses cris. [...] L'image dans l'écriture féminine renoue tout spontanément avec la tradition orale et permet au texte écrit de demeurer parlé ou chanté'. Béatrice Didier, *L'Écriture-femme* (Paris: P.U.F., 1981), 32. My translation.

to be deaf and blind and thus condoned the abuse, from the passers-by who heard the cries of children being beaten in orphanages to the prostitutes' clients who dutifully went back to 'their holy wives and the Rosary' as Bella says (131).[30] As a 'literary ethnologist', Ní Dhuibhne does not only investigate people's behaviour in the past or in the present; she is also careful to interpret the present with a mind turned to the future, on the lookout for present scandals that we would deliberately ignore and that may come out into the open in the future: 'I would perceive my task as a writer simply to put my observations of this type of phenomenon on the record. As a citizen, I often wonder what blind spot we have today. What abuse are we committing that the whole of society blindly condones? [...] it is interesting to speculate as to what terrible injustices being committed right now will be condemned by future generations'.[31] Cases of physical abuse are obviously intolerable and unacceptable but sometimes the abuse can be of a more elusive and perverse nature as in her short story 'The Blind',[32] and it takes all the subtle art and powerful, subversive style of a writer like Ní Dhuibhne to successfully denounce it and to open people's eyes.

30   In an interview with Caitriona Moloney, she attributes this passive and cowardly attitude to a possible impact of the Famine on the Irish psyche: 'We're all descendants of the ones who survived, who were probably involved and turned a blind eye to other people's suffering, probably colluding with all kinds of violence and maybe responsible for it' (Caitriona Moloney and Helen Thompson, 'Éilís Ní Dhuibhne', 14).
31   In Christine St Peter, 'Negotiating the Boundaries', 72. Those reflexions are inspired by questions about 'The Catechism Examination'.
32   Éilís Ní Dhuibhne, 'The Blind', *The Shelter of Neighbours* (Belfast: Blackstaff Press, 2012), 250–65.

PART II

Society in Crisis: Challenges to Authority/ies

MATHEW D. STAUNTON AND NATHALIE SEBBANE

Authority and Child Abuse in Ireland: Rethinking History in a Hostile Field

ABSTRACT

Questions of authority loom large over the historiography of child abuse in Ireland. Chief among these is: who has the authority to decide whether or not abuse took place in the past? And what, if any, authority do historians have to make that decision? Should we accept testimony from survivors as legitimate sources (the religious orders accused of abuse, their representatives and their apologists do not) or craft our histories around 'official' written documents only, even if those documents have been produced, maintained or manipulated by organizations that systematically abused children? At what point should we question the Government's claims that its employees had the authority to treat children in ways we now know were abusive, that the past was simply 'like that'? When do we authorize ourselves to challenge apologists and negationists and frame our own stories historiographically?

In 1974, psychohistorian Lloyd de Mause wrote that 'the history of child-hood is a nightmare from which we have only recently begun to awaken'.[1] At that time there was cause to be optimistic: a new field of historical research was developing around *L'Enfant et la vie familiale sous l'Ancien Régime* by Philippe Ariès[2] and the increasing volume of literature on Henry

---

1   Lloyd de Mause, 'The Evolution of Childhood', in Lloyd de Mause, ed., *The History of Childhood: The Untold Story of Child Abuse* (New York: Peter Bedrick Books, 1974), 1. 'Psychohistory' is the study of the psychological motivations behind past events. It combines psychotherapy with the research methodology of the social sciences to understand the emotional origin of the social and political behavior of groups and nations.

2   Philippe Ariès, *L'Enfant et la vie familiale sous l'Ancien Régime* (Paris: Pion, 1960), was translated into English as *Centuries of Childhood* (1962), earning Ariès a solid reputation throughout the English-speaking world.

Kempe's 'Battered Child Syndrome',[3] including David Bakan's seminal *Slaughter of the Innocents: A Study of the Battered Child Phenomenon*,[4] was beginning to influence policy-making on both sides of the Atlantic. As a result, the decade would see an unprecedented number of public inquiries into child abuse deaths in the UK. In Ireland, too, child abuse was on the agenda and the 1970 *Kennedy Report*[5] shone a beam of light into the darkest, Dickensian corners of the Industrial School system. It seemed that Ireland was, finally, waking up to the suffering of its children and by the time de Mause was publishing his 'Evolution of Childhood' four years later, most of the country's industrial schools had been closed.[6] Unfortunately, this spirit of inquiry and reform did not last very long, the torch sputtered out, and the authorities were soon nodding off again.

The 1980s witnessed a return to a very dark age in terms of child protection and research on child abuse in Ireland. Sociologist Robert Dingwall pointed out in 1986 that: '[i]t is simply incorrect to assume that there is a comprehensive and well-established literature on child abuse. There is a large, heterogeneous body of material which is dispersed through a wide range of professional journals and of extremely variable quality'.[7]

In Dingwall's day, this body of material contained almost nothing that could be considered historiographical and little has changed in the

3   Henry Kempe *et al.*, 'The Battered Child Syndrome', *Journal of the American Medical Association* 181/1 (1962), 17.

4   David Bakan, *Slaughter of the Innocents: A Study of the Battered Child Phenomenon* (Boston: Beacon Press, 1972).

5   This report was the culmination of four years of investigation by the Committee on Reformatory and Industrial Schools which was chaired by Justice Eileen Kennedy. The Committee inspected all of the industrial and reformatory schools in the country and reported that the existing system was far from satisfactory and should be abolished. It also called for law reform and increased oversight of children in institutions.

6   A damning report by the Irish think tank Tuairim in 1966 and the recommendations of the Committee on Reformatory and Industrial Schools in 1970 led to the phasing out of these institutions during the 1970s and a transfer of administrative authority for all aspects of child care to the Department of Health.

7   Robert Dingwall, 'The Jasmine Beckford Affair', *Modern Law Review* 49/4 (1986), 496.

intervening years. Bakan's historical psychology and de Mause's psychohistories of abuse broke important ground in the 1970s but few historians have followed in their footsteps. The absence of a historical discourse on child abuse is even more pronounced in Ireland and, lamentably, there has been no serious attempt by historians of Ireland to challenge the politically expedient myth that the perception of abuse was radically different in the past and that the people of Ireland were collectively to blame for the mistreatment of their children in institutions managed by or in partnership with the State. This is a dangerous situation for, as David Bakan has argued: 'the very abstention from deliberate concern with [child abuse] has played a role in perpetuating it. Child abuse thrives in the shadows of privacy and secrecy. It lives by inattention. Those who have protected themselves from being witness to it have at the same time protected the practice and have thus been a party to it.'[8]

Alarmingly, the Commission to Inquire into Child Abuse (1999–2009)[9] revealed the unexplained but convenient disappearance of many of the documents we now need to understand the institutional child abuse of the past.[10] The few historians who have attempted to engage with this difficult subject have, as a result, found their research compromised in advance by unseen hands.

Since the 1990s, public interest in the subject of child abuse has grown steadily in Ireland. Thanks to the work of investigative journalists, local historians and groups of abuse survivors, hidden narratives have been uncovered, abuse scandals have been mercilessly mediatized, the official discourse of the Irish State has come under increasing scrutiny and overdue law reforms have been implemented. Professional historians, however, have been conspicuously absent from this process and the public sphere has had to muddle through without its experts in the contextualization, analysis and representation of the past as it struggled to find words to express and

---

8   David Bakan, *Slaughter of the Innocents: A Study of the Battered Child Phenomenon*, 3.
9   See below for details of the Commission's *raison d'être* and how it operated.
10   It is impossible to say with any certainty if these documents were deliberately destroyed, were accidentally lost, or simply allowed to biodegrade in the basements in which they were carelessly stored. We can say for sure that the absence of such documents benefits those accused of abuse.

come to terms with the suffering of Irish children throughout the twentieth century. This work has proved slow and often painful and the authority to tell the story of child abuse in Ireland has yet to be fully wrested from the grasp of the representatives of the Irish State.

Questions of authority loom large over the historiography of child abuse in Ireland. Chief among these is: who has the authority to decide whether or not abuse took place in the past? Is it the survivors of abuse? Their abusers? The police? The courts? Or is it the Government? And what, if any, authority do historians have to make that decision? With some academics adopting a self-consciously legalistic stance and prefixing the words 'abuse' and 'victim' with 'alleged' and others accepting research funding from organizations accused of abuse, this question is primordial. But there are other important questions to consider. Should we accept testimony from survivors as legitimate sources (the religious orders accused of abuse, their representatives and their apologists do not) or craft our histories around 'official' written documents only, even if those documents have been produced, maintained or manipulated by organizations that systematically abused children? At what point should we question the Government's claims that its employees had the authority to treat children in ways we now know were abusive, that the past was simply 'like that'? When do we authorize ourselves to challenge apologists and negationists and frame our own stories historiographically?

Renaissance

It is a matter of record that the Irish Government chose to rediscover the child abuse of the past on 31 March 1998. Micheál Martin, the then Fianna Fáil Minister for Education and Science, has been retroactively designated as the driving force behind the year of sporadic policy-making and cabinet discussion that started on that Tuesday.[11] There are a number of reasons

11   *CICA Report*, Vol. 1, Ch. 1, 2009, 1.49.

why things began to move at this time rather than sooner. None of these have anything to do with the work of professional historians.

Firstly, several years of relentless reporting on clerical pedophilia and child abuse cases like the Smythe and Fortune affairs,[12] and of the Church's failure to protect children from its employees made it impossible for the government to continue to turn a blind eye to child abuse. An event horizon of sorts had been crossed. This media coverage led, in turn, to litigation and requests for files on various institutions that put even more pressure on the Government.

It is no coincidence that this was only a week and a half before the signing of the Good Friday Agreement.[13] With the entire country suddenly free to begin to think about something other than the Troubles in Northern Ireland, there was now scope for child abuse to be pushed closer to the top of the agenda and for official action to catch up with the 'rhetoric of empathy', as Minister Martin put it to his Dáil colleagues a year later.[14]

Significantly, the Government's newfound interest in historical child abuse came less than a month after a general apology by the Christian Brothers to all those who had suffered abuse at their hands. The ramifications of such an apology by one of the State's closest educational partners were surely not overlooked by the minister responsible for the schools in which much of this abuse took place.

The renaissance of media-driven State interest in Irish child abuse reached its zenith in 1999. Speaking before Dáil Éireann on 11 May, An Taoiseach Bertie Ahern made a general apology to child abuse victims:

12 During a period of over forty years, Father Brendan Smyth (1927–1997) abused and indecently assaulted over 143 children in Belfast, Dublin and the US. His actions were systematically covered up by Church officials and the controversy this provoked led to the fall of the Irish Government in 1994. Father Seán Fortune (1954–1999) committed suicide in New Ross while awaiting trial for sixty-six charges of sexual abuse against twenty-nine boys.

13 The Good Friday Agreement was a major political development in the Northern Ireland peace process. It established the present devolved system of government and created a number of institutions between Northern Ireland and the Republic of Ireland and between the Republic of Ireland and the United Kingdom.

14 Micheál Martin, *Dáil Éireann* Debate, Vol. 504, No. 6, Thursday, 13 May 1999.

'The Government wishes to make a sincere and long overdue apology to the victims of childhood abuse for our collective failure to intervene, to detect their pain, to come to their rescue'.[15] He went on to outline a number of measures that would be put into place very rapidly, including the establishment of a national counselling service for child abuse survivors, the amendment of the Statute of Limitations[16] to enable them to make claims for compensation and the setting up of a Commission to Inquire into Childhood Abuse.

In April and May of the same year, RTE aired the three-part documentary series *States of Fear*, produced by the investigative journalist and broadcaster Mary Raftery. These programmes described the abuse suffered by children between the 1930s and 1970s in Ireland's Reformatory and Industrial Schools,[17] focused the anger of the public and caused an enormous outcry. The fact that the Taoiseach's apology arrived on the day that episode three was broadcast was retrospectively declared to be coincidental rather than the kneejerk reaction that it appeared to be.

A preliminary version of the commission promised by Bertie Ahern was set up later that year on a non-statutory, administrative footing, with broad terms of reference. High Court judge Mary Laffoy was put in charge and tasked with providing a sympathetic forum in which survivors could recount the abuse they had suffered as well as identifying and reporting on

---

15   *CICA Report*, Vol. 1, Ch. 1, 2009, 1.01.

16   New legislation introduced in 2000 to facilitate civil litigation did not live up to this promise. Rather than unconditionally extend the time limit for bringing a case, the plaintiff must now first prove that he or she has been under a 'disability' while suffering from psychological injury caused by sexual abuse (physical or emotional abuse is not mentioned in the Act) which is of such significance that the victim's will to bring a case or ability to make a reasoned decision to bring a case is substantially impaired. *Statute of Limitations (Amendment) Act*, 2000, section 2.

17   Historically, there is a clear difference between Reformatory and Industrial Schools. Ostensibly, the former aimed to redeem those who had already committed an offence while the latter targeted a younger population that was (entirely subjectively) considered in danger of drifting into crime. It is important to note that both types of school were run as businesses by religious orders and their function as centres of redemption and reform was largely fictive.

the causes, nature and extent of physical and sexual abuse. The recommendations contained in her first two reports were embodied in the *Commission to Inquire into Child Abuse Bill* and subsequent *Act*, and, on 23 May 2000, the Commission became an independent, statutory body.

With hindsight, Tom Boland, the Head of Legal Affairs at the Department of Education and Science, expressed enormous optimism about the Commission, coming very close to describing it as an Irish *Vergangenheitsbewältigung*,[18] a collective working through of the past. There was, he said, a 'folk memory' of widespread abuse but:

> [f]or Irish society the idea was – and this is rather like a truth Commission – that it would establish for Irish society precisely what happened and establish as complete a picture as possible of the causes, nature and extent of childhood abuse including why it happened and also who was responsible. It was very much an important factor that the Commission would establish at least at an institutional level what institutions were responsible for what happened. It was also felt that this kind of process would help Irish society to come to terms with a very negative, very black period in our history.[19]

Very quickly, however, it became clear that the Commission would not inquire into all of the abuse apologized for by the Christian brothers or indeed by Bertie Ahern but would restrict itself to the abuse described by Raftery in her documentary and to the chronological scope she herself had used. Tom Boland's *Vergangenheitsbewältigung* would have to wait. The scope and credibility of the Commission were further diminished when Justice Laffoy resigned on 2 September 2003, claiming that the Government and the Department of Education had frustrated her efforts and slowed the Commission's work.[20]

18 The composite German word *Vergangenheitsbewältigung* describes processes of dealing with the past, which can be translated as the 'struggle to come to terms with the past'.

19 *CICA Report*, Vol. 1, Ch. 1, 2009, 1.64.

20 Laffoy's claims are credible. The Department of Finance was prohibitively slow in responding to the Commission's requests for additional financial resources, the Government was slow to commit itself to compensation for abuse survivors and the Department of Education did not supply requested documents in a timely fashion.

Sean Ryan who had been appointed as Justice Mary Laffoy's replacement concluded that there were major problems facing the Investigation Committee[21] and if it were to continue unchanged, there would be no prospect of its work being completed within a reasonable timeframe and at an acceptable cost. He suggested a number of changes[22] that he felt were needed to overcome these problems. Ostensibly to save money and time, the scope of the inquiry was drastically reduced and the notion of a sympathetic forum for all abuse victims to tell their stories abandoned. The report of the CICA was finally published on 20 May 2009, but, although it documented much of the abuse that took place in residential institutions in the words of abuse survivors themselves, it was evident that there would be no working through of the past. A page was forcefully turned on an embarrassing and difficult subject. Asked how the Government would react to the report, Department of Justice Secretary General Seán Aylward insisted that it had all been a very long time ago: 'Some of the issues that are raised and looked at in the Ryan report and that have been raised in relation to the Magdalene Laundries relate to a very distant, far-off time [...] Many of the people who suffered in that period or were victims of it

---

See Paul Anderson, 'Laffoy resignation letter reported blaming Government', *Irish Times* (7 September 2003) and 'Government response to Laffoy letter', *Irish Times* (10 September 2003).

21   The CICA had three operational axes: a forum for abuse survivors, a redress board and an investigation committee. The latter was hampered by the financial issues raised by Justice Laffoy and the delays caused by the half-hearted cooperation of the Department of Education and its partners in the religious orders which ran the institutions under investigation. Unlike his predecessor, Justice Ryan was prepared to work within these constraints and aim for substantially less than the Commission was initially mandated to achieve.

22   (a) Amendments to the 2000 Act so as to focus the Investigation Committee on its core function, which was to inquire into abuse of children in institutions; (b) at the meeting on 7 May 2004 it was stated that the Inquiry was not going to be able to complete its work if it proceeded on the basis of naming abusers; (c) at a further meeting in June 2004, the Committee announced its decision to proceed on the basis of selection of witnesses from the larger institutions for the hearings; (d) witnesses could be cross-examined.

are no longer with us and it would be very difficult for the State to rewrite its history or right the wrongs that were done.'[23]

Aylward was confusing history with the past as many people do. The past cannot be altered and harms cannot be undone. History, on the other hand, can be written and rewritten *ad infinitum* and our perception of the past incrementally modified. For 'the State' and those who represent it (ministers, senators, senior civil servants, the police, judges, teachers and, of course, Aylward himself) the preservation of an official History that glosses over widespread child abuse in Irish institutions and allows the horrors of the past to slip gently out of folk memory is preferable to litigation, prison time and public opprobrium.

This preference manifests itself discursively in claims that twenty-first-century commentators on child abuse simply cannot understand the conditions that prevailed in the past and that any attempt to apply today's child protection standards to the behaviors of people in former decades would be anachronistic. This was the standard defense of those accused of abuse during the CICA hearings. Historians of Ireland have facilitated this defense by keeping their distance for it is only in the absence of a historiography of abuse that such arguments can be put forward without attracting nationwide derision. Avoiding anachronism is, of course, a valid concern but only up to the point where it is those accused of abuse who demand and acquire the right to define the standards of the past. That the CICA had no direct input from professional historians is, therefore, highly significant. The representatives of the institutions in which abuse was perpetrated and those who facilitated or covered up for them, were allowed to tell their own version of events without fear of historical analysis. There can be no history if the subjects of our inquiries are allowed to construct their own narratives unchallenged.

23   Jamie Smyth, 'State defends response to Ryan report', *Irish Times* (24 May 2011). 'Magdalene Laundries' or 'Magdalene Asylums' were institutions managed by religious orders from the eighteenth to the late twentieth centuries. They were run ostensibly to house 'fallen women' but were essentially businesses employing slave labour. An estimated 30,000 women were unconstitutionally confined in these institutions in Ireland.

Contextualization?

Two accomplished social historians, Moira J. Maguire and Diarmaid Ferriter, have addressed these objections and attempted to establish a contextual framework for what was done to Irish children in the past. Both are archive-based researchers and the archive is, in many ways, the symbol of their rigour and professionalism. Archives, however, can be booby-trapped and readers deliberately manipulated or misdirected. It is worth dwelling on this point for several paragraphs before considering what Maguire and Ferriter have achieved.

Where there is a substantial extant archive, the narrative we piece together from the documents it contains may well be the one we were intended to find. We are familiar with the notion that historians bring their own preoccupations into the archive with them and come away with the story they had already constructed for themselves. To what extent are we prepared to be ambushed by narratives prepared for us by the writers and collators of the archived documents and by the archivists themselves? Carolyn Steedman argues that: 'the historian who goes to the Archive must always be an unintended reader, will always read that which was never intended for his or her eyes'.[24] But this is far from accurate. Archives in Ireland and elsewhere are full of documents that have been altered with pens and razorblades, files with missing pages and books with missing volumes. They are also full of documents that do not correspond in any way to the reality they purport to be describing.[25] Often, then, the researcher is

---

24   Carolyn Steedman, *Dust* (Manchester: Manchester University Press, 2001), 75.
25   The memoir of Red Army tank commander Dmitriy Loza reveals that archives can be very deceptive. In December 1944, a clerical error resulted in an imaginary tank that had already been destroyed going into and returning unscathed from battle after battle, at least on paper. Loza could not record the information that it had been destroyed because he had reached his absolute limit for material losses. When he received a new consignment of tanks, he assigned the serial number of the imaginary tank to the most battered vehicle he could find and sent it out to get deliberately destroyed with the loss of one soldier. This data appears only in his memoir and this

unwittingly guided in his or her reading and should adopt a more critical position vis-à-vis both extant and absent data. That archives cannot give us a complete picture of any situation should come as no surprise: 'The archive is not potentially made up of everything, as is human memory; and is not the fathomless and timeless place in which nothing goes away that is the unconscious. The archive is made from selected and consciously chosen documentation from the past and also the mad fragmentations that no one intended to preserve and that just ended up there.'[26]

Notwithstanding the potential for misdirection, Moira J. Maguire displays an unwavering and unquestioning faith in archival material and a profound suspicion of oral testimony. 'A Good Beating Never Hurt Anyone: The Punishment and Abuse of Children in 20th-Century Ireland'[27] (co-authored with Séamus Ó Cinnéide) and *Cherished Equally? Precarious Childhood in Independent Ireland*,[28] respond explicitly to claims by the administrators of industrial schools that their treatment of children was 'consistent with prevailing practice in homes and schools across the country, and that institutions that catered for such large numbers of neglected, and in some cases delinquent, children could not function without a stringent corporal punishment regime'.[29] Her sources include autobiographies, newspaper articles, the extant files of the Irish Society for the Prevention of Cruelty to Children – ISPCC – and the Department of Education, court records and the records of religious orders.

---

was only published in English in the United States after he handed the manuscript to the American Embassy. Russian military archives, on the other hand, tell only the story of the imaginary tank. Dmitriy Loza, *Commanding the Red Army's Sherman Tanks* (Lincoln: University of Nebraska Press, 1996).

26   Carolyn Steedman, *Dust*, 68.

27   Moira J. Maguire and Séamus Ó Cinnéide, 'A Good Beating Never Hurt Anyone: The Punishment and Abuse of Children in 20th-Century Ireland', *Journal of Social History* (Spring 2005), 635–52.

28   Moira J. Maguire, *Cherished Equally? Precarious Childhood in Independent Ireland* (Manchester: Manchester University Press, 2009).

29   Moira J. Maguire and Séamus Ó Cinnéide, 'A Good Beating Never Hurt Anyone: The Punishment and Abuse of Children in 20th-Century Ireland', *Journal of Social History* (Spring 2005), 635.

Aligning herself with the position of the administrators of the institutions in which abuse took place, she questions the credibility of public discourses (Tom Boland's 'folk memory') and calls for contextualization:

> Media and popular accounts of these allegations have tended to highlight the most salacious and lurid details while silencing alternative memories or accounts and ignoring the historical context. In order to assess these allegations, it is necessary to examine prevailing policy and practice in homes and schools, to see what was regarded as acceptable and legitimate corporal punishment there. It is also necessary to consider public discussions of corporal punishment and of the need to protect children from abuse at the hands of parents and school teachers.[30]

In the introduction to *Cherished Equally?* she develops this distrust of non-archival sources even further and warns her readers to be cautious of testimony from abuse survivors. It is reasonable, she argues, to question the extent to which memories of abuse have been blurred or distorted and the uncritical use of such material by others is a flaw she promises to avoid by placing the memories of survivors in a broader context.[31] In her historiographical practice the context for memory and oral testimony (often called 'allegations') is established by consulting archives (generally called 'evidence'). Regrettably, the archives themselves are neither problematized nor contextualized. Tellingly, the title of chapter five – 'The Abused Child' – is followed by a question mark, echoing typographically and punctuationally the negationist agenda of the representatives of the religious orders during the CICA hearings and questioning the authority of abuse survivors to name their suffering and tell their own stories.[32]

---

30   *Ibid.*
31   Moira J. Maguire, *Cherished Equally? Precarious Childhood in Independent Ireland*, 15.
32   Another product of this unhelpful agenda is Professor Philip Jenkins' *Pedophiles and Priests: Anatomy of a Contemporary Crisis* (Oxford: Oxford University Press, 1996). Essentially a defence of the Catholic Church, this study blames society, exaggerated media reports, therapy, the anti-Catholic tradition, feminism and a voracious culture of litigation for the 'construction of problems and panic' around the issue of clerical abuse. Jenkins is clearly uncomfortable with words like 'survivor' and 'abuse', refraining from prefixing them with the qualifiers 'alleged', 'self-described' and 'purported' for stylistic reasons only.

Much of the material Maguire uses to establish her 'broader context' is highly questionable itself. It is a commonplace that the small number of documents produced by children tend to be ephemeral or inaccessible to researchers. Written accounts of their experiences are produced by adults with a range of personal and corporate agendas, and the sort of administrative records that an archive-based researcher like Maguire would look to for data on abuse and its contexts tend to be maintained by the abusers and those who failed to stop them. As mentioned above, much that might be useful to researchers in these archives has disappeared, been disappeared, or was deliberately not recorded.[33] The archives of the NSPCC/ISPCC exemplify the problematic nature of this issue for the historian of child abuse. Maguire recognizes the limitations of the ISPCC records: 'Until about ten years ago it seemed, indeed, that no case files from the years before the 1970s had survived. Hundreds of case files were eventually discovered in unused closets and cabinets. For some reason that is impossible to explain, these case files all relate to three counties: Wexford, Wicklow, and Mayo, and they are all confined to the period from the late 1930s to the mid-1950s.'[34]

This does not seem to alarm her in any way and without further comment on the inexplicable disappearance of the files, she leaps to the unjustifiable conclusion that they are, nonetheless, representative of the kinds of cases dealt with by the ISPCC and its inspectors. During the hearings of the CICA no such assumption was made and the CEO of the ISPCC was asked for clarification as to the whereabouts of the missing data: 'there are significant limitations in the amount of material available to us, he said.

33   The immense value placed on such records during criminal investigations has resulted in their frequent destruction. The case of the obstetrician Michael Neary who was suspended from Our Lady of Lourdes hospital in Drogheda in 1998 for suspected malpractice on a breathtaking scale is an exemplary one in this regard. While the police investigation was ongoing all of the relevant files were removed from the hospital by the surgeon's colleagues. <http://www.rte.ie/tv/scannal/Neary.html> accessed 1 April 2015.
34   Moira J. Maguire, *Cherished Equally? Precarious Childhood in Independent Ireland*, 14.

Unfortunately, we don't have an explanation as to where the other material has gone, there was a fire in our head office in 1961, perhaps material was destroyed in that'.[35]

This is indeed unfortunate because the extent of the involvement of the NSPCC/ISPCC (National/Irish Society for the Prevention of Cruelty to Children) in committing children to industrial schools cannot now be accurately ascertained.[36] Most of the organizations involved in the Commission had the same story to tell. The Christian Brothers were particularly negligent in their record-keeping and had failed to maintain the legal minimum of files in relation to punishment. And yet, spokesmen for the Christian Brothers have stated that they will concede that there was systematic abuse in their institutions only if documentary evidence can be produced.[37]

Maguire is no less satisfied with the equally problematic Department of Education archives and develops unlikely generalizations from very small amounts of data. Consider the following: 'The available evidence suggests that corporal punishment was commonplace and that parents themselves generally supported a teacher's right to punish their children'.[38]

The 'evidence' for the latter assertion consists of ten case files only. This is, we are told, confirmed by a number of autobiographies.[39] Clearly, however, the Department of Education files can only be interpreted as evidence of the stated opinions of the ten sets of parents, and nothing more. Extrapolating general support for corporal punishment is excessive.

---

35   *CICA Report*, Vol. V, Ch. 1, section 3, 2009, 1.
36   The NSPCC/ISPCC functioned as a silent partner in the Industrial School system
       for several decades, using various pretexts to provide a constant supply of children to
       the religious orders, who, in turn, received per capita funding from the Department
       of Education. The collusion of the Society in the unethical and unconstitutional
       incarceration of children is unquestionable. The extent of this collusion and any
       associated corruption or criminal activity cannot be measured because of the con-
       venient disappearance of the relevant files.
37   *CICA Report*, Vol. 1, Ch. 6, 2009, 6.191.
38   Moira J. Maguire, *Cherished Equally? Precarious Childhood in Independent
       Ireland*, 159.
39   Maguire lists twenty-nine autobiographies in her bibliography.

That this is the case becomes more obvious when we explore the alternative narratives that emerge from a study of the multiple lawsuits against teachers in the 1930s and 40s, from assaults on teachers by outraged parents throughout the twentieth century and from the testimony collected by the School-Children's Protection Organization in the 1950s.[40] Oral testimony from teachers and former pupils[41] reveals a much more complex situation with some parents successfully forbidding teachers from physically punishing their children or negotiating with them to allow transgressions to be dealt with at home rather than in the classroom. The inherent weaknesses of a historiographical approach that champions official archives carefully crafted to disguise an abusive system and protect abusers and their facilitators while rejecting and undervaluing the accounts of the experiences by abuse survivors tend to undermine the otherwise solid research informing Maguire's article and book.

Diarmaid Ferriter, for his part, was commissioned by the lawyers of a group of abuse survivors to provide a historical context for institutional abuse in Ireland and his findings were published in Volume V of the CICA report. He is admirably clear in his introductory statement. His stated aims are to establish a balanced (rather than distorted) sense of historical perspective and 'put more historical context' on events discussed in the public hearings, in order to respond to complaints that abuse was understood differently or not understood at all in the past.[42] He is careful to point out that 'the official record can tell us what happened, but rarely what it felt like'. The obvious conclusion to be drawn from comments made throughout the public hearings of the Commission 'is that the documentation available in the archives of the institutions cannot provide a complete picture'. Memoirs of victims must be treated with caution if they are accepted as

---

40 See: School-Children's Protection Organization, *Punishment in Our Schools* (Dublin: The School-Children's Protection Organization, 1955).

41 M. Staunton has been collecting anonymous testimony on the subject of physical abuse in schools from Irish adults since 2010. The scope of this chapter precludes the inclusion of full transcriptions of interviews but we will give the reference number of relevant testimony and transcriptions will be made available on demand.

42 *CICA Report*, Vol. V, Ferriter Report, 2009, 1.

a source, but 'if enough of them are consulted, it is possible to identify certain common strands that again can help to put the issues revealed in some kind of perspective'.[43]

Arguably, the Ferriter Report falls short of fully achieving these aims. Instead of context for abuse we discover a kaleidoscopic representation of raw data on the social and sexual ills of twentieth-century Ireland, with a particular focus on the interrelation of Church, State, and family. We learn about hiring fairs, unmarried mothers, venereal diseases and other STDs, prostitution, workhouses, poverty, the sodomy of a mare donkey, adoption, children finding comfort in the church, Christian Brothers as victims, emigration, and the Garda Siochana's incredible descriptions of its zealous pursuit of paedophiles, but the report fails to overcome the absence of archival material that it announces in its own preamble and Ferriter resorts *in extremis* to using the text of the Commission hearings as its own context. Opting for breadth rather than depth, he paints a portrait of a very ugly and troubled society that has betrayed its children that could function as a contextual framework for any number of social issues or crimes.

The issue of child abuse is taken up again in his recent book *Occasions of Sin: Sex and Society in Modern Ireland*, in which he acknowledges that 'child sexual abuse simply was not prioritized as an area worthy of immediate political and social action'.[44] Crucially, he goes to great lengths, both in the report and the book, to demonstrate that since the early days of the Irish Free State, many cases of abuse have been referred to the police and the courts, and that it would be inaccurate to claim that no one knew about child sexual abuse. As is the case with Maguire's research, however, it is left to future researchers to establish the deeper context for what happened to Irish children in the past.

43   *CICA Report*, Vol. V, Ferriter Report, 2009, 4.
44   Diarmaid Ferriter, *Occasions of Sin: Sex and Society in Modern Ireland* (London: Profile Books, 2009).

Moving forward

Child abuse in Ireland and elsewhere has always existed in a zone of historical invisibility. The absence of documentation, the institutional and political desire to hide such crimes and criminals, and the repugnance provoked by knowledge of the suffering of children have made this an inhospitable field in which to conduct research. As a result, professional historians have failed to make serious headway into the darkness. In the paragraphs that follow we will suggest methodological strategies for dealing with the issues we have raised, for working through a difficult past and representing Irish child abuse as history.

The historian of children has an advantage over most other historians because he or she was once a child. Many historians have, of course, suffered or witnessed abuse themselves and could use their own experiences to navigate around the gaps in the archive. We might begin, therefore, by structuring our own memories historiographically and collecting the stories of family members, friends, former classmates, colleagues, former teachers and, eventually, complete strangers. It is collection, collation and analysis of raw testimony more than anything else that extends our knowledge of child abuse. The Health Services Research Center in the Royal College of Surgeons in Ireland has been doing groundbreaking research in this area since 1997. Two reports, *The SAVI Report: Sexual Abuse and Violence in Ireland*[45] published in 2002 and *Time to Listen: Confronting Child Sexual Abuse by Catholic Clergy in Ireland*[46] published in 2003 were the first of their kind in the world and involved telephone and postal surveys and qualitative interviews. Such an approach would combine ego-history[47] with oral and local history, and provide useful footholds in the booby-trapped archive.

45 Hannah McGee *et al.*, *The SAVI Report: Sexual Abuse and Violence in Ireland* (Dublin: The Liffey Press, 2002).

46 Helen Goode, Hannah McGee & Ciarán O'Boyle, *Time to Listen: Confronting Child Sexual Abuse by Catholic Clergy in Ireland* (Dublin: The Liffey Press, 2003).

47 'Egohistory' is a field of critical history developed by Pierre Nora. It focuses on the relationship between the personality of historians and their life choices in the process of writing of history.

It should be clear from what we have said above that the problematization of archives and how they have been created, maintained, and sometimes destroyed, is a key element of child abuse historiography. An empty or non-existent archive can be a source itself and we can articulate stories and histories around this empty space just as you would articulate the elements of an image around the empty square in a sliding tile puzzle. As consumers of popular culture and sensational news reports, we are used to the notion that criminals sometimes chop off fingers, remove teeth, burn cars and destroy hard drives to cover their traces, and we enjoy stories of the resourceful detectives who come after them, theorizing the missing information and creating meaning around these acts of destruction. John Le Carré's fictional intelligence officer George Smiley is an excellent role model for the historian of child abuse: he defeats his nemesis by taking the 'back bearings' with his team, looking back from their present position at the gaps in narratives, and identifying the data which have not been recorded by a KGB mole.[48] When historicizing crimes it is perhaps useful to try to think like a detective.

If we consider the methodology of psychohistorian Lloyd de Mause, we can add several types of sources that would enrich a historical contextualization of child abuse. While researching his 'Evolution of Childhood' de Mause studied thousands of paintings, novels, poems, diaries, songs, laws and objects. The latter category provides an excellent insight into what is acceptable or unacceptable in terms of corporal punishment and much can be learned from a careful study of the design, manufacture and commercialization of tools of all sorts for inflicting pain on children.

Another strategy is to abandon the notion that there is something unique about the way children have been treated in Ireland. Children are clearly no safer in Australia, England or the United States. Yes, Catholicism lurks behind the Irish constitution and Irish Common Law and looms large inside Irish schools but is it really the context for abuse? If so, then what of Canada? New Zealand? Zimbabwe? Or South Africa? Ireland has its specificities but we believe that it is more useful to look at abuse across

---

48   John Le Carré, *The Honourable Schoolboy* (New York: Pocket Books, 1989), 59–60.

Europe or in countries that have similar education systems or, to look at the status of schoolchildren in common law jurisdictions and then feed any insights gleaned back into what is known about Ireland.

For the remainder of this paper we will attempt to put some of these strategies into practice in a very neglected area of child abuse history: the widespread physical abuse of schoolchildren at the hands of their teachers.

Towards a history of child abuse in Irish schools

The 1997 *Non-fatal Offences against the Person Act*[49] provides us with a useful starting point for a historical study of physical abuse in the Irish school system. This Act replaced most of an 1861 Act, eliminating obsolete crimes and referencing the most modern ways of hurting and frightening people. Section 24 concerns schoolchildren, and states that: 'The rule of law under which teachers are immune from criminal liability in respect of physical chastisement of pupils is hereby abolished'.[50] The declaratory paragraph of the Children's Act of 1908 that reiterated the Common Law right of teachers to physically punish pupils[51] was thereby obliterated. This right should not have prevented prosecution for instances of common assault that went beyond reasonable and moderate chastisement but the Dublin Metropolitan Police and the Garda Síochána were extremely reluctant throughout the twentieth century to follow up on complaints that were difficult to prove and had little chance of success in court.[52] The result of

---

49 See below for the context of this Act.
50 *Non-fatal Offences against the Person Act*, 1997, section 24.
51 'Nothing in the Part of this Act shall be construed to take away or affect the right of any parent, teacher, or other person having the lawful control or charge of a child or young person to administer punishment to such child or young person'.
52 Even in cases where punishment was clearly excessive and utterly inappropriate tools were used, courts paid 'a tender regard to the nature of the provocation' and, historically, the teacher was generally given the benefit of the doubt. William Clarke

this reluctance is a total absence of criminal case law involving assaults by teachers on pupils in the jurisdictions of the Irish Free State and the Republic of Ireland. Without an evolving body of legal decisions that tested the limits of the rights of teachers and pupils, this potential immunity gradually became absolute and unchallengeable.

What did the 1997 Act mean in practice? While a minority of teachers complained that they were now in danger of being assaulted themselves,[53] most found ways to control their flailing arms. Those who could not control themselves or wanted to continue to use pain and the threat of pain as class management tools, made sure that if they did hit a child it was not in the public and defensible space of the classroom but in one of the many indefensible spaces in school buildings: the room under the stairs, the roof-lit or windowless storage closet, the empty classroom or office.[54] The vice-principal of one north Dublin secondary school used a small room under the stairs for this purpose both before and after the 1997 Act became law.[55] Recent interviews with his colleagues have confirmed that he continued this practice up until his retirement and openly encouraged new recruits to do likewise in order to protect themselves from assault charges.[56]

A 1994 report by the Irish Law Reform Commission[57] that paved the way for the 1997 Act revealed that the legal framework for the relationship

---

Hall & Arnold H. F. Pretty, *The Children Act 1908* (London: Stevens and Sons, 1909), 16.

53   A report on a teacher's union conference reveals that there were still some teachers in 1999 who felt the need for corporal punishment. One used the ridiculous argument that it was teachers who were now at risk of being assaulted by their pupils (*Irish Times*, 9 April 1999).

54   Many adults who were physically or sexually abused as children talk about the rooms in which the abuse took place. Generally these were offices with closed doors, broom closets, book stores, and the various odd and windowless little spaces included in school designs. Interviews TIP1958 (teacher), DUB1972 (teacher) and DUB1973 (former pupil).

55   Interview TIP1958 (teacher).

56   Interviews TIP1958 (teacher) and DUB1973 (former pupil).

57   The Law Reform Commission's role is to keep the law under review and to conduct research with a view to the reform of the law. This includes the development of law,

between teachers and pupils in Ireland was alarmingly nebulous.[58] The breadth of the authority wielded by teachers appeared to be greater than that of parents, to extend out beyond the school gates and up to the child's front door, but this was unclear. The source of this authority was debateable, being based either on a delegation of parental authority, in other words on the Common Law doctrine of *In Loco Parentis*,[59] or on the original power enjoyed by teachers as key actors in the essential sub-society of the school, a sovereign sphere with its own power structure crucial to the healthy evolution of the state.[60] What could be objectively considered as a reasonable punishment was also unclear. Helpfully, the Commission recognized that pointing a loaded gun at a child was unreasonable. As was punishment inflicted by blows to the head. Slaps on the face not likely to cause injury could, however, be interpreted as reasonable, while punishment resulting in temporary pain and discolouration of the flesh would not be considered as excessive.[61]

It is significant that in their report, the Commissioners did not cite Irish Case Law, focusing instead on relevant jurisprudential decisions from England and Wales, and other Common Law jurisdictions like the US, Canada, New Zealand and Australia. This was because in the domain of teacher-pupil relations, Irish Common Law had been frozen since 1908 as cases of criminal assault by teachers were not getting to court and there was no possibility for the law to evolve. There was abundant jurisprudence relating to civil suits that might have provided some clarity but this was not taken into consideration. In the 1920s and 1930s Irish judges faced

---

its codification (including its simplification and modernization) and the revision and consolidation of statute law.

58 Law Reform Commission, *Report on Non-fatal Offences against the Person* (Dublin: Law Reform Commission, 1994), 1.79.

59 *In Loco Parentis* is discussed below.

60 Law Reform Commission, *Report on Non-fatal Offences against the Person* (Dublin: Law Reform Commission, 1994), 1.79.

61 *Ibid.*, 1.84.

with suits for assault struggled to establish a reasonableness standard[62] and reconcile the tensions between Department of Education regulations that were not legally binding on teachers and the civil rights of both teachers and pupils. By the end of the 1930s this struggle began to bear fruit and court records show judges referring tentatively to precedents set by colleagues. These include using the Department of Education's internal rules as the benchmark for reasonableness and finding in favour of the plaintiff when there was sufficient proof to show that these rules had been breached.

Despite the North American, Australian and New Zealand examples offered by the Law Reform Commissioners, it is the Common Law jurisdictions of South Africa, Nigeria and Zimbabwe that most resemble Ireland. In South African schools the authority of the teacher is perceived as two-tiered. Acting *In Loco Parentis*, teachers have as much right to physically chastise a child as any parent. If parents disagree with the punishment and withdraw this delegated authority, teachers can cite their original power which comes from God or the State or both. Discipline in the school is paramount and the civil rights of the child can be restricted for the greater good.[63] For more than a century, United States judges have been trying to determine if *In Loco Parentis* is a fiction invented by teachers to justify corporal punishment and whether children leave their constitutional rights at the school gate.[64] The Constitution of Nigeria is explicit on this subject. Schoolchildren have as much right to liberty as incarcerated felons, persons suffering from infectious or contagious disease, persons of unsound mind, persons addicted to drugs or alcohol, or vagrants.[65]

---

62   The reasonableness standard is a test which asks whether the decisions made were legitimate and designed to remedy a certain issue under the circumstances at the time. Courts using this standard look at both the ultimate decision, and the process by which a party went about making that decision.

63   See I. J. Oosthuizen, 'The *in loco parentis* Role of the Teacher: A Relationship Perspective', *Koers* 57/1 (1992), 121–34.

64   See Alysa B. Koloms, 'Stripping Down the Reasonableness Standard: The Problems with Using *in loco parentis* to Define Students' Fourth Amendment Rights', *Hofstra Law Review* 39 (2012), 169–99.

65   See section 34, sub-section (1) of the *Constitution of the Federal Republic of Nigeria* (1999).

What of Irish Department of Education's rules on corporal punishment? In 1982 the Minister for Education banned its use by circular letter. This was not legally binding in any way but the department now had a good case for suspending or firing teachers who were caught physically punishing children. Unfortunately, teachers had become accustomed to ignoring Department rules and the ban had little impact on the ground. Objects designed specifically for punishment like straps and canes disappeared immediately from the classroom and one North Dublin school ritualistically burned all of its straps in the basement furnace.[66] Those who had not been hitting pupils, and there were many, continued not to do so. Those who had, simply switched to using classroom objects like metre sticks, T-squares, wooden dusters and window poles. In the unlikely event that an inspector entered a classroom unannounced, the teacher would be found with a perfectly explainable implement in his or her hands. School principals were no longer responsible for punishment, so teachers did what they wanted behind closed doors.

Suggestive statistical data on the preceding decade can be found in a report published by the Irish Union of School Students in 1974 which includes a survey of schools in seven of the twenty-six counties.[67] The students found that 84 per cent of schools were using corporal punishment. 92 per cent of these were all male schools. By contrast, only 12 per cent of vocational schools (run by elected committees rather than religious orders) were using corporal punishment.[68] Although the report calls for the abolition of all forms of corporal punishment, section 6 of their findings introduces the subject of abuse:

> The committee found it impossible to establish in what percentages different methods and instruments of corporal punishment were used. The leather strap seemed to be the most common method but others included canes, rulers, bunches of large keys, T-squares, hurleys, tree branches and chair legs. The survey found several instances

---

66   Interview TIP1958 (teacher).
67   Irish Union of School Students, *Corporal Punishment: The Brutal Facts!* (Dublin: The Irish Union of School Students, 1974).
68   *Ibid.*, 9.

of actual physical assault [...] In some schools punishments were administered indis-
criminately to all parts of the body, face, chest, neck, back, arms, legs, etc. [...] it
would seem that there are some sadists and sexual perverts in charge of classes in
Irish schools.[69]

In post-primary schools, this had been the situation since 1967 when
free secondary education was introduced along with free transport for
schoolchildren and the School Attendance (amendment) Act which made
non-attendance much more difficult and costly for parents. This led to an
influx of pupils from families perceived by some teachers as undesirable.
One North Dublin principal appeared in the staff room on the first day of
term with a suitcase full of punishment straps and encouraged his teachers
to use them liberally to deal with the serious disciplinary problems they
were surely about to face.[70] It quickly became evident that the children of
parents with power or those in a position to sue were less likely to suffer at
the hands of their teachers. One North Dublin solicitor, himself the son
of a solicitor, was spared by the teachers in his school after a visit from his
father.[71] One of his teachers was the vice-principal mentioned earlier. A
South Dublin boy was similarly spared because his father was a well-known
local police sergeant.[72]

Between the creation of the independent Irish State and the 1960s,
it was primary school children who were most physically abused. We can
determine this from the large number of lawsuits brought by parents against
teachers in the 1920s, 1930s and 1940s.[73] The Department of Education

69   *Ibid.*, 10.
70   Interview TIP1958 (teacher).
71   Interview TIP1958 (teacher).
72   Interview DUB1973 (former pupil).
73   A survey of newspaper and court reports reveals that there were many civil cases
      brought by parents for their children against teachers across the country during this
      period. The vast majority was dismissed but there were notable exceptions in the
      1930s (see for example McCann v Mannion and McGee v Cunnane, both in 1932)
      and small fines were imposed on teachers. In 1931, Judge Kenny stated at Skibbereen
      Cicuit Court that 'there should be no corporal punishment in any school' and that
      he 'regarded an assault by a teacher on a pupil just the same as an ordinary assault,

generally showed enormous disdain for complaints made by parents and if they bothered to reply at all it was only to inform parents that they should redirect their complaints to the manager of the school, generally the local Parish Priest. In extreme cases when a complaint could not be ignored or deflected (as in 1929 when 120 of 133 pupils were withdrawn from a Mayo school in an effort to force the Department to deal with an abusive teacher)[74] an inspector would be sent. Investigations, however, were generally conducted in secret and the parents never informed of any decisions that were taken. In the Mayo case the police only got involved to start proceedings against the parents who were in breach of the School Attendance Act (1926).[75] With school managers advising parents to complain to the Department, there was no other option but to bring a civil case against the teacher and sue for damages.

Reports of testimony by children during these cases reveal a wide range of abusive behaviours on the part of teachers. Boys and girls as young as nine were being beaten with canes and straps and any other objects that came to hand. They were being locked in cupboards,[76] punched in the face, thrown to the ground, and having their heads banged off walls. One boy had his head actually pushed through the panelling of a wooden door. In court, many judges showed open contempt for plaintiffs and supporting testimony from doctors did little to change that. Even when there was no doubt about the severity of an assault, the best a family could hope for

---

and if he had his way he would treat them the same'. He nonetheless felt bound by the more conservative views of his High Court colleagues to dismiss the case against the teacher before him (*Southern Star*, 21 November 1931, 9).

74　Department of Education, File 20412.

75　*Ibid.*

76　Eight-year-old Michael Mannion of Rosmuck was locked in a cupboard in a schoolroom by his teacher Thomas McDevitt in 1931. The child managed to escape when he heard his mother asking where he was. The judge in the case awarded £20 to the plaintiff as this type of assault was specifically mentioned in the 1908 Act. (*Connacht Tribune*, 7 November 1931, 22).

was a finding of technical assault due to negligence or/and an award of a few pounds.[77]

After the partition of Ireland (1921), we begin to see a very different approach to physical abuse developing in Northern Ireland, with the successful prosecution of abusive teachers and a healthy evolution of the Common Law. By contrast, in the 1940s and 1950s we see an increasing number of assault charges being brought against parents in the South after confrontations with abusive teachers who could not be satisfactorily dealt with by the courts.[78] In this sort of case, the police did not hesitate to get involved and the mother or father was invariably convicted.

In 1955, a group of frustrated parents set up the School-Children's Protection Organization to try to do something a little more constructive about the abuse their children were suffering, abuse that they too had suffered in their own school days. They collected testimony from parents and children across the country, published these in a pamphlet called *Punishment in Our Schools* and calmly lobbied the Minister of Education, asking him to make sure that teachers respected the rules on corporal punishment. The Minister at the time was former General Richard Mulcahy who reacted as if a group of dangerous subversives were attempting a *coup d'etat*. It was, he said: 'an attack by people reared in an alien and in a completely un-Irish atmosphere [...] It is an attack on the whole spirit of our educational system and it is an endeavour to attack our educational roots.'[79]

Not surprisingly, this campaign ultimately failed but the Organization has, nonetheless, left us with a valuable source of information on what was

---

77   A survey of newspaper and court reports between 1930 and 1960 reveals a wide range of abusive behaviors on the part of teachers and the extreme reluctance of judges to intervene.

78   Cases include: an assault on national schoolteacher James Doyle by John Walsh because he had beaten his son. Walsh was sentenced to one month in prison (*The Irish Press*, 24 September 1932, 7). Teacher Miss B. Foley was assaulted by the mother of one of her pupils in County Clare in 1933 (*The Cork Examiner*, 9 May 1993, 5). In 1942 school Principal Patrick Fahey was assaulted by John Moran whose son had, in his opinion, been excessively punished by the plaintiff (*Western People*, 4 July 1942, 3).

79   *Dáil Éireann debates*, vol. 152 (8 July 1955), col. 470.

going on in schools at the time. Collectively, the letters they published in 1955 depict Irish teachers as callous, contemptuous and abusive. Children were beaten for anything and nothing with fists and objects of every kind. They were warned against telling their parents what was happening in class and beaten if word got out. They were beaten if they testified against a teacher in court, if they were late for school, if the teacher did not like a parent, if they did not learn quickly enough. Parents across the country were terrorized into providing or paying for fuel for school buildings, and paying for the upkeep of classrooms.[80] Their children were beaten if they came to school without the money demanded or if they did not sell enough raffle tickets. Parents were misled about Department of Education rules, while teachers, managers, inspectors and department officials conspired to deprive entire families of their rights. Parents who dared to confront teachers risked assault or making matters worse for their children. Principals transferred or threatened to transfer children to other schools to control and punish interfering parents, sometimes obliging children to attend schools far from their homes. They often refused transfers for the same reason. If parents dared to keep their children out of school to protect them, teachers immediately informed the police. Parents could then be fined and their child potentially sent to an industrial school.[81] The power wielded by teachers was enormous and enormously abused. Successive Ministers did nothing to change the situation and their department abandoned parents and children to their fate.

This brief historiographical experiment is an attempt to explore alternative approaches to representing past child abuse in Ireland. We are far from satisfied with the histories which have, so far, emerged from the archives. Abusers do not document their crimes for posterity and accounts written by abused children while they were still children are extremely rare. Folk memory and the voices of adult abuse survivors must, therefore, be

---

80 Heating and maintenance of school buildings was the responsibility of the Department of Education and school managers. It was, nonetheless, a widespread practice in Ireland to extort money and fuel from parents by concealing this fact and physically abusing children who came to school empty-handed.

81 Testimony concerning all of these abuses is contained in *Punishment in our Schools*.

taken seriously and treated as valid historical sources. To do otherwise is to blinker ourselves. The absence of these voices from the work of both Moira J. Maguire and Diarmaid Ferriter has diminished the potential for insight their histories contain. We need to be suspicious of archives and of those who claim that there can be no evidence without documentation. We do not need talk of 'allegations' and 'alleged crimes' when we discuss child abuse. We are not lawyers. Instead, we should heed the warnings and encouragements contained in Amnesty International's 2011 report *In Plain Sight: Responding to the Ferns, Ryan, Murphy and Cloyne Reports*:

> There have been voices that have sought to dismiss systemic and barbaric cruelty as the norm in the Ireland of the time. Such voices must not be permitted to rewrite or diminish this history, neither now nor in the future, and for that reason it is vital that Amnesty International use the language of international law to clearly name the violations inflicted upon children for what they were. Systemic and repeated rape isn't just child sexual abuse and systemic and ritualized beatings are not merely corporal punishment; they amount to torture in certain circumstances [...] But the focus cannot be purely on the past, as if this history has no relevance for our society now. We must consider the degree to which this history reveals vital truths about the nature of our society today. The past only becomes history once we have addressed it, learnt from it and made the changes necessary to ensure that we do not repeat mistakes and wrongdoing.[82]

82   Amnesty International, *In Plain Sight: Responding to the Ferns, Ryan, Murphy and Cloyne Reports* (Dublin: Amnesty International Ireland, 2011), 7. *The Ferns Report* (2005) was the result of an official Irish government inquiry into the allegations of clerical sexual abuse in the Roman Catholic Diocese of Ferns in County Wexford. *The Ryan Report* (2009) is a popular name for the report of the CICA. *The Murphy Report* (2009) was the culmination of a Government inquiry into the sexual abuse scandal in the Catholic Archdiocese of Dublin. The *Cloyne Report* (2011) was the result of an inquiry into child sexual abuse in the Roman Catholic Diocese of Cloyne.

VALERIE PEYRONEL

The Banking Crisis in Ireland and its Resolution: Authority(ies) in Question?

ABSTRACT

From the mid-1990s to 2007, a housing bubble was generated in Ireland, as it was in many other European countries as well as in the United States, as a result of over-easy access to credit facilities. Consequently, bank assets expanded as never before and credit conditions deteriorated. As households were no longer in a position to pay back their loans, banks were faced with abyssal losses. In parallel, a new attitude towards risk handling emerged, while people were losing confidence in the Irish economy. The situation was set to result in the implementation of bailouts and other rescue plans, as well as in the restructuring of the Irish banking system. In the light of the above-mentioned context, this chapter aims to examine the concept of authority both as a cause for the crisis and as an instrument used to remedy the crisis.

From the mid-1990s to 2007, a housing bubble (including both residential and commercial real estate) shaped up in Ireland, as it did in many other European countries as well as in the United States, as a result of an over-easy access to credit facilities. Consequently, bank assets expanded as never before and credit conditions deteriorated. The rise in real estate prices (as demand exceeded supply) further accelerated the demand for credit. Banks became very exposed to the collapse of the real estate market as the value of the properties which backed mortgages was slumping. As households were no longer in a position to pay back their loans, banks were faced with abyssal losses. In parallel, a new attitude towards risk handling emerged, while people were losing confidence in the Irish economy, two elements that made it more difficult for Irish banks to refinance themselves. The situation was going to result in the implementation of bailouts and other rescue plans, as well as in the restructuring of the Irish banking system. In the light of the above-mentioned context, this chapter aims to examine the concept of authority both as a cause for the crisis and as an instrument used to remedy the crisis.

The German sociologist and economist Max Weber identified three distinct kinds of authority:[1]

- traditional authority, shaped by past customs and practices, and which is subordinated to political power;
- the rational authority related to an official position, which an individual can be entrusted with owing to his testified skills and along legally binding publicized fixed rules;
- the charismatic authority of an individual trusted to hold exceptional qualities.

According to French sociologist Michel Crozier,[2] authority is the same as the power which is legitimized by organizational rules. Crossing both definitions, one can conclude that authority is an attribution or a skill which legitimates the power to order and be obeyed. Consequently, authority is likely to be irreparably undermined by any lack of skills, as its exercise rests in the trust of those it is exercised over.

In the case of the Irish banking crisis, this chapter proposes to try and assess to what extent the economic and political context may have undermined the Irish government's authority. It will then examine the Irish government's failures in coping with the crisis and the crisis of confidence these failures fostered. Finally this chapter will analyse the intricate confusion of authorities that prevailed in the remediation processes.

---

1   Max Weber, 'Autorité: de la hiérarchie à la négociation', *Sciences Humaines*, 117 (June 2001).
2   Michel Crozier, *Le phénomène bureaucratique* (Paris: Editions Point Seuil, 1963).

1. The global context for the crisis

To start with one should reflect upon the liberal and globalized context in which the Irish economic and banking systems are inserted, and explore to what extent such a context may have hindered the exercise of a national Irish controlling and supervising authority on these systems.

1.1.

The first difficulty the exercise of a national controlling authority on the Irish banking system entailed for the Irish government and controlling bodies (the Financial Regulator)[3] arose from the fact that, as a result of its open and increasingly globalized structure, Ireland had become a branch-plant economy not only in industrial fields but also in the banking sector. On the eve of the crisis, Ireland was hosting the branches of more than thirty foreign banks[4] and was consequently confronted with a duality of authorities: the domestic regulations of the countries where the branches had their headquarters and the Irish national banking regulations.

Ireland is indeed integrated in a vast network of European and international banking and financial services and can even boast the development of a very successful International Financial Services Centre (IFSC) in Dublin. But, as was reminded in an address by Jonathan McMahon, Assistant Director General for the Financial Institutions Supervision, Central Bank of Ireland, in May 2010, Ireland as a host country to foreign banks holding Irish funds depends on the supervising authorities of the branches and subsidiaries' home countries for a large range of processes: 'To

---

3   The Financial Regulator (Irish Financial Services Regulatory Authority) was the single regulator of financial institutions in the Republic of Ireland between May 2003 and October 2010.

4   Among which AMRO Bank (Netherlands), Bank of America (USA), Barclays (UK), Intesa SanPaolo (Brazil), Helaba Dublin – Landesbank Hessen (Germany), Wachovia Bank International (Poland).

ensure that: (a) the parent banks of Irish branches are prudentially sound; (b) information relevant to financial stability in Ireland is shared with us [them]; (c) in wind down or insolvency situations deposit compensation arrangements are robust'.[5]

As concerns point a) Ireland, considered as a promising destination for foreign investment, including in banking and financial activities at the time of the Celtic Tiger, was indeed exposed to the chances taken by foreign banks willing to develop their activities in Ireland. As regards point b) the crisis has indeed pointed to the question of information asymmetry[6] entailed by the globalization and delocalization (branch structure) of financial and banking activities, on the one hand, between the host country and the investing country, and on the other hand between headquarters and their branches and subsidiaries. All the more so when the foreign partners of a European country do not belong to the European Economic Area. Finally, point c) points out that conflicting interests can oppose host and investing countries when companies decide to safeguard their interests in their home country rather than those of their branches and subsidiaries in host countries: in the case of banking activities, by winding up subsidiaries and branches abroad, part or full repatriation of assets, or, even worse, locating toxic assets (or bad debt)[7] in the foreign subsidiaries to delete them from headquarters' accounts in the home country. As a result of the crisis, some foreign banks operating in Ireland have indeed decided to either close down or sell numerous branches.[8]

---

5 Jonathan McMahon, 'The Irish banking crisis: lessons learned, future challenges', *Address to Mazars Banking Conference, Central Bank and Financial Services Authority of Ireland* (Dublin, 26 May 2010), 7.

6 Condition in which at least some relevant information is known to some but not to all parties involved. Information asymmetry causes markets to become inefficient since all the market participants do not have access to the information they need for their decision-making processes. Investorwords.com: <http://www.investorwords. com/2461/information_asymmetry.html>, accessed 2 June 2013.

7 A toxic asset is an asset which has lost significant value and consequently finds no purchasers.

8 The decision by Ulster Bank (UK) in July 2013 to close thirty-nine branches throughout the Irish territory illustrates this point.

1.2.

Secondly, as was underlined by Jonathan Mc Mahon, in a liberal model, a government's capacity to interfere with economic operations is reduced: 'The particular challenge for Ireland emerges from its chosen model of economic governance which leaves government with fewer levers to pull when risks start to accumulate in the banking system'.[9] In a speech delivered on 17 March 2010, Lord Adair Turner, head of the British Financial Services Authority,[10] underlined that in a very open and competitive global market, it would have been difficult for Ireland to impose too strict rules on credit facilities, for fear of losing business investors in particular: 'If, for instance, Ireland had increased capital requirements for commercial real estate lending counter-cyclically in the years before 2008, the constraint on its own banks would have been partially offset by increased lending from British or other foreign competitors'.[11]

2. Mistakes and failures

However, the Irish banking crisis cannot be attributed to the sole liberalized and globalized economic and financial context, constantly infringing the national authority of the Irish government and of the Irish Financial Regulator. The crisis of the Irish banking sector also stemmed from mistakes,

9 Jonathan McMahon, 'The Irish banking crisis: lessons learned, future challenges', 5.
10 The Financial Services Authority was the body responsible for the regulation of the financial services industry in Britain from 2001 to 2013. It was abolished by the Financial Services Act 2012 and its responsibilities were transferred to two new agencies: the Prudential Regulation Authority (PRA) and the Financial Conduct Authority (FCA).
11 Lord Adair Turner, 'What do banks do, what should they do and what public policies are needed to ensure best results for the real economy?', *CASS Business School Speech* (17 March 2010).

misconducts or errors of judgement by the Irish government and regulators making poor use of the authority related to their function.

2.1.

First of all the Irish government's and regulators' authority was warped by errors of judgment or of appraisal, as again underlined by Jonathan MacMahon: 'It is also clear that numerical estimations of risk came to beguile financial institutions and regulators alike – for example the output of Value at Risk models[12] or Basel II[13] capital calculations'.[14] In particular, the potential consequences of the housing bubble were clearly underestimated, as the following words uttered by the then Minister of Finance Brian Lenihan can attest: 'Under this Government's assured stewardship, the fundamentals of the Irish economy remain strong. Because of this we are well placed to absorb the housing adjustments and external "shocks" so that our medium-term prospects will continue to be favourable. Our public finances are sound, with one of the lowest levels of debt in the euro area. Our markets are flexible allowing us to respond efficiently to adverse developments'.[15] It became known afterwards that a certain number of warning messages by pundits[16] had been neglected if not dodged.

Besides underestimating risks, the Irish government started confusing the solvency crisis with a liquidity crisis. Consequently it started implementing a guarantee scheme (The Credit Institutions Financial

12   'Value at risk' is a statistical technique used to measure and quantify the level of financial risk within a firm or investment portfolio over a specific time frame.
13   Basel II is a framework agreement published in June 2004 to revise the standards governing the capital adequacy of internationally active banks.
14   Jonathan McMahon, 'The Irish banking crisis: lessons learned, future challenges', 11.
15   Brian Lenihan TD, Minister for Finance, 'Speech in front of Seanad Eireann' (14 May 2008): <http://www.finance.gov.ie/viewdoc.asp?DocID=5286>, accessed 4 May 2013.
16   Professor Morgan Kelly, a professor of economics at University College Dublin, or economist Cormac O'Grada, in particular, had laid a particular emphasis on the very gloomy future perspectives of the housing bubble.

Support – CIFS)[17] amounting to €375 billion, that is to say 240% of the Irish Gross Domestic Product. At the time these preliminary measures were considered as adequate, or even innovative, as no other European country had chosen such a scheme. As a result, the Irish government was regarded as a reactive and trustworthy authority.

In January 2009, the Irish government decided to recapitalize Allied Irish Bank (AIB) and Bank of Ireland and took control of Anglo-Irish Bank, operating a reassuring transfer of authority from the private to the public sphere, which was confirmed by a vote in Parliament on 20 January 2009. The Irish government set up a 'bad bank', the National Asset Management Agency (NAMA), to write out the banks' property development loans which, as a result of the burst of the housing bubble, had turned into toxic assets.

Nevertheless, when losses loomed larger than expected the loss of confidence in the Irish banking system deepened, making it more difficult for Irish banks to find funding to recapitalize and offset their losses. As other countries and financial markets were becoming increasingly confronted to similar difficulties, funding capacities were becoming scarcer. It was not until mid-2010 that the Irish government became aware of the 'solvency' status of the crisis, a fact which highlighted the inadequacy and lack of scope of the measures implemented at that point, and the necessity to have recourse to a €90 billion ECB-IMF bailout programme.

Not only had the Irish government lacked the necessary skills and competences which supposedly underlie a political authority and enable it to be obeyed and impose its rules, but considering the drastic budget deficit reduction conditions that were imposed by the ECB and IMF[18] in exchange for the bailout, it was to yield to a superior authority whose rules Ireland would have to abide by to be rescued.

---

17 Credit Institutions (Financial Support) Act 2008, <http://www.irishstatutebook. ie/2008/en/act/pub/0018/>

18 Prime Minister Brian Cowen's 2011 budget was to seek €4.5 billion in spending cuts and to raise an extra €1.5 billion in taxes.

2.2.

Gaps in the supervision and control of access to funding were another identified cause for the crisis. Although such a weakness could also be attributed to globalization and the increasing internationalization of financial operations and financial markets, it was another piece of evidence of the difficulties encountered by the Irish government to fully and satisfactorily exercise its authority on the Irish financial system and of the inadequacy of the Financial Control Authority then in place.

The financial crisis was indeed fostered by the banks' capacity to easily and cheaply have access to funding as, in the years before the crisis, funds had become abundantly available on wholesale markets, increasing credit facilities, a phenomenon known as 'capital flow bonanza', as confirmed by Jonathan McMahon: 'Between December 2004 and December 2007, Irish banks imported deposits at an incremental rate of €22.8 billion annually'.[19] These figures testify that the Irish government decided not to make use of authoritative policies to regulate the increase in credit and preferred favouring free competition and free market forces, as long as these could boost the Irish economy, as pointed by Adalet MacGowan in an OECD report published in November 2011: 'In an environment of lax prudential supervision, fierce competition for market share emerged amongst Irish banks as well as with local affiliates of UK based banks, such as Ulster bank'.[20]

2.3.

Finally the financial scandals which were revealed in the light of the banking crisis, contributed to breaking Irish people's trust in their government's and Financial Supervision bodies' ability to make proper use of the institutional 'rational' authority they were meant to represent. Furthermore, these scandals infringed on the 'charismatic' authority of bank managers, supposed to rely on 'exceptional qualities' according to Max Weber's

19   Jonathan McMahon, 'The Irish banking crisis: lessons learned, future challenges', 2.
20   Muge Adalet McGowan, 'Overcoming the banking crisis', *OECD Economics Department*, Working Papers N°907 (22 November 2011), 7.

definition. Indeed the 'hidden loans' crisis[21] at AIB's, led to the resignation, on 9 January 2009, of top executives among whom Sean Fitzpatrick,
CEO, and Patrick Neary, Financial Regulator. Reports actually revealed
that Neary had been aware of AIB's hidden loans for eight years before the
scandal broke out. A resignation which not only symbolized the failure of
these prominent characters to deal with the crisis, therefore questioning
their rational authority, but also highlighted their lack of exceptional virtues as, at best, careless or incapable people, at worst, ordinary criminals.
The forgery of Anglo-Irish's accounts thanks to circular transactions with
Permanent TSB,[22] which was discovered after Anglo-Irish's nationalization,
was an illustrative example of the lack of control of the banking system by
political authorities – government and Financial Regulator alike.

3. A challenge to financial authorities

In order to rebuild Irish people's as well as foreign investors' trust in the
devastated Irish banking system and in the Irish government's capacity to
solve the crisis, it became urgent to restore a controlling and supervising
authority, whose undisputed skills would enable it to impose new regulatory policies.

3.1.

Since 2003, the Bank of Ireland had been separated from the Financial
Regulator, the Financial Services Authority of Ireland.[23] But the lack
of coordination and communication between the two bodies was to be

21   In December 2008, Sean Fitzpatrick, AIB's CEO, admitted he had hidden €87 billion
     in loans from the bank.
22   Circular transactions are a fraudulent trading scheme of shares.
23   At that time, separating the Central Bank from the Financial Regulator had been con-
     sidered as a better guarantee against any possible misconduct in financial operations.

identified as one of the reasons for the insufficient supervision of macro-financial relations. In the light of the financial crisis, it became essential to offer banks' customers, investors but also Irish people at large, a new uncontested and central banking supervising authority. The role of the Central Bank of Ireland had to be redefined and tightened:

> Further progress is required in how we think about our role as banking supervisors and specifically about how extensively we will intervene in the commercial decisions banks made. In the period preceding the crisis, supervisory culture internationally, with the possible exception of some Asian countries, tended to be too deferential towards free market ideas, and too responsive to critics of regulation and regulators. Our task as the Central Bank is therefore to foster a supervisory culture in which we take judgments on banks' own judgments, and are then prepared to be tenacious, but not pig-headed, in defence of the public interest objectives government has given us.[24]

The Central Bank Act 2010, which was applicable from 1 October 2010, established a new and unique Central Bank in charge of central banking activities as well as financial regulation. Bank supervisors work in close cooperation with the Central Bank departments in charge of markets, payments and financial stability. Besides, the 2010 Act entrusted the new Central Bank with a new function called Prudential Analytics and aimed to analyse risks and business models, thus developing the Central Bank's skills to legitimize its decisions and policies. The Central Bank website presents these skills under the heading 'fit and proper':

> Directors and Managers of financial service providers regulated by the Central Bank are required to meet standards of competence and probity known as the 'fit and proper' standards.
> Under these standards they are required to have the necessary qualifications, skills and experience to perform the duties of their position and to be honest, fair and ethical.
> The Central Bank has developed a common test that applies across most financial service providers subject to our regulation.[25]

24   Jonathan McMahon, 'The Irish banking crisis: lessons learned, future challenges', 11.
25   <http://www.centralbank.ie/regulation/processes/supervision/Pages/how-super-vise.aspx>.

3.2.

Decisions made to restructure the banking sector were also part of rehabilitating the authority of Irish political and financial leaders by showing their capacity to skillfully impose their views. In the presentation of the objectives of this restructuring process in a Government Banking Policy Division document on 30 March 2011, the role to be played by the government was particularly underlined: 'The Irish Government recognizes it is at a critical turning point for restoring the Irish banking system to health and returning it to its basic function of serving the Irish economy and the Irish people'.[26] Among the key actions to be taken, the report laid the emphasis on the necessity to 'revisit the structures of the Irish Authorities to ensure active management of the State's investment in the banking sector'.[27] Furthermore, the document promised a better control and supervision of credit, as a way to avoid the formerly undetected solvency pitfall: 'We will however be rigorously monitoring the banks' activities to ensure this credit is entering the system for borrowers meeting reasonable credit standard requirements'.[28] Finally the report made a special point of banks' governance, reaffirming the authority of government over banking management: 'The Government welcomes the recent developments on governance announced by the Central Bank on enhanced fitness and probity requirements for senior management and directors of banks. The Department of Finance and the National Treasury Management Agency will work closely with the Central Bank to ensure that these requirements are applied to the covered banks as a matter of priority'.[29]

The crisis prompted immediate action by the Irish government and in-depth changes in the structure of the Irish banking sector, touching the three major banks in Ireland (Bank of Ireland – BoI, Allied Irish Bank – AIB, and Anglo-Irish Bank – Anglo-Irish) and three smaller ones (Irish

---

26   John A. Moran, 'Restructuring of the Irish Banking System', *Government Banking Policy Division* (31 March 2011), 3.
27   *Ibid.*, 6.
28   *Ibid.*, 15.
29   *Ibid.*, 36.

Nationwide Building Society – INBS, Irish Life and Permanent – ILP and Education Building Society – EBS). Allied Irish Bank (AIB) was nationalized in December 2010. Bank of Ireland (BoI) was partly recapitalized by the State but also compelled to increase its private recapitalization in parallel (a successful operation which resulted in reducing BoI's indebtedness ratio down from 30 in 2008 to 14.2 in 2011). Anglo-Irish was nationalized in January 2009 before merging with INBS to form the Irish Bank Resolution Corporation (IBRC).[30] Indeed, INBS was nationalized in March 2010 but in February 2011 its deposits finally had to be sold to Irish Life and Permanent. As the latter also had to be partly nationalized in July 2011,[31] INBS's assets and liabilities were transferred to Anglo-Irish Bank, both banks forming IBRC. Finally the Irish government took a participation in EBS's capital in December 2009, but EBS became an AIB branch in July 2011.

4. A challenge to political authority

Such steps were badly needed as in the meantime the Government's authority had been massively challenged. The lack of control and regulation by the political authorities had not been questioned by consumers as long as they could benefit from the system. Indeed the development of consumer credit facilities, with very few regulations and limits such as the Loan To Value ratios[32] used in other countries like France or Germany, also contributed to the destabilization of financial markets.

30   In the meantime, Anglo-Irish filed for bankruptcy in February 2013 and IBRC's remaining assets have been transferred to Bank of Ireland (BoI).
31   The Irish Life Group, part of Irish Life and Permanent, was purchased by the Irish government, and the remaining activities were renamed Permanent TSB Group Holdings.
32   Loan To Value ratio (LTV) consists in calculating the value of a mortgage as a percentage of the estimated value of the real estate property. It enables a bank to make

But as the financial crisis and its consequences were looming larger, as trust in the Government, in bank managers and in the Financial Regulator's skills was fading away, their legitimate authority started being questioned. This was first illustrated by massive reactions to the ECB-IMF bailout plan and against the related four-year austerity plan meant to save up a total of €15 bn. During the November 2010 demonstrations, a protester was reported to have clearly expressed this distrust: 'But today is just the start of a campaign against the plan. This government doesn't have a mandate to govern; they should allow for a general election and let the public say if they are in favour of the four-year plan'.[33]

Sinn Fein's leader Gerry Adams was reported to have denied the Fianna Fail government in power the 'mandate to negotiate such terms and impose such a burden on ordinary Irish taxpayers'.[34] And the popular vote at the general election of 25 February 2011, relegated the crisis party, Fianna Fail, to third position, with only nineteen seats (losing fifty-eight seats as compared to 2007) and 17.45% of the votes (losing 24.11% of the votes as compared to 2007).[35]

However the endorsement of the European fiscal compact by 60.3% of the Irish voters at the referendum organized on May 31, 2012 was a piece of evidence that the Irish were ready to again acknowledge both the Irish government's and European institutions' political authority, in the sense given to 'political authority' by C. W. Cassinelli: 'The exercise of political authority requires the citizen to obey uncritically and without considering the possibility of coercion; the possession of political authority depends

---

sure that if the borrower cannot pay back its debt, the bank will be paid back on the value of the property. It is also used to assess the capacity of the borrower to pay back its loan.

33 Patrick Sawer, 'Thousands protest against the Irish bail-out', Telegraph (27 November 2010): <www.telegraph.co.uk/news/worldnews/europe/ireland/8164714/Thousands-protest-against-Irishbailout.html#disqus_thread>, retrieved on 6 May 2013.

34 *Ibid.*

35 Irish Election, Trinity College Dublin (25 February 2011): <http://www.tcd.ie/Political_Science/staff/michael_gallagher/Election2011.php, retrieved on 11 June 2013>.

upon his critical acceptance of the use of coercion, and it is compatible with his occasional disobedience'.[36]

Though this may have been a vote by necessity, it nevertheless demonstrated the recognition, by the Irish people that their national governing bodies could be worth their trust and could handle the exceptional situation ensuing from the crisis skillfully enough for the rules they were setting to be abided by.

Conclusion

Hannah Arendt defined authority as a hierarchical relationship, but one very distinct from either power or persuasion: 'Since authority always demands obedience, it is commonly mistaken for some form of power or violence. Yet authority precludes the use of external means of coercion: where force is used, authority itself has failed. Authority, on the other hand, is incompatible with persuasion, which presupposes equality and works through a process of argumentation'.[37]

The banking crisis in Ireland, as well as the steps taken to solve it, have illustrated the difficulties and complexity of exercising political authority in a globalized and international context. It has highlighted to what extent trust is an essential ingredient, and that trust builds on the knowledge that those who represent authority are skilled, honest and act in transparency.

36   C. W. Cassinelli, 'Political Authority: Its Exercise and Possession', *The Western Political Quarterly*, Vol. 14, N°3 (September 1961), 635.
37   Hannah Arendt, 'What is authority?', 1954, <https://webspace.utexas.edu/>, accessed 15 May 2013.

MARIE-VIOLAINE LOUVET

Challenging the Authority of the Irish State on the Question of the Middle East: The Two Gaza Flotillas of May 2010 and November 2011

ABSTRACT

In May 2010 and November 2011, the transnational association 'Free Gaza', actively supported by its Irish branch, sent two flotillas to Gaza, as a challenge to the Israeli maritime blockade which was imposed on the area in 2007. In both cases, an Irish ship was part of the flotilla: the *MV Rachel Corrie* in 2010 and the *MV Saoirse* in 2011. 'Free Gaza' is the head of an international network of associations which functions as a transnational movement, without the participation or the consultation of states. The Irish activists who took part in the flotilla bypassed the state and the traditional institutions holding authority over foreign policy, in particular the Department of Foreign Affairs, in order to denounce the Israeli policy towards Gaza.

In May 2010 and November 2011, the transnational association 'Free Gaza', actively supported by its Irish branch, sent two flotillas to Gaza, as a challenge to the Israeli maritime blockade which was imposed on the area in 2007. In both cases, an Irish ship was part of the flotilla: the *MV Rachel Corrie* in 2010 and the *MV Saoirse* in 2011. 'Free Gaza' is the head of an international network of associations which functions as a transnational movement, without the participation or the consultation of states. The Irish activists who took part in the flotilla bypassed the state and the traditional institutions holding authority over foreign policy, in particular the Department of Foreign Affairs, in order to denounce the Israeli policy towards Gaza.

Notwithstanding the international character of the action, the national identities of the activists as Irish citizens, as well as the registration of the boats as Irish boats, committed the Irish state, which was responsible for the security of its nationals. Particularly striking is the fact that this initiative triggered tensions at state level and aroused Israel's anger towards an

Irish state placed in an ambiguous and uncomfortable position.[1] Indeed, in the two cases under scrutiny, Israel called on the Irish state to stop what it considered to be a provocation, and the Irish state found itself obliged to see to the safety of the Irish citizens on the boats, without having supported their action in the first place. The cacophony of voices claiming to express Irish foreign policy gave rise to a crisis and a challenge to the authority of a state confined to the role of mediator between the activists and Israel.

The crisis which was brought about by the conflicting voices of the state and civil associations, when both endeavoured to frame an Irish foreign policy, is what I propose to analyse in this chapter. It is particularly enlightening in that regard to compare the interactions between the Irish state diplomacy, Israel and the civil associations in May 2010 and November 2011, when the two Gaza flotillas set sail. The analysis will begin with a timeline of the events before focusing on the response from the Irish government, all the while questioning the efficiency of such direct action at a national and international level.

Freedom Flotillas as civil society initiatives

The Gaza blockade and the creation of 'Free Gaza'

On 25 January 2006, the Islamic political party Hamas obtained a majority of nineteen seats over Fatah in the Palestinian Parliament. As a result, a coalition government was formed by the two political parties. The new government was led by Ismail Haniyeh who was nominated Prime Minister on 21 February 2006 by President Mahmud Abbas, Yasser Arafat's successor. Israel, which considered Hamas as an enemy faction and a threat to

---

1   Itamar Eichner, 'Ireland most hostile country in Europe', *Ynetnews: Israel News* (16 November 2011).

its security, imposed economic sanctions on Palestine.[2] In June 2007, one and a half year afterwards, in the aftermath of the battle of Gaza between Fatah and Hamas, the latter took control of Gaza, thus ousting its political competitor. As a response, Israel set up a land blockade, which it justified by security reasons, so that Hamas could not be provided with weapons, in particular rockets which could be used over the border to reach Israeli cities like Sderot and Ashkalon. A maritime blockade was in effect off the coast of Gaza as of January 2009. In 2010, the blockade, which stifled the Palestinian economy, was limited to military equipment, including such vital material as cement.[3]

Every semester, the reports of the United Nations Relief and Works Agency (UNRWA)[4] denounced the horrendous impact of the blockade on the economy in Gaza and the appalling living conditions of its 1.6 million inhabitants, amongst whom more than half are children. According to figures provided by the United Nations, the unemployment rate in Gaza reached 45% in 2012, when 79.4% of the population lived under the poverty threshold.[5] The Human Rights Council requested the blockade to be lifted in 2008, without any positive response from Israel.[6] UN resolution 1860, which was adopted in January 2009, during Operation Cast Lead,

---

2   Article 7 of the Hamas Charter, the constitution of the party, is threatening towards Jewish people: 'The prophet, prayer and peace be upon him, said: The time will not come until Muslims will fight the Jews (and kill them); until the Jews hide behind rocks and trees, which will cry: o Muslim! There is a Jew hiding behind me, come on and kill him!'.

3   The border crossing between Egypt and Gaza through Rafah had been closed in 2007, under the rule of President Hosni Mubarak, because he was hostile to Hamas. In May 2011, post-revolutionary Egypt opened the crossing to Gaza again, due to the good relations between Hamas and the Muslim Brotherhood. In 2014, after Abdul Fattah al-Sisi came to power in Egypt, the Rafah border crossing was closed again.

4   UNRWA is the UN agency which was set up in December 1949 to provide assistance to the 750,000 Palestinian refugees displaced during the 1948–1949 Arab-Israeli war.

5   United Nations Development Programme, 'The Gaza Strip – Facts, Figures and UNDP's Response to the Ongoing Crisis', 2012.

6   Nick Cumming-Bruce, 'UN Human Rights Council condemns Israeli blockade of Gaza', *New York Times* (4 February 2008).

expressed grave concern at the deepening humanitarian crisis in Gaza, and emphasized the need to ensure a regular flow of goods and people through the Gaza crossings. It also called for a ceasefire that would lead to the complete withdrawal of Israeli forces from Gaza, as well as an unimpeded provision and distribution throughout Gaza of humanitarian assistance, including food, fuel and medical treatment. Lastly, it welcomed the initiatives to create and open humanitarian corridors and other mechanisms for the sustained delivery of humanitarian aid.[7] In June 2012, fifty international aid groups and United Nations agencies issued a joint appeal urging Israel to lift its blockade of the Gaza Strip.[8]

Given the lack of efficiency of the international community to convince Israel to lift the blockade, an idea dawned on Michail Shaik, an Australian activist, in 2006, and spread among political activists in the International Solidarity Movement, a pro-Palestinian civil association that was set up in 2001. It consisted of the following: 'Charter a big boat to sail from New York. Make it clear that its purpose is to break the siege of Gaza (that can be the slogan of the campaign). It is very important that the boat have a big send off, with speeches by important people that will get it as much publicity as possible.'[9] With this illumination, 'Free Gaza' was founded in 2006, defining itself as a pro-Palestinian coalition of civil associations, all committed to the defence of human rights. Before the 2010 flotilla and the first sending of an Irish boat, the organization had sent eight convoys of boats towards Gaza, five of which had reached their destination. A Northern Irish involvement was noticeable in the flotillas heading for Gaza in October 2008[10] and June 2009,[11] with the presence on board of Mairéad Corrigan-Maguire, the 1976 Nobel Peace Prize winner.

---

7   UN 1860 resolution, 8 January 2009.
8   'NGOs, UN agencies call on Israel to lift Gaza blockade', *Haaretz* (14 June 2012); 'UN agencies join in shared call for end to Israeli blockade of Gaza', *UN News Center* (14 June 2012). <http://www.un.org/apps/news/story.asp?NewsID=42227#.Uc6yo5zvIYA> consulted on 29 June 2013.
9   Elias Harb, 'Interview with Greta Berlin', *Intifada Voice of Palestine* (13 July 2010).
10   'Israel must learn from North says Corrigan', *Irish Times* (20 October 2008).
11   '"Free Gaza" boats stopped in Cyprus', *The Jerusalem Post* (25 June 2009).

One remarkable characteristic of the pro-Palestinian civil associations which were involved in the flotillas was that they acted in a completely independent fashion from the state, but within an international network with sister organizations, be they in the western world or in the Middle East. Keck and Sikkink identify the development of such non-national bodies as 'transnational advocacy networks': 'A transnational advocacy network includes those relevant actors working internationally on an issue, who are bound together by shared values, a common discourse and dense exchanges of information and services'.[12] Transnational networks, such as 'Free Gaza', stand out because of the centrality of the cause that they defend which is the cement between the different associations.

The MV Rachel Corrie and Freedom Flotilla I

In May 2010, 'Free Gaza' participated in the first self-styled 'Freedom Flotilla', a convoy of six ships, with an Irish vessel among them; the *MV Rachel Corrie* was named after a young American member of the International Solidarity Movement who was run over by an Israeli bulldozer in Gaza in 2003.[13] 'Free Gaza' worked in coordination with five other international organizations: IHH Humanitarian Relief Foundation, European Campaign to End the Siege on Gaza, Greek Ship to Gaza Campaign, Swedish Ship to Gaza and International Committee to End the Siege on Gaza. The flotilla was made up of ships coming from the United States, Greece, Ireland and Turkey and carried more than 700 passengers, citizens coming from thirty-six different countries, who had all rallied around the same slogan 'Palestine Our Route. Humanitarian Aid Our Load'. The Irish ship, *MV Rachel Corrie*, had nineteen activists on board, five of them Irish. Mairéad Corrigan-Maguire and Denis Halliday, a previous UN

---

12   Margaret E. Keck & Kathryn Sikkink, *Activists beyond borders* (Ithaca: Cornell University Press), 1998, 2.

13   Chris McGreal, 'Rachel Corrie verdict exposes Israeli military mindset', *The Guardian* (28 August 2012).

Assistant Secretary-General, were among them. Three other Irish citizens were travelling on board *MV Challenger 1*, the American ship. According to the organizers, the ships were carrying a thousand tons of humanitarian goods.[14] Mairéad Corrigan-Maguire used a satellite phone from the Irish boat to confirm that the ship had been inspected so that there were no weapons on board: 'Our cargo was inspected by officials from the Irish government, by trade union officials in Dundalk and officials of the Green Party. Then the cargo was sealed, totally sealed. We don't have anything but humanitarian aid.'[15]

In addition to the humanitarian goal of helping with the Herculean task of reconstructing Gaza, the flotilla was led by a political objective. The expected media coverage would put the blockade of Gaza in the spotlight and would reveal its unfairness to the world, it was hoped. That is one of the reasons why 'Free Gaza' excluded the delivery of their humanitarian goods in the Israeli port of Ashdod, from where they would have been forwarded to Gaza, according to the Israeli government. They chose to stick to the initial plan and to head on towards Gaza instead.[16] Indeed, when the Israeli government proposed the deal to its Irish counterpart, some doubts were expressed by the activists as to the actualization of the promises. On 31 May 2010, Israeli soldiers were winched down from helicopters to stop the ships. Eight Turkish passengers and one American man of Turkish descent were killed on board the *MV Mavi Marmara* during the assault. The UN Human Rights council, which gathered in September 2010, as well as the UN Palmer report released in September 2011, condemned the

14   'Palestine our route, humanitarian aid our load, flotilla campaign summary report', IHH, 2010.
15   Interview, *RTE radio* (4 June 2010).
16   Early in July 2011, when the second Freedom Flotilla ships were forbidden to leave Greece for administrative reasons, the Greek authorities struck a deal with the Israeli government to transport the goods on board the boats to Israel, for later delivery to Gaza. 'Free Gaza' excluded the option with the following explanation given by Greta Berlin, one of the founding members: 'Not a chance that "Free Gaza" will accept that. This [effort] is not about delivering goods but breaking the illegal siege of Gaza', see: 'Gaza flotilla boat is forced back to shore', *Irish Times* (5 July 2011).

level of violence used by the Israeli army, although the latter deemed the blockade legal.[17] The *MV Rachel Corrie*, which had to remain berthed in Malta after it encountered technical difficulties, still decided to head on towards Gaza, only to be stopped a few days afterwards, on 5 June 2010, without any violent resistance from the passengers.

The MV Saoirse and Freedom Flotilla II

As a result of negative press and of the general indignation of the international community, the blockade was slightly eased by the Israeli government in June 2010. Nonetheless, that was not considered to be a sufficient effort by pro-Palestinian civil society. A second flotilla, whose departure was planned for June 2011, was soon under way. On 30 September 2011, fifty Palestinian civil associations, trade unions and NGOs publicly called for a new flotilla, which would uphold their international campaign in favour of BDS[18] against Israel: 'Creative civilian efforts such as the Free Gaza boats that broke through the blockade five times, the Gaza Freedom March, the Gaza Freedom Flotilla, and the many land convoys must never stop their siege-breaking efforts, highlighting the inhumanity of keeping 1.5 million Gazans in an open-air prison'.[19] Once again, Ireland was involved in the initiative and the organization 'Irish Ship to Gaza' was set up on 30 August 2010, in Dublin, with an aim to raise €100,000 so as to buy and send a ship to Gaza.[20] 'Irish Ship' to Gaza was also launched in Northern Ireland on 8 December 2010, with Gerry Adams sitting at the main table in Conway Mill, Belfast. The solidarity movement in the North was all the stronger since a few passengers were meant to come from the republican community in Belfast and Derry: Gerry MacLochlainn, a Sinn

---

17   'Report of the Secretary-General's Panel of Inquiry on the 31 May 2010 Flotilla Incident', July 2011.
18   Boycott, Divestment, Sanctions.
19   'A call from Gaza to the People of Conscience worldwide to break the Israeli Blockade', 1 November 2011, <http://irishshiptogaza.org> consulted on 30 June 2013.
20   '"Irish ship to Gaza" campaign launched in Dublin', *An Phoblacht* (30 August 2010).

Fein Councillor for Derry and co-founder of 'Derry Friends of Palestine',
Charlie McMenamin a member of 'Derry Friends of Palestine', and Philip
McCullough, a journalist from the Belfast Media Group.[21]

The flotilla, which was made up of ten boats, was supposed to set sail
in June 2011. However, some of the boats were forbidden to leave Greece
and to take to the sea because of administrative reasons.[22] This impedi-
ment was explained by Israeli pressure over the Greek government by some
commentators.[23] What is more, the *MV Saoirse*, like the Swedish ship *MV
Juliano*, had its propeller shaft damaged in the Turkish harbour where it
was berthed.[24] The Irish activists accused Israel of having sabotaged the
boats, without being able to provide any material evidence other than the
similarity of the damage that was done to the two boats:

> The Irish-owned ship, the *MV Saoirse*, that was meant to take part in Freedom
> Flotilla 2 has been sabotaged in a dangerous manner in the Turkish coastal town of
> Göcek, where it had been at berth for the past few weeks […] The propeller shaft
> had been weakened by saboteurs who cut, gouged or filed a piece off the shaft. This
> had weakened the integrity of the shaft, causing it to bend badly when put in use.
> The damage was very similar to that caused to the *Juliano*, another flotilla ship, in
> Greece. The consequent damage would have happened gradually as the ship was
> sailing and would have culminated in a breach of the hull.
>
> The Irish Ship to Gaza campaign believes that Israel has questions to answer and
> must be viewed as the chief suspect in this professional and very calculating act of
> sabotage.[25]

21   The list of passengers was changed between June and November 2011.
22   Michael Jansen, 'Gaza flotilla boat is forced back to shore', *Irish Times* (5 July 2011).
23   'After a complaint about improper documentation filed by an Israeli advocacy group,
      the boat had been held in port outside Athens on police orders. Inspectors visited it
      a week ago Friday, but the results of their inspection had yet to be provided. Without
      them, the ship could not legally set sail', see: Scott Sayare, 'Stuck in Dock, Flotilla
      Activists See the Hand of Israel?', *New York Times* (1 July 2011).
24   Pamela Duncan, 'Irish ship will not sail to Gaza after "sabotage"', *Irish Times* (30 June
      2011).
25   'Irish Ship to Gaza' press release: 'Sabotage of MV Saoirse in Turkey "an act of
      international terrorism"', 30 June 2011.

As a consequence of these twists, the 'Free Gaza' steering committee agreed on sending the ships in small successive groups, a strategy which they named 'Freedom Waves to Gaza'.[26] On 2 November 2011, the repaired *MV Saoirse* and the Canadian ship *MV Tahrir* left Turkey with twenty-seven passengers on board, fourteen of whom were Irish. Some prominent characters were part of the trip: Chris Andrews, a former Fianna Fáil TD, Paul Murphy, the Socialist Party/United Left Alliance MEP, Hugh Lewis, a radical left Councillor (People Before Profit Alliance) in Dún Laoghaire and Trevor Hogan, a former rugby player in the Irish national team. The flotilla was arrested by Israel on 4 November 2011, without any violent resistance from the passengers. One person is reported to have been tasered on the Canadian ship, and water cannons as well as a forced collision between the two boats induced serious damage to the *MV Saoirse*.[27] The fourteen Irish activists were held in the Givon Detention Centre, in Israel, for a week, before being sent back.

As well as drawing attention on the Gaza blockade, the flotillas compelled the Irish government to take a stand on the question, thus bringing grist to the mill of domestic debate regarding the Middle East. The Irish state was liable at two levels. First, it had to do its utmost to ensure the security of the citizens and alleviate the concern of their families and organizations. Then, at an international level, it also had to negotiate the return of the activists, as well as that of their belongings and of the boats and freight which had been seized by the Israeli army and never given back. Doing so, the Irish state had to make sure no irremediable damage was done to the bilateral relation with Israel.[28] Between the two flotillas, a change of

26   'Another flotilla sets sail for Gaza', *CNN News* (2 November 2011).
27   Hugh Farrelly, 'Trevor Hogan's mission to Gaza', *Irish Independent* (22 November 2011).
28   Bilateral relations were already strained after Israeli agents used eight Irish passports to assassinate Hamas leader Mahmoud al Mabhouh, in Dubai, on 19 January 2010. One Israeli diplomat from the embassy in Dublin was expelled from the Irish territory as a consequence. See: 'Statement by Minister for Foreign Affairs, Mr Micheál Martin, T. D., regarding the outcome of the investigations into the fraudulent use of Irish passports in the assassination of Mr. Mahmoud al Mabhouh', 15 June 2010.

government had taken place and Fianna Fáil had been replaced by a Fine Gael-Labour coalition in March 2011. Micheál Martin, the Minister for Foreign Affairs at the time of the first Freedom Flotilla, had been replaced by Eamon Gilmore, a member of the Labour Party, and the two men handled the situations in two different fashions.

The Irish State is forced to take a stand

Micheál Martin and Freedom Flotilla I

The first opportunity for the Irish government to regain authority over the matter of foreign policy in the 2010 Freedom Flotilla case was after the death of the Turkish activists on board the *MV Mavi Marmara*, when the *MV Rachel Corrie* had decided to head on towards Gaza despite the threat of an imminent Israeli intervention. Micheál Martin called on the Israeli government to let the ship reach Gaza: 'I again repeat my urgent call to the Israeli government to allow safe passage of the Irish-owned vessel, the *MV Rachel Corrie*, which is still sailing towards Gaza to deliver its consignment of humanitarian aid [...]. It is imperative that there should be no further confrontation or bloodshed arising from what has been all along a purely humanitarian mission by those involved in the Gaza flotilla'.[29] His choice was undoubtedly influenced by the large demonstrations of support for the activists, fuelled by a widespread indignation at the Israeli raid on the *MV Mavi Marmara*. In Dublin on 31 May 2010, 1,700 people gathered together to protest against the level of violence used by the Israeli army.[30] The negotiations which took place before the boarding of the *MV Rachel Corrie* were led by Martin. The Department of Foreign Affairs acted as a

---

29   'Martin appeals to Israel over Irish-owned Gaza aid ship', *Irish Independent* (2 June 2010).

30   'Protests held in Ireland over Israeli attack', *Irish Times* (31 May 2010).

mediator when its Israeli counterpart offered to forward the humanitarian freight from Ashdod to Gaza, but its hands were tied: when 'Free Gaza' refused the compromise, the negotiations abruptly ended. It was obvious at this point that the decisions were not within the prerogatives of the Irish government, whose role was limited to that of crisis management, with the help of the diplomatic personnel of the Irish embassy in Tel Aviv. The Irish consular staff in Israel was very active both in 2010 and 2011, with the same team of people in charge in the two cases.

Incapable of taking practical action, Martin could still be vindictive in his criticism of the way Israel handled the situation and of its general policy in the region regarding the Palestinian population. Martin turned out to be rather supportive of the flotilla, at least vocally, and he denounced the Israeli blockade as being 'illegal' and 'unjust'.[31] The same stance was adopted by the Taoiseach, the Irish Prime Minister, Brian Cowen, who asserted: "The reason this has happened is there's a blockade taking place at the moment in respect of humanitarian assistance being provided to Gaza, to the people of Gaza. [...] I believe that is in violation of international law. People are entitled to have humanitarian assistance."[32]

Eamon Gilmore and Freedom Flotilla II

The situation was dealt with in a very dissimilar manner in 2011. One could find two main explanations for that. Firstly, as there had not been any deaths this time and the first attempt was thwarted, the press coverage was less intense, there was less pressure from civil society and the Department of Foreign Affairs had more leeway. Secondly, the change of government with the replacement of Martin with Gilmore, in a coalition with Fine Gael, certainly played a part in this. From the first attempt of the *MV Saoirse* to

---

31   'Monday's events can be directly attributed to the illegal and unjust blockade of Gaza which Israel has maintained for some three years now', see: 'Cowen demands safe passage for Irish ship', *Irish Times* (2 June 2010).

32   'Cowen condemns Israeli flotilla attack', *Irish Independent* (31 May 2010).

participate in the flotilla in June 2011, Alan Shatter, the Minister for Justice, Equality and Defence, had voiced reservations concerning the relevance of such an action.[33] In 2011, the Department of Foreign Affairs had agreed to meet the activists before they left. Thanks to the support of Richard Boyd Barrett, the 'People Before Profit Alliance' TD for Dún Laoghaire, they had been received by Eamon Gilmore in the Dáil, the Irish Parliament.[34] Despite Gilmore's considering the blockade on Gaza as being 'absolutely unacceptable' in the same arena in April 2011,[35] the Minister was careful to underline the fact that the flotilla was in no way sponsored or supported by the Irish government in June 2011.

The level of violence which was employed during the 2011 flotilla was inferior to that which the activists had faced in 2010, as Israel had learnt its lesson and was extremely careful about media coverage. The diplomatic role of the Irish state focused on trying to hasten the release of the activists who were detained in Givon for a week. The diplomatic staff endeavoured to check that the prisoners were treated with due respect, after it became known that they had not had access to telephones during the first forty-eight hours of their captivity and had been submitted to repeated body searches. The Irish embassy in Tel Aviv lodged two firm complaints against such treatment, while the Minister for Foreign Affairs remained rather discreet.[36] Indeed, Gilmore renewed his condemnation of the blockade but not of the interception of the flotilla, which was an initiative he publicly disavowed:

> My initial reaction is one of relief that there has been no violence and that all the Irish nationals aboard the *MV Saoirse* are safe and well following this ordeal. My views and those of the Government on the Gaza blockade are well known. We do not agree with it, we regard it as contrary to international humanitarian law in its impact on the civilian population of Gaza, and we have repeatedly urged Israel to

33   'Shatter fails to see purpose behind Gaza aid flotilla', *Irish Examiner* (25 June 2011).
34   *Dáil Éireann Debate*, Vol. 734, N°2, 2 June 2011. Interestingly, Eamon Gilmore is a member of the Friends of Palestine parliamentary group in the Oireachtas.
35   *Dáil Éireann Debate*, Vol. 730, N°5, 21 April 2011.
36   Mary Fitzgerald, 'Irish Embassy in Israel complains over treatment of flotilla activists', *Irish Times* (11 November 2011).

end a policy which is unjust, counter-productive and amounts to collective punishment of 1.5 million Palestinians.[37]

The political opponents to the government, whether highly supportive or highly critical of the initiative but rarely indecisive, played an important part on the domestic scene when the 2011 flotilla was arrested. Richard Humphreys, a Labour Councillor, did not mince his words: 'Ultra left politicians such as Dún Laoghaire Rathdown County Councillor Hugh Lewis, and Paul Murphy MEP, would be fulfilling their duties better if they stayed at home and attended to their constituents, rather than heading off for this ill-advised Mediterranean cruise'.[38] The presence on board of political competitors sparked harsh comments. On the other hand, the presence on the *MV Saoirse* of Chris Andrews, a well-respected politician at the time of the flotilla,[39] brought support from his political family, Fianna Fáil and beyond, especially on the left wing, as had been planned by 'Free Gaza' when the strategy to bring prominent people on board was decided. One could quote the vocal support from Richard Boyd Barrett and Joe Higgins, a Socialist TD, who requested the expulsion of the Israeli ambassador and questioned the Taoiseach about the detention conditions in Givon.[40] Significantly, the former Minister for Foreign Affairs, Micheál Martin, who now spoke as the President of Fianna Fáil, defended both the flotilla and his colleague:

37   'Gaza activists await deportation from Israel', *RTÉ News* (7 November 2011). <http://www.rte.ie/news/2011/1105/gaza.html> consulted on 30 June 2013.

38   See Richard Humphreys' press release on the Labour Party website: 'Ultra-left flotilla politicians should heed UN and stay ashore', 26 June 2011, <http://www.labour.ie/richardhumphreys/news/1309094172572251.html>, also published on his blog <http://richardhumphreys.blogspot.ie/2011_06_01_archive.html> consulted on 30 June 2013.

39   The flotilla took place before the twitter incident which led to his resignation from Fianna Fáil in August 2012. Chris Andrews eventually joined Sinn Féin in July 2013.

40   Michael O'Regan, 'Lack of support for Irish flotilla ship a "capitulation"', *Irish Times* (30 June 2011).

I salute the people who undertook this humanitarian mission to Gaza and their efforts
to highlight the plight of the Palestinian people living there. When I was Minister
for Foreign Affairs I visited Gaza and witnessed firsthand the extraordinary conditions people are having to endure. It is a totally unacceptable situation that must
be resolved. Israel's actions in boarding the vessel and detaining citizens are totally
unacceptable. A former Fianna Fáil TD Chris Andrews is among those detained.
Peaceful political protest is entirely legitimate and must be respected. I am calling for
the immediate release all of those detained and a swift and safe journey back home.
I want to commend the work of the Department of Foreign Affairs in this regard.[41]

In a similar fashion, the delegation from Northern Ireland on board
the *MV Saoirse* included members of the republican movement, in particular John Hearne, a Sinn Fein Councillor for Waterford or John Mallon
and Phil McCullough. Their participation unsurprisingly triggered a very
strong support from the nationalist and republican communities in Belfast
and Derry. West Belfast TD, Paul Maskey, and Pat Sheehan, MLA, both
pressed Gilmore so that he made sure the Israeli authorities did not delay
the activists' return from Israel:

> I have been contacted by the family of John Mallon and Phil McCullough, two West
> Belfast passengers who were on board the Gaza bound *MV Saoirse* and are being held
> by Israel. Eamon Gilmore needs to do more to ensure safe return of the Irish citizens
> who were illegally seized in international waters and taken to Israel against their will.
> The 72 hour period that Israel said they would keep them in custody before releasing
> them has now passed yet they are still being held. [Paul Maskey]

> Israel seem intent on playing games regards the repatriation of those passen-
> gers they illegally took hostage. Israel was wrong in the first place and the Irish
> Government must impress upon Israel that their citizens be repatriated immediately.[42]
> [Pat Sheehan]

---

41   'Martin calls for immediate release of Gaza flotilla crew', *Breakingnews.ie* (6 November
      2011): <http://www.breakingnews.ie/ireland/martin-calls-for-immediate-release-
      of-gaza-flotilla-crew-527292.html> consulted on 30 June 2013.
42   'West Belfast Sinn Féin representatives call for the release and repatriation of MV
      Saoirse passengers', Sinn Féin website, 9 November 2011, <http://www.sinnfein.ie/
      contents/21873> consulted on 30 June 2013.

As a matter of fact, even if most of the activists on board the *MV Saoirse* were not republicans, some republican influence was identified in the 2011 flotilla, with for instance the staunch refusal to let the Israelis take down the Irish tricolour flag on the boat and replace it with an Israeli flag, as they had done on the *MV Tahrir*, the signing by all the men in captivity of the book *Irish Rebels* by Morgan Llywelyn,[43] their singing of rebel songs and the manner in which a demand for political status was made in Givon prison.[44] One Canadian activist, Ehab Lotayef, observed this peculiarity and wrote a poem from Givon which he entitled 'With Bobby Sands in an Israeli jail'. Sinn Fein TD, Gerry MacLochlainn, who was meant to be part of the voyage in November, referred to the 'Irishness' of the activists with enthusiasm: 'I call on the Irish Government to contact the Israeli regime immediately and tell them not to interfere with Irish citizens on the high seas and to lift their illegal siege of Gaza. I ask others to join me in this call on our Government to defend our citizens. To the Israelis I say – You will not stop the Irish! We will break your siege! You will not stop the people of Palestine! Palestine will be free!'[45]

The return of the Irish activists was organized in waves, in the same fashion as they were planning to arrive in Gaza. It was followed by obvious attempts from the Irish government to be particularly affable to its Israeli counterpart. Indeed, after a series of actions taken by pro-Palestinian associations, Ireland had been singled out as being the most hostile country to Israel in Europe in the Israeli and Jewish press in November 2011[46] and the government was eager to turn the tide. Eamon Gilmore and Alan Shatter

43   *Irish Rebels* relates Irish myths of resistance involving famous Irish figures from the Celts to Bobby Sands.

44   'Waterford fishermen's lifeline to Gaza', *An Phoblacht*, Vol. 36, N°4 (April 2012).

45   'To the Israelis. I say – You will not stop the Irish! We will break your siege!', *Derry Friends of Palestine* website, 2 November 2011: <http://www.derry-friendsofpalestine.org/2011/11/maclochlainn-sends-message-to-comrade-on-mv-saoirse/> consulted on 30 June 2013.

46   See: Itamar Eichner, 'Ireland most hostile country in Europe', *Yediot Ahrono* (16 November 2011): <http://www.ynetnews.com/articles/0,7340,L-4149059,00.html> consulted on 30 June 2013 and Jessica Elgot, 'Is Ireland the most hostile EU country to Israel?', *The Jewish Chronicle* (17 November 2011).

made a point of going in person to the 'Israeli Film Festival' at Filmbase in Dublin later that month and to condemn the policy of cultural boycott advocated by the Ireland Palestine Solidarity Campaign.[47] In January 2012, Rivlin Reuven, the President of the Knesset was invited to the Dáil by his Irish counterpart, Sean Barrett, a member of Fine Gael.[48] 'Irish Ship to Gaza' dissolved in June 2012 after completing its mission of sending a ship towards Gaza. The activists decided to look for other ways to highlight the disastrous situation in Gaza.

The question of the efficiency of such actions as the flotillas should be raised. If one uses the criteria found by Keck and Sikkink to appraise the short-term efficiency of this type of actions, the flotillas were successful because they framed debates and allowed the issue of Gaza to be better known by the general public and to appear on the political agenda of national governments, as was the case in Ireland. They also encouraged vocal commitments from states and other political actors. Nonetheless, in the short term, they failed to bring about any procedural change at the domestic and international level, or to affect the policies and behaviour of target actors. Indeed, Irish foreign policy, for instance, remained unchanged and even Ban Ki Moon, the UN Secretary, who had supported the first Freedom Flotilla, declared he was wary of a second such initiative.[49] Mostly, the civil associations drew international attention to the humanitarian crisis in Gaza, which was already a satisfaction for the activists involved. This has to be balanced with the huge investment of time and money – around €150,000 had to be collected to support the *MV Saoirse* – which raises the question of a change of strategy in the immediate future. As Greta Berlin, one of the founding members of 'Free Gaza', put it: 'If we had known it would take two years, 150 people, and eventually close to a million dollars

47   'Film fight: how an Israeli festival in Dublin is causing controversy', *Irish Times* (24 November 2011).
48   'Ireland: Activists block Rivlin's way to parliament', *The Jerusalem Post* (19 January 2012).
49   Jennifer Lipman, 'Hillary Clinton: Gaza flotilla is not necessary or useful', *The Jewish Chronicle* (24 June 2011).

to sail two small fishing boats from Greece to Gaza, I'm not sure how many of us would have signed on to this crazy adventure'.[50]

The extraordinary mobilization of resources was the price to pay for civil associations to act as competitors to the state and call into question its authority and legitimacy to speak in the name of citizens as far as foreign policy was concerned. Civil associations created a crisis situation that allowed alternative voices to be heard. They spoke in the name of all the citizens of one country, directly to the international civil society and to the international community. Claiming a moral authority based on the advocacy of human rights, they bypassed the level of states, whose policy they considered limited by compromising, practical politics and general lack of courage. However, it has also been seen that, in the current geopolitical context, they ultimately could not do without states, asking for their help to see to their safety in critical situations. The flexibility and independence of civil associations are assets that allow them to use a wide array of actions, with a unique capacity to change their strategies, as the mushrooming of pro-Palestinian associations in Ireland in the wake of the Freedom Flotillas has demonstrated.

50   Introduction by Greta Berlin to Angela Lano's report: *Towards Gaza, Live from the Freedom Flotilla*, Lulu.com, 2011, 18.

MICHEL SAVARIC

The IRA and 'Civil Administration': A Challenge to the Authority of the State?

ABSTRACT

This chapter explores the way the Provisional IRA challenged the authority of the state in Northern Ireland through the administration of 'law and order' in Catholic neighbourhoods (so-called 'dissident' Republicans still try to apply the same strategy today). It shows that the origins of this phenomenon lie in the fact that the RUC became completely discredited in the wake of the civil rights protests in the 1960s and in the setting up of 'no-go' areas, notably the one known as 'Free Derry'. Paradoxically, the Provisional IRA and Provisional Sinn Féin's control over segregated Catholic areas was somehow encouraged by the British authorities, for instance during the 1975 truce, as a way to push Irish republicans into 'mainstream' politics. Forty years on, Irish republicans have undeniably entered mainstream politics.

In a now celebrated formula, Max Weber defined the State as an entity which 'upholds the claim to the monopoly of the legitimate use of physical force in the enforcement of its order'.[1] Applying this definition to the reality of Northern Ireland, we realize how much more problematic the notion of State may actually turn out to be. In many parts of that territory, the (British) State certainly did not have a 'monopoly of the legitimate use of physical force'. In Catholic areas, it was the 'republican movement' – principally the Irish Republican Army (IRA) and its political wing Sinn Fein – that had endowed itself with the responsibility of maintaining order in place of the established executive and legislative powers. Within Protestant working-class neighbourhoods, loyalist paramilitary organizations tried to exert similar power but their legitimacy always remained a highly

---

1   Max Weber, *Le savant et le politique, Une nouvelle traduction* (Paris: La Découverte, 2003), 118. My translation.

contentious issue. That is why we will focus on the role of the Provisional IRA (PIRA) which appeared in 1970.[2]

This chapter covers mainly the years 1969–2007 but extends in some ways to the present day. It will start by retracing the origins of the undertaking of law and order by the republican movement. It will then examine to what degree such an endeavour was thought through and justified as a challenge to the authority of the State and an attempt at asserting itself as an alternative power. It will go on to argue that from its very outset, this challenge did gain some sort of recognition by the State and that this recognition eventually led the leaders of the republican movement to enter the State apparatus itself.

Origins

As a revolutionary movement, Irish republicanism has by definition always challenged the authority of the State. At various stages in its history – from the Society of United Irishmen to Young Ireland and the Irish Republican Brotherhood – it constituted itself as an armed clandestine movement. Such a mode of organization requires strong internal discipline: the movement has to be sure of the loyalty of its members and it must protect itself from spies, informers and traitors. Over time, republican movements developed their own disciplinary procedures – through 'court martials' for instance. A control on elements outside the movement was initially exerted in relation with the need to protect the movement itself. Thus, during the Irish Civil War in 1921, the Cork IRA suffered many losses. Mary Lindsay, an

---

2   A split occurred within the organization in 1970. The breakaway faction took up the name 'Provisional' IRA from the 1916 proclamation of the Irish Republic signed by the 'Provisional Government' while the other faction became known as the 'Official' IRA. The PIRA saw it as a priority to defend Catholic areas, the OIRA stressed that its fight was non-sectarian and aimed at causing a revolution. In 1972, the OIRA went on a ceasefire and abandoned the battleground to its rival offshoot.

old Protestant woman, suspected of having passed on information to the forces of the Free State, was executed, together with her house-steward, their bodies never recovered. According to Brian Hanley, 'there have been recurring allegations that the IRA was more likely to kill "spies" if they were ex-soldiers, Protestants or marginal figures, such as tramps, rather than "respectable" members of the nationalist community'.[3]

Social control extending to the whole of the 'community', not exclusively in the aim of protecting the movement itself, is a more recent phenomenon linked to the specific social structures of Northern Ireland. During the Stormont years, and until the emergence of the civil rights movement in the 1960s, the IRA had struggled to maintain its existence. Republican parades were forbidden, as were republican newspapers and the wearing of the 'Easter Lily'. The IRA nevertheless remained active in its role as 'protector' of the Catholic community during the riots of the 1920s and in 1935 when sectarian riots erupted again. From 1956 to 1962, it waged the 'border campaign' but decided to end it when it realized it had no support from the population itself.

Free Derry and law and order

A new form of social contest in the 1960s stands as an important historical watershed. As political events unfolded, an initial demand for equal rights for Northern Ireland Catholics gradually led to a complete reappraisal of the authority of the Stormont government, which had been created under the aegis of the British State. This challenge to Stormont expressed itself materially with the setting-up of 'no-go areas'. These were neighbourhoods from which the police, later the police and the British army, were barred. The most famous of these no-go areas was undoubtedly that of Derry,

---

3   Brian Hanley, *The IRA: A Documentary History* (Dublin: Gill & Macmillan, 2010), 18.

called Free Derry, which existed over three distinct periods, the first of
which came into being on 5 January 1969. A few days earlier on 1 January
and taking inspiration from tactics employed by Martin Luther King,
the student movement, People's Democracy, had decided to organize a
long march from Belfast to Derry. But before reaching its destination, the
march was escorted by the Royal Ulster Constabulary (RUC) into a loyalist ambush at Burntollet bridge. Among the attackers were a number of
off-duty B-Special police reservists.[4] When the marchers later arrived in
Derry covered in blood and with their clothes torn off, a riot spontaneously
erupted in the Catholic area of the Bogside. After the riot, members of the
RUC, some of them inebriated, conducted a punitive expedition in the
Bogside, attacking residents and breaking windows. The next day, Bogside
residents set up barricades and some Republicans organized the first patrols:
'The Derry Republicans were active in putting up barricades and mounting
patrols. The challenge to the authority of the RUC which the stewards'
organization had represented was now expressed in the form of vigilante
groups in which Republicans were heavily involved, defended by barricades
and served by its own pirate radio station, "Free Derry" existed with no
RUC presence'.[5] That first experience of 'Free Derry' lasted for five days.

Barricades reappeared briefly in the Bogside and Creggan estates in
April, and again after an Apprentice Boys' parade on 12 August 1969. The
riot which ensued turned into a full-pitch 3-day battle (the 'Battle of the
Bogside'). The police was pushed back and barricades sprang up and stayed
in place until October. On 14 August, British troops replaced a humiliated

4   The Ulster Special Constabulary (USC) was set up in 1920, largely from former
     Ulster Volunteer Force (UVF) units, to give support to the regular Crown forces of
     the Royal Irish Constabulary (RIC). It was divided into three groups: the A-Specials
     who were full-time and used as reinforcement, the B-Specials who were used for local
     patrol duty and the C-Specials who had no regular duties but could be mobilized.
     The Royal Ulster Constabulary (RUC) replaced the RIC in 1922 and the A- and
     C-Specials were dispensed of. However, the B-Specials remained in existence as an
     official loyalist militia until their disbandment in 1970.
5   Niall Ó Dochartaigh, *From Civil Rights to Armalites: Derry and the Birth of the Irish
     Troubles* (Cork: Cork University Press, 1997), 41.

RUC. The army did not try to enter the area. Quite to the contrary, it left the newly formed Derry Citizens' Defence Association in charge of controlling the comings and goings into the neighbourhood. When a small foot patrol, as if by mistake, made a small incursion into Free Derry, the army apologized to Sean Keenan, chair of the association and IRA veteran, and vice-chairman Paddy Doherty, and promised it would never happen again.[6] Regular patrolling was carried out by vigilantes in order to protect the area both from hostile outside elements and from potential internal delinquents. According to the *Derry Journal*, at a public conference on 1 September 1969, Sean Keenan delivered a stark warning to those who might have been tempted to take advantage of the situation to burglarize shops or houses: 'Rumours were still undermining the work. They had heard about "shop-breaking in the Creggan estate" and that shop-keepers "would be put out of business", but the fact was that since 12 August, there was one attempt at a break-in. We have a very successful Defence Committee and we are doing a wonderful job. Anyone breaking into any shop or house will be dealt with in a very hard manner'.[7] Barricades were put down in October when the association gained assurance from the army that the RUC would not enter the area anymore and that law and order would be maintained by the military police.

The last Free Derry commune started on 9 August 1971, when internment without trial was reintroduced, and ended on 31 July 1972, the day of Operation Motorman. It occurred within the context of a significantly altered political landscape. After the Battle of the Bogside, riots had spread to Belfast causing eight deaths and leading to the destruction of entire streets, such as Bombay Street. The IRA, which was very small at the time, had been unable to defend Catholic neighbourhoods effectively, as evidenced by the graffiti stating 'IRA – I Ran Away' which allegedly appeared on the walls of Belfast at the time.[8] A split occurred within the IRA and, by the early 1970s,

---

6   *Ibid.*, 133.
7   'DCDA Chairman Says Disruptive Elements Should Leave Derry', *Derry Journal* (2 September 1969).
8   Mentions of these graffiti appear in many accounts of that period, see for example: Susan McKay, *Bear in Mind These Dead* (London: Faber and Faber, 2008), 21.

a new generation of young, working-class Catholic 'volunteers' had enrolled *en masse* in the new Provisional IRA. By that time, the honeymoon period between the army and the Catholic population was well and truly over. In Derry, the situation was slightly different. The two IRAs, Official and Provisional, coexisted in equal numbers and jointly administered Free Derry. They set up checkpoints and stopped all the cars going into the area. According to activist Eamonn McCann, the two organizations had an 'official' head-quarters where they received local residents: 'Not all callers were on military business. People would come seeking advice, or with minor complaints – on the type of business which in Britain would naturally be taken to the welfare office or to a department of the local council. Provisional supporters would go to the Provisionals. Official supporters to the Officials. Neutralists had a choice.'[9] McCann also claims that law and order were kept independently by the Free Derry Police which was chaired by football player Tony O'Doherty.[10] However, archive footage from that time clearly shows that the two IRAs had taken it upon themselves to act as a police force.[11] With Operation Motorman, which deployed close to 12,000 soldiers, tanks and bulldozers, the British put an end to Free Derry, and caused the deaths of two people.

The 1975 truce and the 'incident report centres'

Two related phenomena characterized law enforcement in the first years of the modern phase of the Northern Irish conflict, designated as 'the Troubles': the local police force was completely discredited and policing

---

However, their existence has been hotly disputed by Hanley and Millar who suggest it was used in Protestant areas but not in Catholic ones: Brian Hanley and Scott Millar, *The Lost Revolution: The Story of the Official IRA and the Workers' Party* (London: Penguin, 2009), 136.

9   Eamonn McCann, *War and an Irish Town* (London: Pluto Press, 1993 [1974]), 155–6.
10   *Ibid.*, 156.
11   <http://youtube/aQS5IzQpi6g>

functions were progressively carried out by the IRA in barricaded Catholic neighbourhoods, as they briefly and precariously lived beyond the control of Stormont, the Protestant unionist 'Statelet'. The major crisis Northern Ireland went through then pushed the British State to reveal itself as the real power: when the army intervened on 14 August 1969, the RUC immediately deserted the edge of the Bogside and Creggan estates. That State which, for nearly fifty years, had left the Unionist Party completely in charge of running the Northern Irish territory was very briefly able to abandon some of its regalian functions as it pragmatically adapted to changes in the balance of power. When the RUC was forced to step aside, it left a void which was immediately filled by the IRA, who thereby gained tacit recognition. In his book dedicated to the year 1972, Malachi O'Doherty recalls that the building of Andersonstown Leisure Centre had to be stopped because of the difficulty in finding an insurer willing to cover the construction companies. This resulted in the IRA being asked to safeguard the building site: 'So though the Provisional IRA was an illegal revolutionary organization, intent on murder and destruction on a massive scale, even as early as 1972 it was acquiring a recognized role within the institutions of the state; local government representatives have asked it to provide safe passage for workers and protection for building projects, and presumably trusted its undertakings'.[12]

This recognition awarded to the IRA as a belligerent force by the official authority also manifested itself several times during secret negotiations, such as at the beginning of the summer of 1972, leading to a short-lived truce from 26 June to 9 July. In 1975, further secret negotiations brought about a renewed ceasefire from 10 February to 12 November. On 12 February, Northern Ireland Secretary of State Merlyn Rees announced the opening of 'incident report centres'. There would be seven of such centres in North Belfast, West Belfast, Derry, Newry, Armagh, Enniskillen and Dungannon.[13] Entirely funded by the State, they would house Sinn Fein

---

12   Malachi O'Doherty, *The Telling Year: Belfast 1972* (Dublin: Gill & Macmillan, 2007), 141.

13   'Hot Lines to Peace Soon in 14 Centres', *Irish News* (13 February 1975).

202   MICHEL SAVARIC

members with a direct telephone and telex links – tapped of course – to the
Northern Ireland Office in Stormont. The official goal of these centres was
to ensure the ceasefire was kept and prevent misunderstanding between the
various parties concerned. In the House of Lords, Parliamentary Under-
Secretary of State Lord Donaldson explained on 11 February that 'if developments occur which seem to threaten the ceasefire, these incident centres
will act as a point of contact in either direction'.[14] According to former
IRA member Tom Hartley, quoted by Peter Taylor, the first consequence
of the opening of these incident centres was to give Sinn Fein a visibility
it had hitherto been denied:

> They began a trend of actually taking Sinn Fein out of the back room and putting it
> onto the main arterial routes. As long as we were in the back rooms, people wouldn't
> see us. We wouldn't be seen as a political force. As the old saying goes, out of sight out
> of mind. In 1975, the whole of West Belfast knew where the Sinn Fein rooms were.
> Every day they passed the office as they passed by in a black taxi [the 'People's Taxis'
> that provided cheap transport] up and down the Falls Road and people would say,
> 'there's the Sinn Fein office'. The incident centres gave the party a physical presence.[15]

The real goal of the government was to push Republicans onto a political
and 'constitutional' road by bringing Sinn Fein into the limelight. As for
the leadership of the IRA at the time, they genuinely believed in an imminent British withdrawal from Northern Ireland.

The fact that Sinn Fein was able to benefit from offices supplied for
free by the State while they did not have a single elected representative
infuriated the other political parties, unionist and nationalist alike. The
controversy became even fiercer when it was reported that the centres were
being used as alternative police stations by Republicans. Both the Secretary
of State and Sinn Fein's president had to issue a statement denying this was
the case: 'Secretary of State Merlyn Rees and Sinn Fein organizer Seamus
Loughran both denied yesterday that the incident centres being opened to

14 *Hansard*, Lords Sitting, 11 February 1975: <http://hansard.millbanksystems.com/
    lords/1975/feb/11/northern-irelandceasefire#S5LV0356P0_19750211_HOL_90>
15 Peter Taylor, *Provos: The IRA and Sinn Fein* (London: Bloomsbury, 1997), 186.

help maintain peace will be used for policing republican areas'.[16] However, Sinn Fein quite readily agreed that the IRA was in charge of law and order in those neighbourhoods where centres had been set up: 'Mr Loughran said that small groups of men were doing vigilante duty in some parts of the city, including Andersonstown, Falls, New Lodge, Ardoyne and the Markets. 'They are not all members of the republican movement – just volunteers who want to make sure there is no widespread violence.' He added that the idea of vigilantes was to protect the areas but said that anyone who was to be punished would be handed over to the Provisional IRA'.[17] The way the IRA maintained order was spelled out a few days later:

> The spokesman at a centre in West Belfast was speaking in a BBC Radio 'World At One' interview.
> He said that the Republicans had been wrongly accused of acting as a community service. We have no co-operation with the Royal Ulster Constabulary.
> 'These are lies that we hand over complaints to the RUC. We take care of these incidents ourselves. Usually it means going round and talking to the people concerned. If there is a robbery, we go round and get the money back. We just take care of it in our own way and make sure these things don't happen again.' Asked what 'their own way' was, he replied 'No comment'.[18]

As the controversy raged, the Ulster Defence Association also started patrolling Protestant neighbourhoods from 28 February.[19] This ended on 5 March when Merlyn Rees gave his assurance the government had not given over the policing of Catholic areas to the Provisional IRA.[20] As for the Official IRA, which still enjoyed a relatively high membership in 1975, it disdainfully dismissed those incident centres as 'Provo Police Stations'. A feud between the two IRA factions caused twelve deaths towards the end of the year. In November, the PIRA announced the closure of the Derry centre, as a protest against renewed house searches by

16   'Incident Centres "Not for Policing"', *Irish News* (14 February 1975).
17   'Row Looming over Policing of Truce', *Belfast Telegraph* (13 February 1975).
18   'Centres "Not for Policing" – Rees', *Irish News* (26 February 1975).
19   'Loyalists "to Start Policing" Tonight', *Irish News* (28 February 1975).
20   'UDA Suspend Policing after Rees Pledge', *Irish News* (6 March 1975).

the British army.[21] In fact, it was the sign that a decision had been made to end the ceasefire. In most cases however, Sinn Fein decided to keep the centres open for they had greatly strengthened its influence in Catholic areas. These incident report centres became Sinn Fein's Advice Centres and considerable resources were allocated to them. Their creation by the British government in 1975 therefore paved the way for the IRA to take control of Catholic neighbourhoods. Paradoxically then, in wanting to reduce terrorist violence, the government had actually widely contributed to consolidating IRA presence in Catholic working-class areas. This very fact is evidence enough that the State's main priority was simply to protect itself. Another instance of this may be found in the British soldiers' common practice of sheltering themselves behind children,[22] going as far as letting them climb onto tanks or play with military material.

The IRA as an alternative to the State in the 'Brownie' articles

After the 1975 ceasefire, the IRA underwent major changes both in terms of internal organization and strategy. Such changes were carried out under the leadership of Gerry Adams who had been interned at Long Kesh from 1973 to 1976. While in prison, he had outlined his vision of the future for the republican movement in a series of articles published in *Republican News* under the pseudonym Brownie. In particular, he advocated intensifying the challenge to the authority of the State:

21   "'Due to Increase in British Army Activity" Provisionals Close Derry Incident Centre', *Derry Journal* (11 November 1975).
22   See: <http://www.gettyimages.ae/detail/news-photo/british-army-soldiers-in-nationalist-west-belfast-news-photo/183109104>, <http://www.gettyimages.ca/detail/photo/northern-ireland-west-belfast-british-army-high-res-stock-photography/200561341-001> or <http://flashbak.com/photos-of-the-british-army-in-northern-ireland-1969-1979-27624/>

'Why go to the local councillors about houses?' Squat!!! 'Why go to parks Committees about facilities for youngsters?' Build!!!!! Why complain about anything to committees and councils? Organise!!!!! Ignore the British Government's systems, boycott them, abstain from them – and build our own. [...] We must build an alternative. We have isolated the Brit terrorists and their system from the people, we must now replace them with a peoples' civil administration. [...] And the Republican Movement has the structure and the blueprint to make local government outside the British system not alone feasible but necessary. ACTIVE ABSTENTION.[23]

This article, with its almost libertarian undertones, appears simply to be calling for collective self-management. In reality, however, Adams was pleading for the republican movement to substitute itself totally to the services of the British State. His point was to re-create the State within the confines of the ghetto. At the root of the State, there is physical force – that is the gist of Weber's definition. As an armed group, the IRA and Sinn Fein could then constitute the State within a context where the Northern Ireland police and the British army had lost all form of legitimacy.

In another article, Adams transcribed a debate he had organized in Cage 11 at Long Kesh camp on the way to building this alternative to the British State he had in mind. The process was described in a very detailed manner:

The attacks from outside the area led to welfare committees and refugee groups, defence rotas, first aid posts and things like that all became necessities. School children became involved and people came forward to look after their special needs. Then of course we had the issue of the RUC and this affected all areas. When the RUC was refused entry a vacuum in local policing had to be filled. Like this was hard to do because of pressure from the Brits and because wanted men find it hard to tie themselves down.[24]

The eviction of the police from Catholic areas was the starting point to the setting-up of alternative structures. Further on, one of the protagonists staged by Adams described the new role of the IRA volunteers as amounting to building a 'mini Republic' in their neighbourhoods. The place of IRA

---

23   'Active Abstentionism by Brownie Long Kesh', *Republican News* (18 October 1975).
24   'The National Alternative', *Republican News* (3 April 1976).

members was therefore central in this conception: 'I reckon every one of us has to examine ways and means of turning our local war machine into an alternative to the Brit system. An alternative in keeping with people's needs, with the war effort and with national policy'.[25] When he came out of prison, Gerry Adams undertook to restructure the IRA. Until then, it had been organized on the model of the British army with battalions, companies and brigades. With the help of Brendan Hughes and Ivor Bell, Adams imposed the 'cell' structure in the aim of fighting infiltration from the secret services.[26] This restructuration led to a reduction in the number of 'operators' really involved in the armed struggle as well as greater specialization. A distinction was made between the élite of the movement, regrouped in 'Active Service Units' (ASU) and the rank and file who were put in charge of 'civil administration'.

'Civil administration'

In the testimony he gave to journalist Brian Feeney, former IRA member Gerry Bradley was very specific about what such specialization entailed within the hierarchical structure of the IRA:

> 'Guys from the civil administration did the batterings etc.', that is to say punishment beatings and shootings of people involved in 'anti-social behavior' and criminal activity. Like other ASU members, Bradley took no part in any of that. 'ASU men tended to remain separate from the civil administration. If someone came to you and reported something, you would pass it on to one of the guys in the civil administration. Operators would have a kind of seniority in the district. People looked up to them'.[27]

---

25   'The National Alternative', *Republican News* (3 April 1976).
26   Ed Moloney, *Voices from the Grave: Two Men's War in Ireland* (London: Faber and Faber, 2010), 183.
27   Gerry Bradley with Brian Feeney, *Insider: Gerry Bradley's Life in the IRA* (Dublin: The O'Brien Press, 2009), 248.

Units in charge of civil administration, that is to say policing neighbour-hoods, were less respected because for them risks were minimal. In contrast, the IRA's internal police, whose job was to hunt down informers and enemy agents who had infiltrated the organization, was very highly placed within the hierarchy. According to Brendan Hughes' testimony published by Ed Moloney, those units frequently resorted to torture: '[...] these people tortured guys. There was a friend of mine who owns a bar, Paddy McDaid, an IRA volunteer who was taken away by these people and tortured. I mean they burned him with cigarettes, they put his head in water, they kept him starved for four or five days in an old [...] barn somewhere across the border. Paddy McDaid came to me not long after I got out of prison and told me what happened to him [...] he was accused of being a tout'.[28] Only much later was it revealed that the internal security unit was in fact infiltrated by British secret service agents.

The civil administration envisioned by Gerry Adams in his Brownie articles was a logical extension of the incident report centres set up by the British government during the 1975 ceasefire. The reduction in the number of members actively involved in the struggle swelled the ranks of those in charge of policing Catholic neighbourhoods. As the techniques of social control became more refined, so a gradation of punishments inflicted became defined and generalized. Criminologist Andrew Silke has classified them from the least to the most serious: verbal warning, imposition of a curfew (mostly for teenagers), fines and restitution of stolen goods, public humiliation (from tar and feathers at the beginning of the 1970s, the IRA went on to use paint in the 1990s), battering, bullets shot in the joints (including kneecappings), banishment and death.[29] In a 1999 article, Silke estimated that about 40,000 people had been subjected to physical violence

28   Ed Moloney, *Voices from the Grave: Two Men's War in Ireland*, 280.
29   Andrew Silke, 'The Lords of Discipline: The Methods and Motives of Paramilitary Vigilantism in Northern Ireland', *Low Intensity Conflict and Law Enforcement*, 7/2 (Autumn 1998), 124.

by paramilitaries in Northern Ireland.[30] Civil administration became the
backbone of Sinn Fein who, by the late 1980s, gained priority over the
'military' side of the movement until it eventually relinquished the armed
struggle. Silke insisted, however, that the repressive policy pursued by the
IRA proved ineffectual in deterring acts of delinquency, comparing it to
the American states that had reintroduced the death penalty. But acting
as a deterrent was perhaps not the main point anyway. The death penalty
in American states and physical violence in all its guises assuage desires
for revenge that are widespread in society. And the IRA's maintaining of
law and order in Catholic neighbourhoods was also a means of asserting
its authority.

The Peace Process: From DAAD to RAAD

During the first years of the Peace Process after the 1994 ceasefire, there was
a sharp increase in the number of acts of violence carried out against young
delinquents. This trend partly reflected the need to keep IRA members
occupied. It was also supposed to illustrate continuity: although on ceasefire, the IRA still maintained law and order and its authority was intact.[31]
Republicans thus launched an extremely aggressive campaign against drug
dealers. Numerous attacks were carried out and several 'unintentional'
deaths were claimed by a group calling itself Direct Action Against Drugs
(DAAD). There was no doubt this was in fact the IRA. But the choice
of name meant that it could automatically associate any of its victims to
drug trafficking without having to prove anything, as Eamonn McCann
wryly notes:

30   Andrew Silke, 'Rebel's Dilemma: The Changing Relationship between the IRA,
      Sinn Féin and Paramilitary Vigilantism in Northern Ireland', *Terrorism and Political
      Violence* 11/1 (Spring 1999), 56.
31   Kiran Sarma, 'Defensive Propaganda and IRA Political Control in Republican
      Communities', *Studies in Conflict and Terrorism* 30 (2007), 1089.

The broad justification for the 'DAAD' death campaigns is that its targets are doing the community damage. The campaign is, therefore, being waged for the community's good, in a sense on the community's own behalf. [...] Strange all the same that we haven't heard from Direct Action Against Sweatshop Employers. Or Direct Action Against Pederast Priests. Or even Direct Action Against The Minister Responsible For Abolishing Lone Parents' Allowance and thus plunging thousands of the most vulnerable members of the community deeper into poverty.[32]

From the point of view of the British government and Northern Ireland's main political parties, the fact that these attacks did not have a 'sectarian' character, or that they were not perpetrated in the name of the fight against 'British imperialism', were reason enough to maintain there was no breach of the ceasefire. So we can identify the same attitude from the British government as during the 1975 ceasefire: the State was ready to delegate some of its policing duties to the IRA as long as its own integrity was preserved.

On 22 November 2006, Sinn Fein signed the St Andrews agreement whereby it accepted the legitimacy of the Police Service of Northern Ireland. From then on, the summary justice carried out by the IRA could no longer be justified (or excused as a necessary evil). Since then, given that Sinn Fein is now fully integrated into the State, it may be argued that the State seems to have regained its monopoly of the legitimate use of physical force. However, dissident Republicans still wage their war against young delinquents and drug dealers. One such group calling itself Republican Action Against Drugs (RAAD) has emerged, and is particularly active in the city of Derry. Interviewed by the *Derry Journal* in August 2009, one of its spokespersons claimed: 'we are involved in a battle against ruthless individuals who have no respect or loyalty to the very community in which they have been reared'.[33]

On 9 February 2012 in Buncrana, Co. Donegal, RAAD killed Andrew Allen, a 24-year old boxer from Derry whom they accused of being a drug dealer. Allen had been banished from Derry but he had come back one day.

32   Eamonn McCann, 'The Worm at the Heart of Direct Action Against Drugs', *Hot Press* (15 January 1996).
33   'Only Way to Eradicate Drugs Scourge is to Remove the Dealers', *Derry Journal* (18 August 2009).

On his return to Buncrana, he was shot through the window of his house by RAAD's 'Donegal unit'.[34] The murder was duly condemned by Sinn Fein.[35] On 26 April 2012, a mother was forced to bring her 18-year old son to an appointment to be shot in the legs. According to the Derry Journal, 'Asked why she did not contact the PSNI after receiving the threat, the mother said only: "We hold staunch republican views"'.[36] The existence of a dissident republican paramilitary organization solely dedicated to punishing alleged drug dealers and juvenile delinquents is an arresting phenomenon. RAAD, which recruited former members of the Provisional IRA, seemed initially to have retained only the 'civil administration' side of the IRA's structures that was so despised by former 'operators' like Gerry Bradley.

But on 26 July 2012, Republican Action Against Drugs announced it was merging with the Real IRA, the Continuity IRA[37] and former Provisionals to form a new paramilitary organization simply called the IRA. So it seems that vigilantism was only one aspect of a wider strategy aimed at gaining respectability and support within the Catholic working-class community. Being in charge of law and order remains the main priority for those dissident groups because it enables them to assert their power practically while challenging the authority of the State (including the authority of 'mainstream' Republicans) at the same time.

Irish republicanism's challenge to the authority of the State in Northern Ireland from the late 1960s onward involved gradually taking control of Catholic working-class neighbourhoods. Control over what became 'republican strongholds' formed the very basis of Sinn Fein's political strategy which led it to enter the State apparatus. Sinn Fein today has accepted the legitimacy of the police and governs Northern Ireland in partnership with

---

34   'RAAD behind Andrew Allen shooting in Buncrana', BBC News (22 February 2012): <http://www.bbc.co.uk/news/uknorthern-ireland-17125572>

35   'Dissidents Condemned Over Murder', Belfast Telegraph (13 February 2012).

36   '"I hope he listens now" – Mum ordered to bring son to be shot', Derry Journal (30 April 2012).

37   The Continuity IRA resulted from a split in 1986 over the issue of taking up seats in the Irish Parliament while the Real IRA was created in 1997 by Provisionals who were unhappy with the peace process.

the Democratic Unionist Party (DUP). Its electoral successes rest on its abandonment of the 'armed struggle'. As for the British State, its priority was always to ensure its own security. In that sense, it could yield part of its control over the Northern Irish territory in so far as it was conducive to an appeasement of the political violence directed against it. The British State has always recognized the might of its adversary. States know how to negotiate with armed movements, especially when they are as well-structured and hierarchical as the IRA. Its strategy invariably consisted in swapping that recognition for a commitment to falling back into line and adopting the parliamentary and 'political' route. So far, it is a strategy that has proved fruitful.

FABRICE MOURLON

The Crisis of Authority in *You, Me and Marley*

ABSTRACT

In the early 1990s, as negotiations were taking on a new turn to find a settlement to end the conflict in Northern Ireland, the BBC commissioned a series of TV drama that dealt with issues that characterized a society which seemed at a crossroads. *You, Me and Marley*, screened in September 1992, captures the mood of war-weariness in Northern Ireland at that period all forms of authority are shown to be challenged and/or collapsing. This crisis is analysed through the concepts developed by Hannah Arendt and René Girard which demonstrate that the end of authority can explain the increase in disorder and violence in society and its institutions. Viewed from this perspective, *You, Me and Marley* is characteristic of the end of an era, when the conflict in Northern Ireland had reached a dead-end.

In an essay entitled 'What is authority?' Hannah Arendt claims that 'authority has vanished from the modern world';[1] she further argues that the 'disappearance of practically all traditionally established authorities has been one of the most spectacular characteristics of the modern world'.[2] She contends that the true source of authority lies in the 'Roman experience of foundation' and warns against the confusion frequently made when seeking to define authority: 'Since authority always demands obedience, it is commonly mistaken for some form of power or violence. Yet authority precludes the use of external means of coercion; where force is used, authority itself has failed. Authority, on the other hand, is incompatible with persuasion, which presupposes equality and works through a process of argumentation.'[3]

1   Hannah Arendt, *Between Past and Future* (New York: Viking Press, 1961), 91.
2   *Ibid.*, 100.
3   *Ibid.*, 92–3.

Her analysis, which dates back to the 1960s seems particularly relevant for my analysis of the representation of the Northern Ireland conflict given in the TV drama *You, Me and Marley*.[4] The film was commissioned and produced by the BBC and first screened on television on 30 September 1992. It depicts a chaotic society where authority is either rejected or abused through violence, a situation symptomatic of a state without a firm foundation; this could aptly characterize the creation and development of the Northern Ireland statelet. Indeed, from the outset its legitimacy was questioned and contested as exemplified by the rejection of the Government of Ireland Act 1920[5] by Dail Eireann the same year, and the sectarian violence that subsequently developed in Northern Ireland in the early 1920s. Tensions resulting from the instability created by the Anglo-Irish War (1919–21)[6] followed by the Civil War (1922–23)[7] led to the setting up of emergency measures and institutions in Northern Ireland to ensure the viability of the statelet, e.g. the creation of the almost exclusively Protestant reserve police force, the Ulster Special Constabulary, and the passing of the Civil Authorities (Special Powers) Act (Northern Ireland) 1922.[8]

René Girard's approach to the nature and process of violence also provides an interesting point of view through which to analyse this film.[9] One

4   *You, Me and Marley*, Director: Richard Spence. Script: Graham Reid, 1992.
5   This Act actually partitioned the island of Ireland creating two Home Rule institutions, one for the six north-eastern counties and the other for the twenty-six counties. These arrangements were accepted by Unionists in what would become Northern Ireland but rejected by the Republicans in Dail Eireann who had declared Irish Independence on 21 January 1919.
6   The Irish War of Independence was fought by the Irish Republicans who had formed a breakaway government in 1919 against Great Britain.
7   The conflict between Republicans and the British government was settled by the Anglo-Irish Treaty signed on 6 December 1921. However a fraction of the Republicans refused the Treaty and a civil war ensued between the pro-Treaty and the anti-Treaty Republicans.
8   This Act gave sweeping powers to the Home Affairs Minister to maintain order. These included internment without trial.
9   René Girard, *Le bouc émissaire* (Paris: Grasset, 1982).
     René Girard, *La violence et le sacré* (Paris: Albin Michel, 1990).

particular aspect of his theory is that when 'undifferentiation' characterizes social order, *i. e.*, when social and individual roles are not defined, violence is unleashed against a scapegoat. This applies to the situation depicted in *You, Me and Marley* where this violence is turned against young people in the community.

The analysis of this work of fiction through these theoretical lenses will attempt to demonstrate how the crisis of authority that Northern Irish society is shown to experience can explain disorder and violence and to what extent the film highlights aspects of the conflict in Northern Ireland in the early 1990s.

TV drama as a challenge to news reports

You, Me and Marley is part of a long tradition of TV drama commissioned and produced by the BBC – either the central BBC or BBC Northern Ireland. Since the 1960s over 100 TV dramas or series have given accounts of Northern Irish society. In the period predating the conflict, the films explored issues such as sectarian tensions in the workplace and the relationships between Britain and the Northern-Irish Unionist population with a focus on the world of the working-classes.[10]

When violence erupted in the late 1960s, the conflict started to dominate the news on British television as pictures by RTE and UTV of the Civil Rights march attacked by the Royal Ulster Constabulary (RUC) in October 1968 were shown internationally. From then on and until the mid-1990s, debates on media representations of Northern Ireland focused on news and current affairs coverage.[11] However, with journalists confronted

10   Martin McLoone, 'Drama Out of a Crisis: BBC Television Drama and the Northern Ireland Troubles', in Martin McLoone, ed., *Broadcasting in a Divided Community: Seventy years of the BBC in Northern Ireland* (Belfast: Institute of Irish Studies, QUB, 1996), 73–92.
11   *Ibid.*, 80.

with indirect and direct censorship and self-censorship,[12] several academics argued that 'drama could paint a more accurate picture of the situation in Northern Ireland and could provide imaginative insights into the complexity of the conflict'.[13]

After the 1994 ceasefires two film specialists, Lance Pettitt and Martin McLoone,[14] tried to assess whether TV drama was able to offer alternative visions that journalists were unwilling or unable to explore. Both concluded that, to a large extent, this had not been the case except in a few instances when script-writers and directors had questioned their own cultural and political ideological standpoints. Lance Pettitt added: 'While most drama has followed the terrain of the Troubles, marking out a representational middle-ground, in a few cases drama has challenged viewers' minds by imagining events that could not be countenanced by factual television. Fictional representations, therefore, have played a major role in the maintenance and reshaping of perceptions about the Troubles and to this extent they have performed a political function.'[15]

In 1998 Graham Reid,[16] who wrote the script for *You, Me and Marley*, argued that what was important about Northern Ireland was to show that people there were not different from people in the rest of the UK. He claimed that 'as a dramatist, whatever subject I tackle, I will do through human beings and through human relationships'. He avoided taking sides

12   David Miller, *Don't Mention the War* (London: Pluto Press, 1994).
13   K. Cully, 'Nationalist attitudes', *The Tribune* (23 February 1979), quoted in Lance Pettitt, *Screening Ireland: Film and television representation* (Manchester: Manchester University Press, 2000), 229.
14   Martin McLoone, 'Drama Out of a Crisis: BBC Television Drama and the Northern Ireland Troubles'.
     Lance Pettitt, *Screening Ireland: Film and television representation*, 227–45.
15   Lance Pettitt, *Screening Ireland: Film and television representation*, 245.
16   Graham Reid is a Belfast-born playwright famous for his trilogy 'the Billy plays' shown on the BBC in the early 1980s and starring young Kenneth Branagh.

and did not try to offer any solution: 'In Northern Ireland there is no solution as such. There is a need for toleration.'[17]

Whether the film offered an alternative vision of the conflict is difficult to say. However it exposed to a wide audience a dysfunctional society in which violence had no purpose and its agents had no political reasons to engage in it. Set in West Belfast in 1992, it depicted the nationalist community acting like 'scorpions in a bottle'[18] since its population directed violence towards its own younger generation, thus underlining the level of absurdity that the conflict in Northern Ireland had reached. The idea that this community was 'fighting for a cause' was clearly challenged. Pillars of authority and their motivations from within the community – parents, the Church, the paramilitary organizations – and from the state apparatus – the police and the army – were questioned. Furthermore, the film focused on an issue that drew attention and concern, notably among researchers, in the 1990s: the issue of paramilitary organizations 'policing' their own area and targeting young people through the use of 'punishment beatings and shootings.'[19]

17   Eamonn McCann and Graham Reid, 'Drama Out of a Crisis', *Broadcast* (9 September 1988), 17–19, cited in Martin McLoone, 'Drama Out of a Crisis: BBC Television Drama and the Northern Ireland Troubles', 88.

18   John Darby, *Scorpions in a Bottle, Conflicting Cultures in Northern Ireland* (London: Minority Rights Publications), 1997.

19   See Colin Knox, '"See no evil, Hear no evil" Insidious Paramilitary Violence in Northern Ireland', *British Journal of Criminology*, vol. 42 (2002), 164–85; Liam Kennedy, '"They Shoot Children, Don't They?" An Analysis of the Age and Gender of Victims of Paramilitary "Punishments" in Northern Ireland', *Report prepared for the Northern Ireland Committee Against Terror (NICAT) and the Northern Ireland Affairs Committee of the House of Commons*, 2001. <http://cain.ulst.ac.uk/issues/violence/docs/kennedy01.htm> accessed 31 July 2013; Marie Therese Fay *et al.*, *The Cost of the Troubles Study, Report on the Northern Ireland Survey: The Experience and Impact of the Troubles* (Derry: INCORE, 1999).

Refusing authority

In the few reviews written on *You, Me and Marley*, critics have focused their analysis on the negative image given to West Belfast and on the stereotypical portrayal of the republican movement.[20] One could argue that the image of the nationalist community was indeed tarnished, especially at a time when political talks were under way to find a settlement to end the conflict and when Sinn Fein had launched a document entitled *Towards A Lasting Peace* in Ireland (17 February 1992 *Ard Fheis*). Nevertheless, as later research showed, one could claim that 'punishment beatings/shootings' had been carried out to a greater extent by the Provisional Irish Republican Army (PIRA)[21] against the youngest population of their community.[22]

Bearing in mind Graham Reid's 'neutral' position regarding the conflict, the message of the film goes far beyond that particular community, which is only an example of a society where the social fabric and moral values are falling apart. Authority is constantly challenged by a new generation of young people who come up against adults, who though they are supposedly legitimate figures of authority, either do not act responsibly or abuse their authority by resorting to violence.

Alternating tragic and comic scenes, *You, Me and Marley* tells the story of three young people, Sean, Frances and Marley who engage in anti-social activities, mainly joyriding, on the streets of their estate, much to the dissatisfaction of the whole community. Sean lives in a fatherless

---

20   Paul Nolan, 'Images of a wild west', *Fortnight* (November 1992), 42; Neil Jarman, 'Violent Men, Violent Land: Dramatising the Troubles and the Landscape of Ulster', *Journal of Material Culture* 1, 39–61.

21   The Provisional IRA was set up after a split in the IRA in 1969 due to differing opinions on the future strategy of the organization. See for example: Richard English, *Armed Struggle: A History of the IRA* (London: Macmillan, 2003); Agnès Maillot, *IRA: les républicains irlandais* (Caen: Presses Universitaires de Caen, 2001).

22   Liam Kennedy, '"They Shoot Children, Don't They?" An Analysis of the Age and Gender of Victims of Paramilitary "Punishments" in Northern Ireland'.

household with his mother, who is striving to hold the family together, and his sister, a bulimic girl who is trying to set up her own family by going out with older men. Sean's two brothers had joined the Irish Republican Army (IRA) and were killed respectively by the army and by the member of a Loyalist paramilitary organization. Frances, Sean's girlfriend, is a bright sixth-former with a promising future. Marley is a harmless character – his short-sightedness is a symbol of his naivety – who lives with his old-fashioned and respectable family.

The opening scenes of the film are devoted to the presentation of the trio and to their disruptive activities. The plot starts when an angry resident has just tried to stop a car race by throwing a brick at one of the cars, almost killing the driver. He is beaten up by a group of young people in violent retaliation. The following days see the local IRA intent on policing the young people and planning to put an end to their anti-social activities. The priests organize a meeting with local residents to attempt to find a peaceful and responsible solution to the problem. However, the local residents prefer to adopt the immediate violent solution offered by the IRA. The young are then victims of punishment beatings, tar and feathering as well as kneecapping. Because Sean and his friends refuse to take heed of these warnings and continue to challenge the IRA, the local leader of the organization decides that Sean will be exiled to England.

The rejection of authority is embodied by the three protagonists and their friends. Throughout the film, their main activity consists of going joyriding with no particular purpose. As the term 'joyriding' explicitly suggests, they just want to have fun. One of the priests actually claims: 'After all maybe they are joy riders'. Indeed they represent typical teenagers of the 1990s when a joyriding culture was developing in Ireland and Britain. They are normal teenagers in the sense that they refuse social conventions and the established social order. Like James Dean in the 1957 Hollywood movie they are 'Rebels without a cause'. They reject the IRA and the republican cause, as made clear by Sean: 'We don't need the IRA for protection', 'Who gives a shit about the Provies'?

They keep playing cat and mouse with official authority figures, such as the RUC, and they defy the IRA. In the first scene, Sean, Frances and Marley are driving a stolen car on a main road with techno music blasting from the car stereo when they see an RUC armoured car. The trio decides to go and confront the police laughing and yelling 'Oh yes go on!' and 'Go for it!' They start whirling their car in front of the RUC in defiance, but the two police officers fail to react and start drinking Coke. The senior police officer says it is not worthwhile intervening as the youth are only 'wee bastards'. To test the RUC further, the trio bumps the rear of their car and in the process injures the younger policeman who gets out and shoots at them but they make a safe get-away.

Provoking the adults and testing their limits is a staple ingredient of this story of reckless teenagers going through the 'crisis' typical of their age. They steal cars at the Royal Hospital and give the nurses the finger, almost running them over. When the meeting is organized by the community to find a solution to anti-social activities, joyriders come to defy them driving their cars noisily. When the IRA Chief-of-Staff arrives at the meeting, he is surrounded by their cars just like Indians would encircle cowboys in Western movies and as a result his authority is called into question.

The young generation is portrayed as having no faith in adults and they seem to be very much left to their own devices. They try and create their own society away from adults and away from the Northern Ireland conflict. This alternative micro-society is materialized by the various places where they meet, either on waste ground or outside the city, symbolizing a new start built both on the ruins of the actual decayed society and outside any signs of civilization. This microcosm has its own internal makeshift economy based on goods trafficking (car spare parts – smuggled prescription drugs), a way for young people to survive and learn to become adults on their own somewhat dangerous terms.

One scene shows Sean and Frances having a quiet conversation on the hills on the outskirts of Belfast. They chat about their teachers and about their everyday life in the way teenagers do. Sean claims that 'it's boring around here'. Frances tells him that her teacher said she 'could have a career' and that she is contemplating studying in England. When she asks him if he would follow her, he replies 'I like it here, my mates are here'. The image of the mature girl and less mature boy is a stereotype of teenagers' development. And so is their conversation about their future as a married couple with children who could end up being 'wee joyriders' when Sean, playing the responsible father, replies 'I'll break their arse!'

The characteristics of teenage life, either contesting authority or learning to become adults through creating their own microcosm, are embodied by the protagonists of the film. They want to enjoy freedom and turn their backs on the conflict-ridden society that the adults have created.

Abusing authority

If young people refuse traditional structures and values, it is largely, the film suggests, because authority figures do not play their role. The state and the law-enforcement apparatus are shown to be dysfunctional and bear most of the negative characteristics that were commonly held against them in the 1990s. Common stereotypes of the 'security forces' – both the British Army and the Royal Ulster Constabulary – emphasize their ruthlessness against the Catholic/nationalist community, as well as their lack of commitment to solving tensions and enforcing law and order.

The presence of the British army in Northern Ireland is severely challenged in the story. In one of the early scenes of the film, a soldier is posted at the entrance of a corner shop where Sean goes to buy his cigarettes. The soldier is kneeling and 'striking a pose' with his gun reminiscent of so many newspaper photographs from Northern Ireland. He is in the foreground and is looking towards the spectator, as if expecting trouble from that quarter, when in fact real action is happening behind him: Sean enters the shop and looks down on him as if questioning the need for his presence. In the shop Sean is punched by a local resident who then drags him out to hand him over to the army. As they come out the soldier leaves his position and walks away. The resident runs after him yelling 'Here is your joyrider'. But the soldier is not interested; he only half turns back and orders him to 'piss off!' Sean escapes the grasp of the resident, runs across the street stopping an army tank that nearly stalls, and then moves on as if nothing was the matter.

In another scene, Sean is driving a stolen car at full speed in full view of a group of soldiers performing their routine duty and in front of an army tank and no one takes any heed of him. The scene is shot from a central point and shows a crossroads in wide angle. Sean's car, after whirling in front of the army in defiance, turns one way, while the tank goes the other way. The soldiers on patrol perform a sort of ballet walking aimlessly without noticing the trouble right in front of them.

The only moment in the story when the army intervenes is at the end of the film. While trying to intercept the joyriders who did not stop at a checkpoint, several soldiers fire at the car mistaking the youth for terrorists and killing them. When one of the soldiers realizes he has killed teenagers, he starts crying 'They're all fucking dead!' and vomits. The soldier is himself young and inexperienced, echoing many critics of the British presence in Northern Ireland.[23] The image of the army in the film reflects the feeling of war weariness of the British governments in the early 1990s and proves that the presence of the army was considered pointless and illegitimate. Viewed in the light of Arendt's theory exposed earlier, the British Army's use of violence is a sign that it has no genuine authority.

The film shows an equally uninvolved or abusive police force with officers failing to take action and sounding cynical and disillusioned. The experienced police officers even make it clear at several points that the people in West Belfast should be left to sort out their problems by themselves. Thus when the IRA members arrive at the meeting:

YOUNG POLICEMAN: Who's that?
OLDER POLICEMAN: That, my son, is Reggie Devine
YOUNG POLICEMAN: Reggie Devine, Chief of Staff?
OLDER POLICEMAN: Ex ... ex-Chief of Staff
YOUNG POLICEMAN: Let's go and get the bastard
OLDER POLICEMAN: What for? 4 hours up at Castlereagh and he walks away... Leave him to these wee bastards. They cause them more grief than we can at the moment.

23 John Lindsay, *Brits Speak Out: British Soldiers' Impressions of the Northern Ireland Conflict* (Derry: Guildhall Press, 1998). See also the film '71, directed by Yann Demange, screenplay by Gregory Burke, Crab Apple Film/Warp Film, UK, 2014.

YOUNG POLICEMAN: (Taking his gun) I could put one right between his eyes.
OLDER POLICEMAN: Put that bloody gun away. You don't have a current vermin licence.
YOUNG POLICEMAN: How can you sit here and calmly watch him?
OLDER POLICEMAN: It's called experience!

They drink Coke as they chat, thereby signaling to the spectator that they are behaving like teenagers themselves. They are also prone to the general senseless violence as in the scene when they arrest and brutally beat up Sean and his friends revealing that they have been drawn into the routine and meaningless violence they are supposed to fight. A police officer later tries to recruit Sean as an informer. He makes a speech about the perversity of the IRA who use their own people to do the dirty work for them, although he actually does exactly the same thing with Sean. Institutions like the police or the army who are entrusted to enforce the law are totally discredited either for their ineffectiveness or for their brutality. The foundations of the state are undermined, which can only lead to chaos.

The only people who still seem to have moral values in the community are the two priests. They hold the community together and support people in hardship. At times they embody the function of the 'Greek chorus',[24] commenting on their decaying society and usually adopting a distanced and sometimes cynical point of view. After the meeting the young priest, Father Tom, comments: 'If those thugs who were in here beat the tripe out of those thugs who were out there and the RUC thugs in turn beat the tripe out of both sets of thugs, will you lose any sleep?' Father Murphy, the oldest priest, replies: 'You've been here too long!' They are sometimes more lucid. Talking about institutions they remark: 'At times I think, they don't take this place seriously enough'.

During the meeting the priests organize with the local residents, they try to give a clear and articulate social and political analysis of the problem the community is facing with its youth: 'What I see in West Belfast is a society literally tearing itself apart, a society literally being eaten up by its own youth. The paramilitaries can't solve the problem and the RUC won't

24   Paul Nolan, 'Images of a wild west', *Fortnight* (November 1992), 42.

solve it. Violence is not the way. We've got to show our young people a better way. We're not fighting aliens. We're not fighting an invading army. An invading army would be quieter (*commenting on racing cars outside*). These are our own young people'. However their position as moral beacons is not guaranteed within the population anymore. They are not listened to by the audience at the meeting and are greeted by someone with 'Long time no see'. Very few people acknowledge them when they arrive at the meeting room. Their speech is interrupted by the joyriders outside and their position is challenged by the local IRA team who eventually win over the public.

Although they care for their own community they are depicted as distant characters who do not seem to be anchored in reality. When the meeting is over they realize they failed to convince the local residents. They stroll home, smoking a cigarette and saying 'what a beautiful night', an attitude which reinforces their ambivalence towards what is happening in their community. These characters both embody a clear insight into the situation their community experiences and the temptation to steer away from that situation. Their contradictory attitude is then denounced by the filmmaker who ironically undermines their credibility by showing them 'stealing' cars that have been previously stolen by joyriders in order to give them back to their real owners.

Except for Sean's and Marley's parents, the adults in the film usually act as a group. At the meeting they applaud the speech delivered by the IRA leader. They look like a wild mob whose basic instincts have been aroused by the paramilitaries. The control that the local IRA exercises over the population is based on fear and intimidation and on a discourse that appeals to their basic instinct for revenge. When the IRA men walk into the meeting room, silence falls upon the audience. Reggie Devine, the ex-Chief of Staff of the organization, is portrayed as a mafia godfather with no political cause left to defend. His staff pushes people aside and he nods to start the meeting but remains silent. The image of importance is conveyed by the fact that he is the only person who wears a suit and he is followed by a group of bodyguards. His name itself seems to reinforce his important status, Reginald meaning the person who rules, and the clear phonetic association of 'Devine' with 'divine'. However, his aura is undermined by the diminutive form 'Reggie'. His character may recall the cold, calculating and ruthless Dan Gallagher in Liam O'Flaherty's novel *The Informer*. His enemies are no longer the British but the young generation within his own community. At the meeting he lets one of his men react to the priest's speech. His henchman explains that it is not important to try and find the causes of young people's behaviour. He declares: 'These are hoods! They are not bored deprived young teenagers. These are hoods! I propose to drive them off the streets. We'll hound them night and day... and make their lives an even bigger misery'. His solution is clearly the cycle of violence and revenge. When the priest accuses him, 'It's YOU who's the cause of everybody's misery, they are your monsters', Reggie Devine eventually seizes the opportunity to turn the situation to his advantage: 'Ladies and Gentlemen, I don't know anything about the IRA or about its involvement in all of this. But let's agree with Father Murphy. Let's accept that they are indeed our monsters, and I guess our responsibility. So let's deal with them in our own way. Let's go and get them. (*People cheer and stand up*)'.

To try and get at Sean, Devine first focuses on Marley, the weakest member of the trio, savagely beaten up by his men who have broken every joint in his body. This scene is also presented as a sacrificial ceremony with people shown hitting Marley who thus becomes the scapegoat, according to Girard's theory. Reggie Devine feels remorse and expresses his doubts after the beating: 'Look at what we've done. What are we doing? Some of these lads are lads of comrades; some are orphans of men who died for Ireland. What's gone wrong? What in the name of God is going wrong?' He is unable to make sense of the causes of the social and political deterioration of the situation in which he is a protagonist. Thus all the archetypes of authority discussed so far have a blurred or distorted understanding of their own society. This lack of vision undermines their authority which is further challenged as they are either not respected or shown as not respectable. Their involvement in a vicious circle of violence and revenge to establish their own contested power confirms Arendt's theory of the failure of authority.

Marley's parents seem to provide the only alternative to the violent adult mob. They are traditional parents who want to pass on moral values to their son. Marley's real name is Desmond and his mother is adamant that he should not address her as 'Ma' which to her is a 'corner boy's expression' but 'Mother'. They do not want to be involved in politics and live in a parallel world. The interior decoration of their house dates back to the 1950s. The father's vision is heavily impaired and his main activity is to have the weather forecast read by his son out of the local newspaper. They are not aware of their son's activities. They are in total denial of reality. When the IRA come and fetch Marley to beat him up, the father says: 'Are they from the youth club he belongs to?'

Marley's parents are strikingly contrasted with Sean's mother, Sarah, a strong figure who dares confront Reggie Devine. When he comes to her house to get Sean, she calmly recalls the past: 'It's changed times. I remember the ould days when we were all in this together. When the Brits used to raid us… But the Brits, as bad and all as they were, never left anybody in the mess you left young Marley'. Sarah and her son Sean are actually the strongest and most articulate characters in the fiction as they have come to the realization that the society in which they live is dysfunctional. Sarah has paid a heavy sacrifice to the republican cause, having lost two sons, but tries to hold the family together and refuses to be intimidated by the IRA. At the end of the film, when Reggie Devine changes his mind and decides to allow him to stay, it is Sean who decides that he will go anyway as leaving the country seems to be the only way to escape the chaos and violence. The only characters who try to survive the dysfunctional society represented in the film are those who either stay aloof (the priests, Marley's parents) or refuse the unfounded authority of supposedly authoritative institutions. Sarah and the young people stand for this latter category.

Conclusion

You, Me and Marley fits Arendt's and Girard's theories since it depicts Northern Ireland as lacking any true source of authority. This is reinforced by the 'undifferentiated'[25] roles of the characters. This inexorably leads to

---

25   According to Girard's theory of 'indifferenciation'.

the use of violence, which in turn is a sign that authority has failed. The film represents a society that has reached a deadlock. The once clearly defined enemies do not exist anymore and explaining the conflict is much more complex than traditional nationalist and unionist readings of the situation suggest.[26] In the film, none of these traditional explanations has been adopted and no authoritative historical account is offered. As McGarry and O'Leary, two leading political scientists, claimed: 'There is conflict in Northern Ireland, and we seek to explain it. This task is complicated because there are multiple disagreements over what kind of conflict it is, and about whether it is "one" or "many"; in short there is a "meta-conflict", a conflict about what the conflict is about.'[27] So with no agreed version of the past,[28] the foundation of society in Northern Ireland is uncertain and lacks the authority theorized by Arendt. Authority figures in the film are undermined either by the young generation or by their own nature and functioning.

The film grasped the feeling of weariness about the conflict and underlined that Northern Ireland was reaching the end of an era. Both the British government and many Republicans were aware that they would not win the war they were waging against each other. With negotiations underway since the late 1980s that would lead to the 1994 ceasefires and the subsequent Belfast Agreement of 1998, *You, Me and Marley* caught the prevailing mood of the time.

---

26   John Whyte, *Interpreting Northern Ireland* (Oxford: Oxford University Press, 1990), 113–75.
27   John McGarry, Brendan O'Leary, *Explaining Northern Ireland* (Oxford: Blackwell, 1995), 1.
28   The issue of dealing with the past is still dividing Northern Ireland although a last minute agreement was reached on the subject on 23 December 2014. The Stormont House Agreement has yet to be implemented. <https://www.gov.uk/government/publications/the-stormont-house-agreement> accessed 9 January 2015.

CLAIRE DUBOIS

'Through Darkest Obstruction': Challenging the British Representation of Ireland (1880–1910)

ABSTRACT

The purpose of this chapter is to analyse a series of chromolithographs published between 1880 and 1910 in Irish nationalist newspapers such as the *Weekly Freeman*, the *Nation* and *United Ireland*, the aim of which was to challenge the derogatory representation of Ireland in British satirical newspapers. Irish nationalist chromolithographs often appropriated and altered models from *Punch* or other British comic weeklies, thus undermining the British perception of Ireland. This chapter shows that this visual strategy contributed to the shaping of an Irish identity through the subversion of British authority. The Irish satirical press played a critical role in shaping Irish public opinion and mobilizing the people for the nationalist cause in the context of the Home Rule crisis.

In the nineteenth century, the particularly strained British-Irish relationship was well illustrated in the political cartoons and caricatures published in newspapers and periodicals. If the British visual representation of Ireland has been studied extensively,[1] the nationalist representations on the Irish side have yet to be analysed thoroughly.[2]

---

1   See Lewis Perry Curtis, *Apes and Angels, the Irishman in Victorian Caricature* (Washington, DC: Smithsonian Institution Press, 2nd ed., 1997); Roy F. Foster, *Paddy and Mr Punch, Connections in English and Irish History* (Harmondsworth: Penguin Books, 1995); Michael de Nie, *The Eternal Paddy: Irish Identity and the British Press 1798–1882* (Madison: University of Wisconsin Press, 2004).

2   The following books and articles tackle different aspects of Irish nationalist political cartoons: Lawrence McBride, *Images, Icons and the Irish Nationalist Imagination 1870–1925* (Dublin: Four Courts Press, 1999); 'Historical Imagery in Irish Political Illustrations 1880–1910', *New Hibernia Review* 2/1 (1998), 9–25; Joel A. Hollander, 'Parnell in Irish Political Cartoons 1880–1891', *New Hibernia Review* 4/4 (2000),

The purpose of this chapter is to analyse a series of chromolithographs published between 1880 and 1910 in Irish nationalist newspapers such as the *Weekly Freeman*, the *Nation*, or *United Ireland* the aim of which was to challenge the derogatory representation of Ireland in British satirical newspapers. The most famous British cartoons, from *Punch* or *Judy*, would be available for sale or in the windows of Dublin print shops. Before the emergence of chromolithography, Irish cartoonists had already challenged the British perception of Ireland with hand-coloured or black and white Dublin-produced cartoons, even if the Dublin market was smaller and poorer than the London market. The most famous example is probably the satirical series 'Hints and Hits' published on a weekly basis during the trial of Daniel O'Connell at the beginning of 1844. The series aimed at supporting O'Connell in this troubled period and reassuring his followers, legitimizing the Liberator's actions and presenting the ultimate success of the Repeal cause as inevitable.[3]

There were virtually no political cartoons published in Ireland after this series until the 1860s because of the decline of the Repeal cause and probably also of the Great Famine and its political and social consequences.[4] In the 1860s, political cartoons were first introduced in the *Weekly News* issued by Alexander Martin Sullivan, also editor of the *Nation* and *Zozimus*. In 1867, a series of cartoons was used as part of Sullivan's campaign to support the 'Manchester Martyrs', three Fenians who had killed a

53–65; Lewis Perry Curtis, *Images of Erin in the Age of Parnell* (Dublin: National Library of Ireland, 2000).

3   After the Clontarf meeting for the Repeal of the Act of Union was banned by the government and subsequently called off by Daniel O'Connell in October 1843, O'Connell was charged with high treason and sentenced to imprisonment. For a detailed analysis of the satirical series see Peter Gray, 'Hints and Hits: Irish caricature and the trial of Daniel O'Connell, 1843–4', *History Ireland* 12/4 (Winter 2004), 45–51.

4   During the Great Famine (1845–1850), more than a million people died and another million emigrated, hastening the failure of the Repeal Movement and the 1848 uprising and numbing the country into inaction for decades. See Peter Gray, 'Hints and Hits: Irish caricature and the trial of Daniel O'Connell, 1843–4', *History Ireland* 12/4 (Winter 2004), 50–1.

policeman while rescuing their comrades from a police van and who were
finally executed. The satirical weekly *Zozimus* (1870–1872), named after
the pseudonym of the musician Michael Moran, was intended as an Irish
answer to *Punch* and *Judy* as the first cover suggested – the cover drawn by
John Fergus O'Hea showed the musician Zozimus chasing the characters
representing *Punch*, *Fun* and *Judy*. It seems that from the beginning Irish
caricatures and political cartoons aimed both at supporting the nationalist cause and lampooning the British perception of Ireland as advertised
in English satirical weeklies. This need for an 'Irish consciousness' moving
away from British patronage could also be found in a form of economic
nationalism with the 'Buy Irish' campaigns.[5]

The first poster-sized chromolithographs were published in the
Christmas issues of the *Shamrock* and *Young Ireland* at the beginning of the
1880s. The *Freeman's Journal* was the first broadsheet to introduce a colour
cartoon on a weekly basis in its weekend edition. From the beginning of the
1880s to 1910 when the chromolithograph was gradually replaced by black
and white photographs, more than 2,000 cartoons were published – mainly
by five illustrators: John Fergus O'Hea, Thomas Fitzpatrick, Phil Blake,
W. T. O'Shea and W. C. Mills. The cartoons focused on current political
issues and on historical events of the Irish past, especially in special issues
such as on St Patrick's Day or the Christmas issue.

I wish first to study the interest of this new technique and try to show
that its use implied both a larger audience as the cartoon came as a free
weekly or monthly supplement and a more elaborate artwork. I will then
try to analyse the elements of the composition, which often appropriated
and altered models from *Punch* or other British comic weeklies, thus undermining the British perception of Ireland. Finally, I wish to show that this
visual strategy played a critical role in shaping Irish public opinion and
mobilizing the people for the nationalist cause, closely linking the visual

5   To understand how the period 1840–1920 witnessed attempts to foster 'home' indus-
     tries with the Dublin Exhibition for instance where Irish products on display could
     be bought see John Strachan and Claire Nally, *Advertising, Literature and Print
     Culture in Ireland 1891–1922* (London: Palgrave MacMillan, 2012).

arts and patriotism in a nationalist construct aimed at subverting British authority in the context of the Home Rule crisis.

Chromolithography: A modern technique

The technique of chromolithography was created at the beginning of the nineteenth century. A French printer from Mulhouse was awarded one of the first patents for chromolithography in 1837 for example. In Ireland, it was first introduced in Belfast in 1870 and rapidly spread across the country. The process consists in a series of very precise stages. First the design is drawn onto stone, then inked with oil-based paint and passed through a printing press for the image to be transferred onto paper. Each colour is applied to the paper one at a time and it was not unusual to find up to twenty or twenty-five different colours on the same design.

This new technique allowed to lower the production costs and to mass-produce the colour prints as compared with hand-coloured caricatures such as 'Hints and Hits' (1844) for which the caricature was printed in black and white and then hand-coloured, which was an expensive and time-consuming process.

During the Victorian era, chromolithography became very popular, being frequently used in advertising posters, children's books and other forms of books and popular prints. This was a real revolution in graphic art as the production costs were relatively low especially thanks to the steam-driven printing press and more affordable paper stock from the 1850s. It thus allowed the production of large-sized posters inexpensively.

The heyday of chromolithography was approximately from 1860 to 1900 when it was gradually replaced by even cheaper printing techniques and by black and white photographs. This technique made art and printing more accessible for middle-class families who bought them from print shops. Thanks to colour prints in the newspapers, this technique brought colour to the masses and thus revolutionized communication and perceptions.

The Irish nationalist newspapers published chromolithographs from 1880 to 1910 on a weekly or monthly basis depending on the publication. They sold issues nationally and also to Irish communities abroad. If the Unionist *Irish Times* sold 45,000 copies, the nationalist publications combined sold about 50,000 issues a week: that is to say 24,000 to 30,000 for the *Freeman's Journal*, 13,000 for the *Independent* and 13,500 for the *Nation* in 1900 according to the Royal Irish Constabulary Crime Branch Special Unit.[6] This of course does not include the monthlies that were on offer by subscription or at newsagents.

The colour illustrations came as a poster-sized free supplement in the weekend issue or on special occasions such as Christmas or St Patrick's Day. The bright colours made the prints very attractive as compared to the black and white British cartoons. The different layers of colours made such prints pieces of artwork, sometimes even close to the quality of an oil painting. As they were printed on card or on heavier paper, they were meant to be saved and posted in the readers' homes or in shop windows even if some considered them as a low form of art and questioned their authenticity and creativity.[7] Some of them can still be found and purchased in antique shops and bookstores.

The use of colour and of this new technique demonstrated the publishers' desire to leave an imprint in the minds of their nationalist readership. The regular publication of colour prints was meant to serve a nationalist interest alongside articles and other media in the campaign for Home Rule.[8]

6   Lawrence McBride, *Images, Icons and the Irish Nationalist Imagination 1870–1925*, 9.
7   Michael Clapper, 'I was Once a Barefoot Boy: Cultural Tensions in a Popular Chromo', *American Art 16* (2002), 16–39.
8   For instance, the products advertised in Ireland were often defined in terms of Irishness as the national campaign for Home Rule gathered pace.

A propagandist visual strategy

The illustrations were first intended as an answer to the British image of Ireland as advertised in *Punch* and *Judy* as the omnipresence and authority of this image needed to be challenged. The first caricatures from *Zozimus* (1870–1872) or *Ireland's Eye* (1874–1876) clearly state this ambition: each *Ireland's Eye* issue featured a caricature of a prominent character such as John Spencer[9] or Prime Minister Benjamin Disraeli. *Zozimus*, later revived as *Zoz* (1876–1878), featured political satire. Later cartoons such as 'The English Vampire' published in the *Pilot* in 1885 (Figure 1) are direct answers to *Punch* or other British satirical weeklies – as can be seen in the caption reading 'Reply to Punch's "Irish" Vampire October 24th'. In the *Punch* cartoon Hibernia[10] was lying on the ground at the mercy of a vampire bat about to drain her of her blood; here she has been replaced by Erin who looks well able – and fully determined – to defend herself against British rule, leaving the British bat comically startled and a little scared.

In the 1870s, the cartoonist John Fergus O'Hea was at the centre of a boom of sorts in Dublin-published satirical periodicals, as he participated in the *Weekly News*, *Zozimus*, *Ireland's Eye* and *Pat*, among others. Political cartooning was becoming a very popular nationalist strategy of communication as the introduction of a weekly cartoon in the *Weekly Freeman* followed by other nationalist newspapers (*United Ireland* and the *Nation*

9   John Spencer served as Lord President in Gladstone's third government.
10   During the seventeenth century, a feminine allegory of Ireland came to be used by Irish and English artists alike. Following the Act of Union, two different images of Hibernia developed. The one used by English cartoonists was often portrayed as a passive victim of Irish rebels while Erin, used by Irish artists, came to represent the Irish nation's desire to escape the British yoke. Male figures were also used to represent Ireland: Paddy, the stereotypical Irish rebel sometimes simianized. John Bull was used as a personification of England's conservatism. For more details on Erin, see Lewis Perry Curtis, *Images of Erin in the Age of Parnell*.

Figure 1: 'The English Vampire', The *Pilot* (7 November 1885)
Courtesy of the National Library of Ireland.

mainly) at the beginning of the 1880s shows.[11] The cartoons supported
Charles Stewart Parnell, his land reform and Home Rule campaigns[12] with
sophisticated satire and very high-quality designs, taking advantage of the
new technique of chromolithography.

The cartoons that were published regularly in the *Weekly Freeman*,
the *Nation* or *United Ireland* were more propagandist than humorous in

11   Other cartoonists were openly anti-nationalist like Richard Moynan who published
      his work in the *Union*, see Maebh O'Regan, 'Richard Moynan: Irish Artist and
      Unionist Propagandist', *Éire-Ireland* 39 (2004), 59–80.
12   Charles Stewart Parnell was the leader of the Irish Parliamentary Party and the
      president of the Irish National Land League from 1879. He campaigned for a reform
      abolishing landlordism in Ireland and for Irish self-government. Despite a scandal
      about his private life in 1890, he has been admired by subsequent Irish nationalists.

tone. They featured caricatures of political figures together with the female and male personifications of Ireland: Erin and Pat. Erin is represented as a dark-haired beauty usually dressed in classical outfit, whereas Pat is a handsome farmer, sometimes armed with a shillelagh.[13] The cartoons dealt both with issues of the day and historical episodes, especially in special issues and commemorations of historical events.

There was an obvious inter-textuality with both British and Irish sources. Cartoons from *Punch*, *Fun* or *Judy* were often used as an inspiration as 'The Rivals' (Figure 2) suggests. Originally issued in *Punch* on 13 August 1881, the cartoon by Tenniel satirized the Irish situation at the moment when the Second Land Bill was introduced by Gladstone, then Liberal Prime Minister.[14] The characters represent Parnell's Land League, Hibernia and Gladstone respectively. Gladstone is offering a bunch of flowers labelled 'Land Bill' to Hibernia who is about to accept this measure which was seen as largely favourable to Irish tenant farmers. The Land Leaguer behind Hibernia seems disappointed but he has not yet renounced his opposition to British rule in Ireland. In O'Hea's 1888 cartoon, 'The Rivals', Erin has chosen Pat and not Arthur Balfour.[15] The latter says: 'Confound that fellow, he is taking all the gals from me. I must get him another six months', which is an allusion to the Coercion Acts under which many Irish nationalists were imprisoned. At the time the cartoon was published, Balfour, Chief Secretary for Ireland of the Salisbury administration, was aiming to 'kill Home Rule with kindness', solving Irish social problems to undermine the demand for Home Rule.[16] This policy is here satirized with the representation of Arthur Balfour, holding a bunch of flowers labelled 'Coercion'.

---

13   The shillelagh is an Irish wooden cudgel or club.
14   The Second Land Bill (1881) gave Irish tenants more security, allowing them to take their rents to the Land Court for reduction. Gladstone's aim was also to undermine the Land League and its influence.
15   Arthur Balfour was Chief Secretary for Ireland under the Salisbury Conservative administration (1887–1891). His introduction of the Coercion Acts (1887) and his ruthless enforcement of the Acts earned him the nickname of 'Bloody Balfour'.
16   'Killing Home Rule by kindness' or Constructive Unionism are the names given to the policy enforced by the Conservative governments in the last fifteen years of

Figure 2: John Fergus O'Hea, 'The Rivals', the *Weekly Freeman* (2 June 1888)
Courtesy of the National Library of Ireland.

Many cartoonists were inspired by the satire of the British weeklies, turning it to their advantage. According to Joel A. Hollander, this should not be considered as a sign of 'intellectual inferiority',[17] as the reader can understand both the meaning of the caricature and the reference to the source it lampoons. The viewers that read the British press could indeed understand the references. The other viewers did not know about them but perceived the anti-British criticism anyway. The cartoons can thus be said to have multiple layers of understanding, depending on the viewers' knowledge of the visual representation of the Anglo-Irish relationship, its *clichés* and symbols.

---

the nineteenth century. Land and local government reforms were implemented in an attempt to make the Home Rule movement less popular. The 1887 Land Act increased the protection of tenants, as a first concession to win more support.

17   Joel A. Hollander, 'Parnell in Irish Political Cartoons 1880–1891', *New Hibernia Review* 4/4 (2000), 59.

In the cartoons dealing with current events Charles Stewart Parnell often featured prominently, contributing to his representation as a hero, up to the point when his adulterous relationship with Kitty O'Shea was revealed in 1890. If the majority of his own Irish Parliamentary Party stopped supporting him, some cartoonists added to the Parnell myth even after his death with cartoons commending his determination to bring about political change through constitutional action only.[18]

The subversive portrayal of their political enemies was certainly meant to entertain the nationalist viewer. British politicians such as Arthur Balfour or Lord Salisbury[19] were portrayed as unable to understand the Irish situation, useless and ridiculous figures whose authority could thus be undermined. For instance, in a cartoon published in 1884, Salisbury and Gladstone, Tory leader and Liberal Prime Minister respectively, are shown as Erin's tormentors, discussing her fate while she is tied to a tree.[20] After the defeat of the First Home Rule Bill,[21] the leaders of the Unionist Coalition – Lord Salisbury, Hartington, Randolph Churchill – together with Joseph Chamberlain, are portrayed as murderers about to cut Erin to pieces on a dissecting table.[22]

Gladstone was generally treated with more respect than other British politicians, especially after Irish nationalists understood in 1884 that he was in favour of Home Rule and that he would work with the Nationalist Party to secure the measure. He is represented as Erin's 'ardent admirer' in the 1887 cartoon 'In the Lion's Den' (Figure 3), the one that

18   'He Fought for Freedom, not for Faction', *Irish Weekly Independent* (7 October 1893).
19   Lord Salisbury was a British Conservative politician who served as Prime Minister three times. He opposed Irish self-government.
20   'The Reason Why', *Weekly Freeman* (11 October 1884).
21   The First Home Rule Bill (1886) was introduced in the House of Commons by Gladstone's Liberal Government but was never passed. If the Bill was rejected by the Conservatives under the leadership of Randolph Churchill, Gladstone also alienated some Liberals like Chamberlain. Lord Hartington broke with the Liberals and opposed the Bill because his younger brother was murdered in Dublin during the debate in the House of Commons.
22   'On a Dissecting Table – Again, Perhaps', *Weekly Freeman* (31 July 1886).

will save Erin from the Tory lion about to devour her – in the context of Arthur Balfour ruthlessly enforcing the 1887 Coercion Acts. Erin seems forgotten by all except Gladstone and yet she is clinging to the green crown of Home Rule.

Figure 3: John Fergus O'Hea, 'In the Lion's Den', the *Weekly Freeman* (23 July 1887) Courtesy of the National Library of Ireland.

The cartoon 'Through Darkest Obstruction' (Figure 4), was published in 1893 and refers to Conservative/Unionist attempts to delay the passage of Gladstone's Second Home Rule Bill through the House of Commons by talking it out. Gladstone (appearing here as a young man) is shown with a tree-felling axe, accompanied by 'Pat' the stereotypical honest Irishman. The black shapes with red lips lurking behind trees include Arthur Balfour (Conservative leader in the Commons; higher of the two faces on the right, with sideburns and open mouth) and Liberal Unionist leader Joseph Chamberlain (with eyeglass) while the monkey with long moustaches on the branch overhead represents the Ulster Unionist leader Edward

Figure 4: Thomas Fitzpatrick, 'Through Darkest Obstruction',
the *Weekly Freeman* (26 August 1893)
Courtesy of the National Library of Ireland.

Saunderson.[23] Here the 'anti-nationalists' are represented as ape-like – reversing the traditional stereotype used by British satirical weeklies – and the colours offered by the technique of chromolithography are exploited to the full, especially with the contrast between red, green and dark colours.

If Erin and Pat are used as positive representations of Ireland – contrary to Hibernia and Paddy – John Bull is generally portrayed as an unattractive man who fails to understand Erin and the Irish cause. For instance, he recoils with fear from the vision of Erin emerging triumphantly from her grave at the top of a snow-covered mountain holding a cross and the crown of Home Rule.[24] Inscribed on the tombstone behind her are the words 'Ireland Buried Here 1171', *i.e.*, the year of the arrival of King Henry II.

As could be expected, Britannia and Erin seem unable to understand each other. Thus when Britannia invites Erin to join her in the celebrations for Queen Victoria's Jubilee, the latter refuses, preferring to mourn the death of the heroes of the 1798 uprising.[25] The setting is a cemetery which includes the graves of 1798 revolutionary heroes such as Robert Emmet or Lord Edward Fitzgerald.[26]

Some cartoons dealt even more directly with the historical past of Ireland, generally in special issues for Christmas or anniversaries, often losing their humorous tone and satirical outlook. They could deal for instance with the 1798 rebellion[27] or with the living conditions during

---

23   After Gladstone became Prime Minister again in 1892, he introduced the Second Home Rule Bill in the House of Commons in 1893. If the Conservatives and Unionists used obstructionist tactics to oppose it, almost rejecting it word for word, the Bill was passed in the House of Commons, but rejected by the Conservative-dominated House of Lords.
24   'John Bull beholds a vision of the near future', *Weekly Freeman* (1884).
25   'Who fears to speak of '98', *Weekly Freeman* (26 June 1897).
26   The 1798 uprising was a rebellion against British rule in Ireland. Lord Edward Fitzgerald was killed during his arrest on charges of treason. Robert Emmet participated in the 1798 uprising and then tried to organize another one in 1803 after which he was sentenced to death for high treason and executed.
27   This was exemplified by a female insurgent on watch in: 'A Scout of '98 – The Yeos', *Weekly Freeman* (19 December 1891).

the Penal Days when Catholic masses were forbidden.[28] Those cartoons were obviously not meant to entertain, but rather to commemorate past events, and to remind the viewers of past grievances to strengthen their nationalist opinions.[29] The cartoons thus transported the viewers back to the past affecting their collective memory, sometimes with a melodramatic tone. Other cartoons were meant to be reassuring, conveying the idea that the future would be bright thanks to hopeful imagery, with for instance Erin – with harp and wolfhound by her side – dreaming of Home Rule and a vision of Parliament emerging in the smoke.[30] The hopeful imagery used by Thomas Fitzpatrick ten years later in the cartoon 'The Dawn of Freedom' (Figure 5) is quite similar. Erin is sitting by a Celtic cross with harp and wolfhound by her side again. She is looking towards the rainbow and the rising sun in the distance, with a hopeful expression on her face. We can see ruined houses and churches in the landscape which may mean that Erin is used to sorrows and suffering and yet she still seems full of hope.

Shaping Irish public opinion

The cartoons presented, however varied in tone and subject, all share the ambition to strengthen and pander to the readers' nationalist opinions, in the context of the struggle for Home Rule. When dealing with current events, the cartoonists kept to the editorial line of the newspapers seeking to entertain readers by criticizing the British government's Irish policy, be

28   The Penal Legislation was a set of laws imposed to force Irish Catholics and Presbyterians to conform to Anglicanism. See: 'Mass in the mountains, A Picture of the Penal Days', *Weekly Freeman*, Christmas issue 1884 (date uncertain).
29   Lawrence McBride, *Images, Icons and the Irish Nationalist Imagination 1870–1925*, 16–18.
30   'A Vision of Coming Events', *Weekly Freeman* (16 December 1882).

Figure 5: Thomas Fitzpatrick, 'The Dawn of Freedom',
the *Weekly Freeman* (24 December 1892)
Courtesy of the National Library of Ireland.

it Liberal or Conservative.[31] The numerous caricatures depicting Erin as a victim, enchained or caught between two malevolent British politicians, appealed to a public that was probably deeply resentful over the way the advocates of Irish self-government were treated. This image also left no doubt concerning the obstacles remaining on the way to Home Rule. Even if British politicians were generally criticized, Gladstone, after it became clear that he would support Home Rule, was mostly portrayed positively as in the cartoon 'In the Lion's Den' (1887).[32]

The image of Erin as a victim surrounded with threatening male characters can be said to be ambiguous, as it fails to challenge the subservient

31 Some cartoonists such as Fitzpatrick worked for unionist newspapers before being hired by nationalist papers.
32 See Figure 3.

role ascribed to Ireland in the colonial relationship. Were the cartoonists reinforcing the British perception of Ireland as weak and female? According to Joel Hollander quoting Baudelaire, this can be seen as a form of *comique absolu* as the cartoon becomes a sort of enigma for the viewer – the caption often being in total contradiction with the design and revealing the satirical intentions of the cartoonist.[33] In his satirical cartoon, the artist thus mocks appearances to re-establish the truth, which can then be considered as a way to subvert British authority, reversing its imperialist images.

Other images feature Erin or Pat as strong characters, challenging British rule and possessing the necessary strength to lead the Irish out of subjection. Such cartoons were mostly issued during the rise and prominence of Parnell in the 1880s. The best example is probably the *Irish Pilot*'s reply to Tenniel's *Irish Vampire* published in 1885, 'The English Vampire', in which the Irish cartoonist reversed the imagery used in *Punch*, portraying British rule as an evil bat (Figure 1).

Another way to influence Irish public opinion was to remind them of episodes of Irish history, especially the 1798 rebellion and life in the Penal Days. This nationalist visual history provided lessons for the viewer, influencing their collective memory. The cartoonists thus tackled various issues and subjects, always with the aim of responding to their nation's critics and exposing the distortions and stereotypes produced in London.

When in tune with other media and political speeches, the cartoonists played a key role in the shaping of an Irish nationalist identity, making the link between the idea and the action more visible.[34] The cartoons reinvented an Irish national identity, through a series of carefully chosen episodes taken from the Irish past, reinforcing the readers' hope for self-government and resentment towards British mistreatment.

33   Joel A. Hollander, 'Parnell in Irish Political Cartoons 1880–1891', *New Hibernia Review* 4/4 (2000), 59–60. Hollander is referring to Charles Baudelaire's essay *De l'essence du rire et généralement du comique dans les arts plastiques* (1855).

34   Taking the example of Cuchulain and ancient Irish heroes, Kiberd shows the power of images and ideas when they are appropriated by people and expressed in direct action, such as the Easter R. Declan Kiberd, *Inventing Ireland: The Literature of the Modern Nation* (London: Vintage, 1996), 196.

At the end of the nineteenth century, the role of the press gradually took a new turn. The élite and educated classes had dominated the editorial press up to the 1840s, taking very seriously their 'mission' to guide the people thanks to their *penny papers* but they gradually lost this sense of having a mission to fulfil – especially because of a rising class-consciousness. The contents of the newspapers became more politicized and they became the voice of political movements or parties, the masses also becoming more politicized thanks to suffrage movements and reforms extending the franchise such as in 1884.[35] The nationalist newspapers thus tried to mobilize the people around common goals and ideas, advertising and illustrating British wrongs and Irish rights. According to Jürgen Habermas, the press took advantage of the political awareness of the masses that were gradually emancipating to use the productive force created by communication, in other words, use the media in a manipulative way.[36] They aimed at producing political effects thanks to their influence on the people and on their opinion. The *Freeman's Journal* for instance was owned by the Gray family from 1841 to 1892. Initially a Protestant family, the Grays successively supported Repeal, the Church of Ireland disestablishment, Home Rule and Parnell until his fall in 1891. The then Lord Lieutenant, Earl Spencer, condemned Edmund Dwyer Gray for supporting Parnell only in order to sell copies of his paper, in a letter to Gladstone dated 25 August 1882: 'Gray is a man who plays a game & that a false game for he does not at heart believe in the policy of the extreme men in Irish politics & yet he is always pandering and flattering their policy & themselves'.[37]

The cartoons helped the audience understand the present situation thanks to elements drawn from the Irish past; they helped to challenge

35   After the 1884 Representation of the People Act, approximately 30% of the adult male population could vote in Ireland.

36   See Jürgen Habermas, *L'espace public. Archéologie de la publicité comme dimension constitutive de la société bourgeoise* (Paris: Payot, 1962), 164, 190; *Théorie de l'agir communicationnel* (Paris: Fayard, 1987), 174, 429. Also see: 'L'espace public, 30 ans après', *Quaderni*, 18 (Fall 1992), 161–91.

37   See Felix M. Larkin, 'A Great Daily Organ: the *Freeman's Journal*, 1763–1924', *History Ireland*, 14, 3 (May/June 2006), 44–9.

British preconceptions about Ireland and gathered the people around collective memories and common hopes. There is sadly little information about the impact of such cartoons on the readers. But at a time of acute tension between London and Dublin, they probably strengthened Irish nationalism, also contributing to the rejection by many of any British influence and rule. However we do know about the success of the 'Buy Irish' campaigns with ads to be found in the newspapers. Such ads stressed the virtues of Irishness and linked the literary and cultural revivalist movement with a form of economic nationalism in a wider Irish self-representation. The cartoons probably contributed to the shaping of this Irish identity through the subversion of British authority. If the British government used different tactics to undermine the movement for Home Rule, they systematically failed and the Irish satirical press no doubt played its part in encouraging resistance and campaigning for constitutional change.

CIARAN BRADY

An Old Kind of History: The Anglo-Irish Writing of Irish History, 1840–1910

ABSTRACT

Two exceptional features characterize the evolution of history writing in late nineteenth-century Ireland, both of which may be expressed in the negative. One is the absence of any trend toward the so-called 'professionalization' of historical study which is such a marked feature of cultural development in Europe and America in this period. And the second, closely related, but by no means identical process was the unwillingness of Irish scholars and intellectuals to participate overtly in the absorption of the widespread conviction that the study of history could be transformed into an authoritative scientific discipline. This essay examines the Anglo-Irish reconstruction of Irish history and the resulting successful refurbishment of an old kind of history which served more effectively than any pretension to scientific models to reassert their claim to cultural leadership.

Two exceptional features characterize the evolution of history writing in late nineteenth-century Ireland, both of which may be expressed in the negative. One is the absence of any trend toward the so-called 'professionalization' of historical study which is such a marked feature of cultural development in Europe and America in this period. And the second, closely related, but by no means identical process was the unwillingness of Irish scholars and intellectuals to participate overtly in the absorption of the widespread conviction that the study of history could be transformed into an authoritative scientific discipline.[1] In what follows I shall attempt to explain the forces underlying this strange case of Irish exceptionalism.

---

[1]   On the development of these two inter-related processes see: Georg G. Iggers, 'The Intellectual Foundations of Nineteenth-Century "Scientific" History: the German model' and Gabriele Lingelbach 'The institutionalisation and professionalization of history in Europe and the United States', in Stuart Macintyre et al., eds, The Oxford

Resistance to the professionalization of history

Ireland's divergence from this common pattern of Western historiography has complex roots. Concerning the failure of history to emerge within the Irish university sector as a distinct academic discipline, in the manner in which it had done in European and North American universities by the last quarter of the nineteenth century, several institutional, structural and cultural factors may be considered. In the later nineteenth century, it might be said, Ireland was oversupplied with third-level institutions, for in addition to the relatively ancient colleges Trinity College (founded in 1592) and the Catholic seminary of St Patrick's College Maynooth (founded in 1796), three state-endowed 'queen's colleges' (in Belfast, Galway and Cork) had been founded after much intense political argument between proponents of secular and denominational education, and a distinctively Catholic University had enjoyed a short and halting existence in Dublin. At a time of chronic economic and demographic recession in post-Famine Ireland, demand for such an expanded supply of tertiary institutions was very low, and state funding correspondingly so.[2] By 1870 (at a time when the population of Scotland was considerably below that of Ireland), it has been estimated there were as many students on the books in either the universities of Edinburgh and Glasgow as were attending all of the Irish colleges.[3]

    History of Historical Writing: Volume 4: 1800–1945 (Oxford: Oxford University Press, 2011), 41–58, 78–96.

2   Susan M. Parkes, 'Higher Education, 1793–1908', in W. E. Vaughan, ed., *A New History of Ireland: Volume VI: Ireland Under the Union, 1870–1921* (Oxford: Oxford University Press, 1989), 539–570; Ciaran Brady, '*Arrested Development*: Competing Histories and the Formation of the Irish Historical Profession, 1801–1938' in Tibor Frank and Frank Hadler, eds, *Disputed Territories and Shared Pasts: Overlapping National Histories in Modern Europe* (London: Palgrave, 2011), 275–97.

3   W. E. Vaughan, 'Ireland c. 1870' in Vaughan, ed., *A New History of Ireland: Volume VI: Ireland Under the Union, 1870–1921* (Oxford: Oxford University Press, 1989), 797–9.

The rudimentary and impoverished character of the Irish tertiary sector did not encourage any developments whatever within their walls, let alone the establishment of distinctive departments for the teaching and study of history as an independent discipline. 'Professors' of History were indeed appointed in the Queen's Colleges, but invariably they were lone scholars – invariably teachers rather than researchers or writers of history, and they were normally engaged in teaching other disciplines such as philosophy, and geography as well. In fact the first of such departments appeared only in the twentieth century. In the meantime, however, original research on Irish history continued to be conducted and published by figures working within the older institutions, such as James Henthorn Todd, George Thomas Stokes and Alexander Ritchie in Trinity and by Patrick F. Moran and Charles W. Russell in Maynooth. But, with the exception of Ritchie, who was an academic lawyer, all of the others were ecclesiastics who, unlike several of their counterparts in Britain, evinced no interest in developing their historical studies within an independent departmental framework. And, perhaps just as significantly, few expressed a desire to move outside their own individual institutions to establish the kind of inter-institutional organs, associations, committees and joint journals which were becoming the hallmark of a distinctive academic discipline.

The internal structural stagnation of Irish third-level education had deeper roots than financial underfunding and demographic decline. The deep confessional divisions of Irish society which had bedevilled attempts at the reform and development of Irish education in general since the later eighteenth century continued to operate in the century thereafter. The Catholic hierarchy's virulent opposition to the 'godless' queen's colleges ensured that attendance of members from the majority Catholic population would be restricted. And after the failure of the Catholic University in Dublin, those few Catholic families interested in, and able to afford, a higher education for their offspring looked instead to a select number of Catholic colleges in Britain and on the Continent. Meanwhile in Trinity, the threat of establishing a second college under the umbrella of the University of Dublin which would be entirely Catholic in its ethos having been averted, a calm of sectarian complacency was restored, and Catholic entrances diminished. And finally, the success of the demand in

Belfast that the Queen's College there should have a close relationship with
the Presbyterian seminarian College having been accepted, the possibility
that third-level education in Ireland might lead to a non-denominational
and secular mode of education was dismissed.[4]

Structural, economic and above all cultural (largely religious) factors
thus contributed greatly to inhibiting any tendency toward the professionalization of history as an academic discipline within Irish third-level colleges. Yet, while it cannot be discounted, such a simple structural-functional
account is in itself insufficient on several grounds. For in no less important
ways Ireland in the early nineteenth century can be shown to have possessed all of the pre-conditions which have commonly been identified as
essential to the transformation of history from a branch of *belles-lettres*
into a rigorous academic discipline.[5]

One of these preconditions was the existence of a strong antiquarian
culture among the leisured classes which found expression in the establishment and maintenance of local or dedicated papers. Indeed, reading
societies and clubs funded regularly appearing journals or magazines in
which the research of their members was given permanent form in print. A
second was the existence within the universities and colleges of traditional
disciplines or faculties with a pre-existing historical dimension, such as
classical studies, theology or divinity and law. A third was the acknowledged place within the broader public sphere of political and moral debate
of works supplying historical narrative and interpretation. And finally, at

4   Susan M. Parkes, 'Higher Education, 1793–1908', in W. E. Vaughan, ed., *A New History
     of Ireland: Volume VI: Ireland Under the Union, 1870–1921*; T. W. Moody, 'The Irish
     university question in the nineteenth century', *History* vol. 43 (1958), 90–109; R. B.
     Mc Dowell and D. A. Webb, *Trinity College Dublin, 1592–1952: an academic history*
     (Cambridge: Cambridge University Press, 1982), T. W. Moody and J. C. Beckett,
     Queen's Belfast 1845–1949: the History of a University (2 vols, London: Faber and
     Faber, 1950).
5   See among many, Philippa Levine, *The Amateur and the Professional: Antiquarians,
     Historians and Archaeologists in Victorian England 1838–1886* (Cambridge: Cambridge
     University Press, 1986), Peter Novick, *That Noble Dream: The 'Objectivity Question'
     and the American Historical Profession* (Cambridge: Cambridge University Press,
     1988).

the centre of such public debates was the question of national identity: a contemporary and forward-looking question as to the character of a particular culture in regard to which historical writing was regarded as essential.

From these pre-existing conditions, the process of transformation took one of several courses. In the case of Germany, where the university community was in an especially strong position, the academics took the lead, quickly establishing their authority over the amateur antiquarians, and appropriating for themselves the role of public arbiter in debates on politics, morals and national identity.[6] Elsewhere more complex struggles took place. In England and in the United States, for example, the move to the academy was closely related to a disillusion with or hostility toward prevailing Romantic modes of public history writing, which sought to effect a transformation of individual readers through inspiration, in the face of both powerful political and economic realities and of the formidable challenges posed to traditional forms of belief by discoveries in physics, geology and biology.[7] In France, where similar pressures applied, the process was made more complex still due to intensive competition and boundary disputes within the walls of the academic institutions.[8] But in all cases a similar result was ultimately achieved: proponents of history

6   Georg G. Iggers, 'The Intellectual Foundations of Nineteenth-Century "Scientific" History: the German model'; Leonard Krieger, *Ranke: The Meaning of History* (Chicago: University of Chicago Press, 1977); Fritz K. Ringer, *The Decline of the German Mandarins: The German Academic Community, 1890–1933* (Cambridge, MA: Harvard University Press, 1969).

7   J. W. Burrow, *A liberal descent: Victorian historians and the English past* (Cambridge: Cambridge University Press, 1981); Philippa Levine, *The Amateur and the Professional: Antiquarians, Historians and Archaeologists in Victorian England 1838–1886; Peter R. H. Slee, Learning and a Liberal Education: The Study of Modern History in the Universities of Oxford, Cambridge, and Manchester, 1800–1914* (Manchester: Manchester University Press, 1986); *Reba M. Soffer, Discipline and Power: The University, History, and the Making of an English Elite, 1870–1930* (Stanford: Stanford University Press, 1994)

8   William R. Keylor, *Academy and community: the foundation of the French historical profession.*

withdrew from the high claims of the Romantic prophets, renounced a place in the arena of literary discourse, and settled instead for a modest but firm contention that history was a form of knowledge, equipped with methods, procedures, systems of validation and falsification which freed it from the charge of individual bias and caprice, and entitled it to be recognized as a science. But in Ireland nothing of the kind happened at all.

The strange divergence of history writing in Ireland from the pattern of development elsewhere in the later nineteenth century is all the more curious because in Ireland all these conditions applied to a greater or lesser degree. A strong intellectual interest in antiquities had emerged in the early seventeenth century, in keeping with the European pattern, it had been developed greatly over the course of the eighteenth century, and continued to flourish in the nineteenth century.[9] Despite its reputation in the eighteenth century as 'the silent sister' Trinity in the early nineteenth century had established a considerable reputation in classical studies; while a little later St Patrick's Maynooth began to build a reputation for scholarship based on the continental education of its leading faculty.[10] And historical writing continued to feature as a central element in Irish public debate, at least as much as anywhere in Europe.[11] In the aftermath of the bloody rebellion of 1798 and the consequent abolition of Irish constitutional independence in the Act of Union (1801), a vigorous debate opened

9   Clare O'Halloran, *Golden Ages and Barbarous Nations: Antiquarian Debate and Cultural Politics in Ireland, c. 1750–1800* (Cork: Cork University Press, 2004); Damien Murray, *Romanticism, Nationalism and Irish Antiquarian Societies, 1840–8* (Maynooth: The Department of Old and Middle Irish National University of Ireland Maynooth, 2000); Elizabeth Tilley, 'The Royal Irish Academy and antiquarianism', in James H. Murphy, ed., *The Oxford History of the Irish Book Vol. IV* (Oxford: Oxford University Press, 2011), 463–76.

10   R. B. McDowell and D. A. Webb, *Trinity College Dublin, 1592–1952: an academic history* (Cambridge: Cambridge University Press, 1982); Patrick J. Corish, *Maynooth College, 1795–1995* (Dublin: Gill & Macmillan, 1995).

11   *Jacqueline Hill*, 'The Intelligentsia and Irish Nationalism in the 1840s', *Studia Hibernica* 20 (1980), 73–109; Donald McCartney, 'The Writing of History in Ireland, 1800–1830', *Irish Historical Studies* X, n° 40 (1957), 347–62.

up about Ireland's current situation, largely on historical grounds. Richard Musgrave's pro-Union and highly Protestant account of the '98 Rebellion, entitled significantly *Memoirs of the different rebellions in Ireland since the arrival of the English* (1802) which placed the events of 1798 against a background of previous Irish rebellions arguing that the Catholic Irish were by definition rebellious, provoked a storm of controversy which was largely conducted historically through publications such as Denis Taaffe's *Impartial History of Ireland* (1809–11) which directly challenged Musgrave's sectarian thesis.[12] In the 1820s and 1830s, as the anti-Union argument revived and grew in influence, arguments in favour of repeal of the Act of Union began to appear in the form of extended narratives of Irish history.[13] Under the influence first of Scott and later of Carlyle, the Romantic perspective on history's meaning and purpose added greatly to this movement as the re-establishment of Ireland's constitutional independence was presented as crucial to the fashioning of a new and united Irish identity. Romantic history as expressed both in historical prose and in fiction and poetry reached its zenith in the early 1840s in the pages of the *Nation* a weekly newspaper edited and written by a group of young intellectuals styled 'Young Ireland'. Combining ballads, poems and stories with straightforward essays on historical topics, the *Nation* and its ancillary publications sought to provide their readers and their listeners, (for the paper was intended to be read aloud in public reading-rooms) with an entirely fresh and dramatic experience of absorbing history in a manner that was intended to be personally inspiring and transformative.[14] Finally, in the later 1840s, in

---

12   On Musgrave see: James Kelly, *Sir Richard Musgrave 1746–1818: Ultra-Protestant Ideologue* (Dublin: Four Courts Press, 2009); Taaffe's *Impartial History* is available on-line through archive.org at: <https://archive.org/details/impartialhistory03taafiala>

13   Donald McCartney, 'The Writing of History in Ireland, 1800–1830'; Clare O'Halloran, 'Historical writing, 1690–1900', in Margaret Kelleher and Philip O'Learey, eds, *The Cambridge History of Irish Literature Vol. I* (Cambridge: Cambridge University Press, 2008).

14   See *inter alia*, Patrick Rafroidi, *Irish Literature in English: The Romantic Period, 1789–1850* (2 vols, Gerrards Cross: Colin Smythe, 1980); Helen Mulvey, *Thomas Davis and Ireland: a biographical study* (Washington DC: The Catholic University

the midst of the Great Famine and the subsequent dissolution of 'Young Ireland' through the debacle of the rebellion of 1848, this Irish version of Romantic history was to be engulfed by an economic and political crisis which was even more severe than those which were to overwhelm similar movements in the rest of Europe and later in the United States.

But in contrast to other experiences, the failure of Romantic history did not lead to the retreat into the academy and the concomitant redefinition of history writing as a scientific discipline. Instead, the successors of 'Young Ireland' remained resolutely outside the academy, composed no methodological or epistemological claims for their work, and seemed increasingly to devote themselves to the composition of chronological narratives. It is in this that the peculiarity of the Irish experience within the context of Western historiography lies. Given the existence in Ireland of the several conditions conducive into the transformation of history writing from a form of literature to an academic discipline with scientific pretensions – antiquarianism, academic institutions, the ideological uses of history writing in a debate over national identity, and the failure of the last great attempt of shaping history as a literary art –, an outcome similar to that which took place in Europe and America seems quite predictable. But in Ireland, for some reason, the convergence of these factors failed to take place, the transformation did not occur. And the question is why?

William Edward Hartpole Lecky

The problem is, moreover, deepened by the fact that this process of divergence took place not within an atmosphere of torpor or degeneration, but amidst a veritable renaissance of serious historical research and writing

---

of America Press, 2003); James Quinn, *Young Ireland and the Writing of Irish History* (Dublin: UCD Press, 2015).

which arose outside university walls and continued throughout the later nineteenth century. For these years witnessed a huge increase in the scholarly output on the part of individual and largely amateur (that is to say non-academic) historians concentrating on the reinterpretation of Irish history.[15]

Pre-eminent among these was William Edward Hartpole Lecky (1838–1903). Having begun his publishing career as an essayist on Irish history, Lecky early abandoned the subject in favour of work on European intellectual and cultural history from the Middle Ages to the eighteenth century. It was on the basis of his cosmopolitan reputation, rather than his Irish origins, that Lecky was invited by his publishers, Longmans, to write on the history of England in the eighteenth century. It was only in that context, and for reasons that will be discussed below, that Lecky returned to Irish history in a manner that would transform his image and reputation as a historian. When Lecky's *The Leaders of Public Opinion in Ireland* appeared first in 1861, it was at first hardly noticed.[16] But the unprecedented space which he devoted to Irish history in the eighteenth century in the midst of his multi-volume history of England in the eighteenth century changed everything.[17] Universally praised by Irish reviewers, it was to become a model for subsequent narrators of the Irish historical record, such as Richard Bagwell who first devoted three thoroughly researched volumes to a sustained narrative history of *Ireland under the Tudors* (1886–92), and a further three-volume set on *Ireland under the Stuarts (1890–1890)*. Lecky's model was followed by Goddard Henry Orpen whose four-volume *Ireland under the Normans* (1910–1920) completed what was almost a comprehensive narrative history

---

15   For a brief and selective survey see Marc Caball, 'History and politics: interpretations of early modern conquest and reformation in Victorian Ireland' in Stefan Berger and Chris Lorenz, eds, *Nationalizing the past: historians as nation builders in modern Europe* (London: Palgrave Macmillan, 2010), 149–69.

16   William Edward Hartpole Lecky, *The Leaders of Public Opinion in Ireland: Swift, Flood, Grattan, O'Connell* (London: Saunders, 1861).

17   Lecky's *A History of England in the Eighteenth Century* first appeared in an eight-volume edition (1878–1890); a twelve-volume cabinet edition of 1892 which separated out the Irish chapters into five separate volumes made clear the extraordinary space which he had given to Irish history in the original.

of Ireland from the twelfth century down to the early nineteenth century. At the same time many other scholars were enriching the Irish historical record through monographs based upon deep archival research and the publication of major collections of edited manuscripts.[18]

Yet not one of these figures held an academic post of any kind and Lecky turned down the offer of a chair in Trinity. They were all, in a distinction that was now becoming notable, avowedly amateurs rather than professionals. Furthermore, and distinguishing Irish historiographical culture from contemporary international patterns elsewhere, was the complete absence in their writing of any speculation or comment regarding the epistemological status of historical research, and in particular any indication on their part of the claim, now becoming familiar among both 'amateur' and 'professional' scholars that history was a science.

This is not to say that the Irish historians eschewed the value of a profound knowledge of primary archival sources or that they rejected the aspiration to write unbiased, dispassionate history. For clearly they did both. The real point is that they refused to go further. None gave any explicit allegiance to the philosophical – historicist – foundations of the scientific model. None showed any interest in supporting the institutions associated with 'scientific' history, seminars, postgraduate theses, peer-reviewed journals. And above all, none showed any enthusiasm for concepts of constitutional development, community development and state formation which was a characteristic of the 'scientific' approach elsewhere.[19]

18   In the 1850s, for example, John T. Gilbert opened a distinguished scholarly career
      with the publication of his three-volume *History of Dublin* based on topographical
      principles. In 1865 John P. Prendergast published his highly influential study of *The
      Cromwellian Settlement in Ireland* and in 1881 Prendergast prepared for the press
      lifelong researches of Charles Haliday into the history of *The Scandanavian Kingdom
      of Dublin*. Both Gilbert and Prendergast were tireless editors of historical documents,
      and throughout this period an impressive body of original, archive-based research
      continued to appear in the pages of Ireland's several local historical and archaeologi-
      cal journals.
19   Georg G. Iggers, 'The Intellectual Foundations of Nineteenth-Century "Scientific"
      History: the German model'; for a fascinating and contrasting account of the devel-
      opment of the 'scientific' model in another peripheral European country, see Effi

To this Lecky is partially an exception; but an exception that proves the rule. In his relatively early work, his *History of European Morals from Augustus to Charlemagne* (1869) and most particularly his *History of the Rise and Influence of Rationalism in Europe* (1865), where he shows some indication of being influenced by the English historical sociologist, H. T. Buckle, Lecky may have been working on a largely implicit model of the manner in which human history progressed through key intellectual frameworks by which the world was perceived. Yet on his resumption of the study of Irish history any such model was dropped in favour of a detailed interpretative narrative form in which his modes of causation, explanation and judgement were derived from a close analysis of events, the specificity of individual character motivation and interest, and sheer contingency. When Lecky returned to Ireland, he reverted to narrative.

A partial explanation for this curious divergence may be found in the very event which influenced so much historical writing and argument in the first half of the nineteenth century, the Act of Union itself. The centrality of questions of national origins and nation-state development to nineteenth-century European historiography is well known. Concentration on such questions as to why some nations progressed into powerful states while others declined, encouraged historians to seek certain patterns in the histories of nations, certain stages of development, certain key turning points that were to determine their destiny. In pursuit of this predetermined and intrinsically comparative goal, it was essential, they believed, that a standardized and uniform approach to the inspection of the historical record be developed. This was to be achieved through the articulation of a clear and explicit method by which secondary sources should be firmly separated from primary ones; that in the case of the latter refined distinctions should be made in the selection, assessment and application of such sources, and that in general the archives of the state, whether failed or successful, should be prioritized over others. Following this practice, the historians should be able to derive firm and objective explanations of the

Gazi, *Scientific national history: the Greek case in comparative perspective, 1850–1920* (Frankfurt am Main: Peter Lang, 2000).

course of one nation's history in contrast to another's. Rational and testable conclusions would rest on a rigorous and uniform method.[20] The success of this 'scientific' approach was most obvious in diplomatic history, or in the history of the inter-relationship between states generally. But it was scarcely less attractive in terms of domestic history where such a method in the hands, say of a Stubbs or Maitland in England, or a Fustel de Coulanges in France served to supply a greater methodological rigour to traditional 'Whig' accounts of the inexorable triumph of freedom, by replacing the latter's speculative emphasis on individual heroes and villains with solid institutional history based on acute documentary analysis.[21]

Seen against this background, the Irish Act of Union presented Irish historians with multiple challenges. In the first instance the 'state archive' was itself intrinsically problematic. The accumulated remains of so many revolutions in Irish government since the twelfth century, the identity of the Irish state and the character of its archive was itself a subject of the most profound dispute: a contention made more complex still by the arbitrary and massive destruction of large bodies of the Irish historical record, the proliferation of forgeries and embezzled texts, and a long tradition of highly polemical historical narratives. The Union which appeared to claim that the real identity of Ireland lay not in original Celtic culture, nor in the Anglo-Norman colony, nor in the Irish kingdom (established by statute in 1541) but as part of the United Kingdom of Great Britain and Ireland now greatly intensified the complication. For all those engaged with the question of the origins and character of the nation-state, the Union raised deeply divisive issues. Was it, as Musgrave and other pro-Unionists argued,

20   For a wide survey see: Stefan Berger and Chris Lorenz, eds, *Nationalizing the Past: Historians as Nation Builders in Modern Europe*; John Breuilly, *Myth-making or myth-breaking: nationalism and history* (lecture at Birmingham University, 1997); Stefan Berger, 'The invention of European national traditions in European Romanticism', in Stuart Macintyre *et al.*, eds, *The Oxford History of Historical Writing: Volume IV: 1800–1945*, 19–40.
21   In addition to the sources cited in notes 6–8 above, see G. R. Elton, *F. W. Maitland* (New Haven: Yale University Press, 1985) and Pim Den Boer, *History as a profession: the study of history in France, 1818–1914* (Princeton: Princeton University Press, 1998).

the natural and inexplicably long-delayed destiny of the island of Ireland? Or was it, as its opponents insisted, an un-natural deviation forced upon Ireland amidst violence and tumult which ought to be overturned as soon as possible? If it were the former, why was this destiny delayed for so long (over 600 years) and why was its eventual attainment secured only through violence, corruption and repression? But if it was the latter, why was it allowed to happen at all, and as it happened was it not a sign that the pre-Union kingdom was a polity in decline?[22]

These were serious enough challenges to the writing of Irish history within the prevailing paradigm of the rise of the nation-state. Yet they were not in themselves insurmountable. The problem of the biased and corrupt nature of the Irish archive had been grasped early on, even by the Young Irelanders, and in the subsequent decades the expansion, recovery and reform of the Irish historical record was the driving force behind much of the work of Gilbert and Prendergast.[23] Elsewhere in Europe, within the Austro-Hungarian Empire, for example, profound disagreement over the origins and character of national identity did not of necessity inhibit the evolution of historical research and thought. Indeed it often positively encouraged it.[24] And in Ireland itself as the century progressed the debate among historical writers was turning increasingly against the Unionists and toward those who were in favour of some sort of restored Home Rule.

---

22   Daire Keogh and Kevin Whelan, eds, *Acts of Union: The Causes, Contexts, and Consequences of the Act of Union* (Dublin: Four Courts Press, 2001); Michael Brown *et al.*, eds, *The Irish Act of Union* (Dublin: Irish Academic Press, 2003).

23   Gilbert in particular was intensely engaged with the exposure of the biased and unbalanced nature of the official state sources for Irish history; see *inter alia* the series of public letters published by him under the thinly veiled pseudonym of 'An Irish archivist': *Record revelations: A letter on the Public records of Ireland* (London, 1863); *Record Revelations Resumed: A letter on the Public records of Ireland* (London, 1864); *English Commissioners and Irish Records: A letter* (London, 1865).

24   See Monika Baár, 'East-Central European historical writing' in Stuart Macintyre *et al.*, eds, *The Oxford History of Historical Writing: Volume IV: 1800–1945*, 326–48.

Lecky's *Leaders of Public Opinion in Ireland*

Though it appeared quite late in the period, and initially exercised little
enough influence, Lecky's *Leaders of Public Opinion in Ireland* was in many
ways emblematic of the kind of self-confident anti-Union history-writing
that had developed over the previous six decades. Through a set of four
interlocking biographical studies – on Swift, Flood, Grattan in the eighteenth century and on O'Connell in the nineteenth, followed by a more
contemporary survey on 'Clerical influences' – Lecky sought to provide
a coherent interpretative narrative of Irish history over the previous one
hundred and fifty years. Both the format and the title of his study are
revealing of Lecky's underlying assumptions and his overt intent. His focus
on biography asserted that the real motive forces of Irish history lay in
the character and achievements of specific powerful individuals. 'In diseased and undeveloped nations', Lecky wrote in the Preface to his work,
'history [...] resolves itself into biography. The national life radiates from
a single individual'.[25] Why this must be so he leaves unexplained. From
this it might be surmised that there is more than a hint of Macaulayesque
Whiggism in Lecky's approach to history. His portrait of Grattan seems
to fit entirely in this mould. For Grattan was a Whig hero, a tireless pro-
ponent and defender of liberty, a believer in progress, a fearless opponent
of tyranny and corruption. But even Grattan is not unblemished: he grew
tired, sometimes in his care for others lost sight of his true objectives, and
died neglected and almost forgotten. Other figures in the set are even
more ambiguously assessed. For all his courage and generosity, Swift was
a sceptical and bitter man whose 'mind was positively diseased'. 'A morbid
melancholy, a ceaseless irritability continually preyed on him, and disco-
loured and distorted every object in his path preyed on him'.[26] Flood too,
though 'a consummate master of political tactics [...] after one brilliant flash
of defiant glory' regressed into 'insignificance', his life was one long series of

25   Lecky, *The Leaders of Public Opinion in Ireland*, 1.
26   *Ibid.*, 58.

disappointments and reverses'.[27] For Daniel O'Connell, Lecky reserved his severest criticisms. Though he possessed the sagacity of a statesman and the independence of a patriot, he 'was pre-eminently a peasant character who continually spoke on impulse and was betrayed into the grossest vulgarisms'. O'Connell did his country great service by the manner in which he contributed to the development of its public opinion. But his legacy was profoundly ambivalent. And: 'when to the great services he rendered to his country we oppose the sectarian and class warfare that resulted from his policy, the fearful elements of discord he evoked, and which he alone could in some degree control, we cannot but doubt whether his life was a blessing or a curse to Ireland'.[28]

The qualified assessments of his biographical essays indicate that Lecky was less concerned with individual leadership than the way in which strong figures influence for the good, or the bad the growth of a phenomenon which as his title suggests was the real underlying subject in his book: the emergence and growth of 'public opinion' in Ireland. Though it is invoked on multiple occasions throughout the book, Lecky nowhere gave a clear definition of the concept as he understood it. But a general sense of his grasp of the term can be derived. Public opinion was a central force in modern politics and society which contained a massive potential for good:

> That lively interest in public affairs, that healthy action of public opinion which we call the national sentiment, is the true essence of all national prosperity. [...] When public opinion is most vigorous, and the political condition of a country most satisfactory, the moral and intellectual development of the people will be highest. When public opinion grows faint, when patriotism dies, and factious or personal motives sway the state, a corresponding decadence will be exhibited in every branch.[29]

But it was of recent origin; and it was a fragile and unstable force. In Ireland 'public opinion' was not an intrinsic cultural development arising 'from any spontaneous movement among the people'. It was entirely an extraneous

27   Lecky, *The Leaders of Public Opinion in Ireland*, 207.
28   *Ibid.*, 266.
29   *Ibid.*, 207.

development 'the work of a few transcendent intellects, and reflected in all its phases their opinions, and even their characters':[30]

> Under Swift public opinion first acquired a definite form and an imposing influence. Under Flood it penetrated into the debates of Parliament. Under Grattan it triumphed in 1782; it succumbed in 1800; it assumed a more expansive and catholic character. Under O'Connell its dominion became still wider, but its spirit more narrow. It became democratical, and at the same time sectarian, and on his death the political was almost absorbed in the religious element.[31]

In this Lecky was silently endorsing the general concept of 'public opinion' which had gradually been taking shape since the later seventeenth century. In contrast to the pejorative connotations of simple individual 'opinion' or worse 'vulgar opinion', 'public opinion' began to be conceived as a force that was opposed and potentially superior to both. Emerging from a combination of surviving ideas of republican virtue and duty, of Lockean sensationalism, and of the widespread support for franchise extension and reform, public opinion came to be perceived as a political force that was at once inescapable, and capable of bringing great strength or great weakness to any polity. Whether it worked for good or for ill was to be determined by how it was managed and channelled by those in authority.[32]

But in regard to this, Ireland represented an exceptional problem. For since the Union those in authority cared little for public opinion in Ireland; indeed the public opinion they cared for, in England itself, had shown itself remarkably hostile to Ireland. Moreover the emergence of a 'healthy' public opinion before the Union had been halting and uncertain. 'Swift had created a public opinion [...] but had not provided for its continuance'. Through the exertions of Flood and Grattan, 'public opinion began to show itself outside the walls of Parliament, and a powerful opposition was organised within'. In time it might be expected that 'the progress of education and of public opinion would regenerate and reform the Irish Parliament as it

---

30   Lecky, *The Leaders of Public Opinion in Ireland*, 2.
31   *Ibid.*
32   See in particular, Hans Speier, 'Historical Development of Public Opinion', *American Journal of Sociology* 55 (January 1950), 376–88.

regenerated and reformed the Parliament of England; and every year the sense of independence grew that the reform of Parliament should be the result of the development of public opinion within the nation, not of the interposition of an external power'.[33]

But such a process had been violently disrupted by the Union. O'Connell's agitations had resuscitated it, but at a very considerable cost of surrendering its development into the hands of 'a bigoted priesthood'. Thus at present: 'public opinion is diseased – diseased to the very core. Instead of circulating in healthy action through the land, it stagnates, it coagulates, it corrupts'.[34] Yet all was not quite lost. Lecky professed to believe that 'all the elements of a great movement exist among the people – a restless, nervous consciousness of the evil of their present condition, a deep disgust at the cant and the imbecility that are dominant'. All they needed was a leader such as in times before they had risen to follow:

> Should a political leader arise whose character was above suspicion, and whose intellect was above cavil, who was neither a lawyer nor a lay preacher, who could read the signs of the times, and make his eloquence a power in Europe, his influence with the people would be unbounded [...] The waves of sectarian strife would sink to silence at his voice; the aspirations and the patriotism of Ireland would recognize him as the prophet of the future. [...] We look forward with unshaken confidence to the advent of such a leader. The mantle of Grattan is not destined to be for ever unclaimed.[35]

From whence was such a leader likely to arise? Lecky had no doubt: 'the landlords, who are chiefly Protestants, are obviously the natural leaders of the people [...] Protestantism is eminently adapted, from its character to coalesce with every form of Liberalism [...] the Reformation was the dawn of the government of public opinion [...] every subsequent step towards the emancipation of mankind may be distinctly traced to its influence [...] and the Church of Rome has associated herself indissolubly with the despotic theory of government'.[36]

33   Lecky, *The Leaders of Public Opinion in Ireland*, 61, 66, 150.
34   *Ibid.*, 273.
35   *Ibid.*, 306.
36   *Ibid.*, 283.

The layers of elitism revealed here are multiple. That public opinion, especially in Ireland, must be created, rather than allowed to emerge, that it could be developed only by leading individuals rather than by social movements, that it was persistently susceptible to corruption, by demagogues, self-seekers, and especially in Ireland by priests, that only landlords and Protestants (rather than coarse 'peasant' Catholic characters like O'Connell) were equipped for the task of leadership are all expressions of a monumental and naïve condescension of which Lecky himself seems to have been quite unaware. The superiority of its attitude toward the Catholic majority, and its outright hostility toward the Roman Catholic Church no doubt accounted in good part for the failure of the work to sell until its late editions. But the text is none the less remarkable for the innocent manner in which it makes explicit the operating assumptions of so many of those writing Irish history from an anti-Union perspective, including even the Young Irelanders.

Lecky's attitude toward the Young Irelanders was ambiguous. He deplored their willingness to contemplate rebellion (especially in its aftermath). But in other regards he had nothing but praise. Composed mainly of Protestants (Lecky thought somewhat inaccurately), Young Ireland was far more independent of the priests than O'Connell, and was little swayed by theological censure. Unlike O'Connell and Flood they were much opposed to accepting offers of government office. He admired also their resistance to O'Connell. But above all he praised their ambition to be in the tradition of Irish public opinion's leaders. The 'columns' of the *Nation* 'maintained with unqualified zeal the cause of liberty and nationality in every land [...] Seldom has there been a more striking evidence of the effect of a great enthusiasm in evoking the latent genius of a nation; seldom has any journal of the kind exhibited a more splendid combination of eloquence, of poetry, and of reasoning.'[37]

Here was a succinct summary of Young Ireland's aspirations, if not its achievements. As would-be leaders of Irish public opinion, the Young Irelanders had sought to construct by essays, ballads and songs a new

37   Lecky, *The Leaders of Public Opinion in Ireland*, 242.

narrative of Irish history intended not only to rebut the disparaging and condescending narratives of English and pro-Union writers, but to inspire in its receivers a renewed sense of the distinct and proud national identity.[38] The character of this episodic and fragmented new narrative is interesting as much for what it omits as for what it includes. A major emphasis was given to Ireland's wars and rebellions and the heroic individuals associated with them. This may seem quite in accord with the principles of Romantic historiography, but even by such standards, the principle of selection is remarkably narrow. Chieftains, lords and soldiers abound but non-violent defenders of the people are rare; and there are no saints, no religious martyrs, and, despite their own intense literary preoccupations, precious few writers. These restrictions reflect the limitations of the Young Irelanders' specific view of the central themes of Irish history. Their rejection of sectarianism which Lecky among others thought admirable also entailed a severe diminution of the role of religion and religious conflict in Ireland's history, since the twelfth, and certainly since the sixteenth century. Similarly, despite their enthusiasm for stories, myths and poems relating to 'ancient Ireland' the Young Irelanders displayed little interest in the revival of the Irish language itself. Though not overtly opposed to it, and while showing a consistently benevolent attitude toward those scholars who were actually engaged in the recovery of early Irish literature, it is significant that the *Nation* made no attempt to publish items in Irish, and that in its presentation of what it termed 'Celtic' culture it gave over-riding prominence to translations of the most free degree. Young Ireland historiography's diminution of Gaelic culture was accompanied by a parallel celebration of the importance of the Anglo-Irish. Their audacious 'speaking of '98' centred around figures such as Wolfe Tone, Lord Edward Fitzgerald and the Shields brothers, rather than Father Murphy. And further back, it was Anglo-Irish rather than Gaelic Irish exponents of resistance to England that attracted most attention. Principal among these were 'the Geraldines', the Fitzgeralds, founders of the great Anglo-Norman feudal houses of Desmond and Kildare, who

---

38   See especially Thomas Davis, *Literary and Historical Essays* (Dublin: James Duffy, 1845).

had been memorably celebrated in Thomas Davis's poem first published in the *Nation* in June 1843 and reprinted many times after. 'The Geraldines', embodied the great Anglo-Irish tradition of resistance to English rule that was for Davis the central theme of Irish history. And it pointed to the future. Having in successive stanzas emphasized the centrality of 'the Geraldines' to all of the great movements against English rule in Ireland, the poem concluded with a call toward the future:

> The Geraldines! the Geraldines!—and are there any fears
> Within the sons of conquerors for full a thousand years?
> Can treason spring from out a soil bedewed with martyr's blood?
> Or has that grown a purling brook which long rushed down a flood?—
> By Desmond swept with sword and fire—by clan and keep laid low—
> By Silken Thomas and his kin,—by sainted Edward! No!
> The forms of centuries rise up, and in the Irish line
> Command their son to take the post that fits the Geraldine![39]

Young Ireland's intrinsically elitist attitude toward the people they aimed to inspire was largely obscured first by the populism of their appeal and the enthusiasm with which they pursued their project, and then by the feeble and pathetic nature of their failure in the midst of the Famine. But the underlying elitist assumptions of the Protestant anti-Union historians continued to operate after the Famine in the writings of a figure whose popularity and influence as an Irish historian in the 1850s and 1860s far exceeded any other. This was John P. Prendergast.

---

39   Davis was not the only Young Irelander to celebrate the Geraldines. Before Davis's poem appeared, a drama entitled 'Silken Thomas' was performed on the Dublin stage in the summer of 1843. In July 1848 a lengthy poem by Eva (pseudonym for Mary Izod O'Doherty) celebrating 'Silken Thomas' unambiguously as a hero was also published in the *Nation*. It was reprinted again in 1849. In a fiery speech delivered in the Rotunda in 1847 John Mitchel listed several Fitzgeralds in a long list of patriot martyrs. Significantly perhaps, Young Ireland clubs established in Dublin, in Bradford and in London in 1848 to promote Repeal of the Union, were named in honour of the tragic Geraldine rebel Thomas, Lord Offaly or 'Silken Thomas'.

John P. Prendergast

A barrister by training, and an estate agent by profession, Prendergast was a frequent contributor to antiquarian and local journals, and he was an inveterate editor of original manuscripts.[40] But he was also intensely engaged with contemporary politics. Early articles on 'The Ulster Creaghts', on the failed Caroline attempt at plantation in Ormond and on 'The Clearing of Kilkenny in 1654' castigated English administrators and English adventurers in Ireland. But his most powerful account of England's brutal exploitation of Ireland was presented in *The Cromwellian Settlement* (published in 1865) which, though based on deep scholarly research, presented an unwavering condemnation of English policy in Ireland from the sixteenth century down to the present.[41] Published to a rapturous reception by Irish nationalist opinion, *The Cromwellian Settlement* established its author's reputation as the foremost authority of Irish history from a nationalist side.[42] Indignant and unwaveringly critical of the English government in all its aspects, Prendergast's *The Cromwellian Settlement of Ireland* is an unrestrained protest against injustice and repression. Yet he also details the confusion and incompetence of the Cromwellians striving to fit the

---

40 On Prendergast in general, see the entry in *Dictionary of Irish Biography* (Cambridge: Cambridge University Press, 2009).

41 See for example, 'On the projected plantation of Ormond by King Charles I', *Transactions of the Kilkenny Archaeological Society*, 1, 3 (1851), 39–409; 'The Ulster Creaghts' in *Proceedings and transactions of the Kilkenny and South-East of Ireland Archaeological Society* vol. 3 (1854–5), 420–30; 'The Clearing of Kilkenny, anno 1654' in *Proceedings and transactions of the Kilkenny and South-East of Ireland Archaeological Society* new series, 3 (1860), 326–44.

42 Prendergast consolidated his reputation with a series of articles in the *Nation* including: 'Conquest Oppression: The Irish in the 698th year of the rule of the English in Ireland, and in the year of our lord 1869', *Nation*, 26 June 1869; 3, 10 July 1869, 716–7, 732–3, 747; 'Sir Phelim O'Neill and Charlemont fort', 9, 16, 23 April 1870, the *Nation*, 536, 539–40, 571–2; 'English parliament and the Irish nation', the *Nation*, 20 August 1870, 27; 'English legislation and Irish crime', the *Nation*, 6 May 1871, 422–3; 'Ireland's long agony but certain victory', the *Nation*, 21 October 1871, 422–3.

realities of Ireland's land divisions into their procrustean surveys, and how the officers cheated the soldiers and were in turned cheated by the adventurers who were in turn abandoned by the English Parliament. For all the radical and brutal character of its intent, the Cromwellian conquest was a failure. In this the so-called 'Cromwellian settlement' was merely one of the several failed English attempts to conquer Ireland. And it was one which, like all the rest, had been endured and coped with by those suffering underneath, and which had gradually had its worst effects reduced by the same combination of natural recurring impulses and reasonable procedures arising from titular and tenurial disputes, conveyances, dowries, mortgages and leases wills and inheritances, all of which had been regularly achieved through the mediating practice of law.[43]

Here is another version of the elitist Anglo-Irish history. For it was the Anglo-Irish who conducted this process of mediation and reconstruction. They were not necessarily of the same ethnic or genealogical origins: the remains of each botched English conquest, they were generally descendants of the original agents of that failed conquest. What they held in common was a recognition that, the original aim of total conquest having been abandoned, it was necessary to find a sustaining accommodation with the unreconciled natives in their everyday intercourse without becoming swamped by them, or even losing the position of authority which the early phases of conquest had given them.[44]

Prendergast's identification of law and lawyers as a central force in the driving of Irish historical development offers a more specific interpretation of the evolution of public opinion in Ireland than Lecky's heroic narrative. In part, no doubt, it has roots in Prendergast's own profession as a barrister. It lay also in the intense private study he had made as a young man of the way in which the Penal Codes enforced in the years after the defeat of the Jacobites had, through a set of unforeseen problems arising out of disputes

43   Ciaran Brady, 'John Patrick Prendergast and the problems of history writing in nineteenth-century Ireland' in *Irish Historical Studies* (forthcoming).
44   Prendergast's thesis is most succinctly set out in the preface and extended introduction to *The Cromwellian Settlement* (New York: Clachan, 2014), vii–x; see also: 52, 110, 139, 148, 168–202.

over property, marriage and inheritance, their original intent gradually overthrown.[45] But a further source for the development of his conception of the character and role of the Anglo-Irish lay, according to Prendergast himself, in his reading of Augustin Thierry's *Histoire de la conquête de l'Angleterre par les Normands.*[46]

The attraction of Thierry to advanced literary and cultural circles in Ireland in the 1830s and 1840s has been noted before. The first translation of his *Histoire de la conquête* had been produced by an Irishman, Charles Claude Hamilton, as early as 1825 and several of his contributions from *Le Censeur Européen* and other studies collected in his *Dix ans d'études historiques* (Paris, 1835), notably his essays on 'Chants Irlandais' and on 'Sur l'esprit national des Irlandais', exercised a broad influence over the literary generation of the 1830s and 1840s, especially over 'Young Ireland'. Thomas Davis was a great admirer, and John Mitchel was said to have kept Thierry's *Norman Conquest* on his shelves beside a manual on the uses of artillery.[47] The Young Irelander's attraction to Thierry has frequently been put down to his strongly romantic celebration of Irish stories and songs, especially the songs.

This was in some part true. The *Norman Conquest* contained a substantial section devoted to Irish history since the twelfth century which

45 Among the Prendergast papers in the King's Inn Library is a manuscript volume entitled 'Mss by John Patrick Prendergast on Howard's Popery cases' [Gorges E. Howard, *Several special cases on the laws against the further growth of popery in Ireland* (Dublin, 1775)] dated 2 Dec. 1844; indications of Prendergast's ironic readings of Howard's commentary can be seen on the following pages: 20, 23, 33, 48.

46 A second edition (1830) in the original French remains in Prendergast's papers in King's Inn.

47 Davis contributed two essays on Thierry to the *Nation* on 26 November and 3 December 1842. Richard Davis, *The Young Ireland Movement* (Dublin: Gill and Macmillan, 1987) chapter 7; Malcolm Brown, *The Politics of Irish Literature: from Thomas Davis to W. B. Yeats* (Seattle: University of Washington Press, 1973), 46, 86, 121; Augustin Thierry, *History of the Conquest of England by the Normans*, trans, C. C. Hamilton (3 vols, London: Whittaker, 1825); this edition was however rare; and it is likely that, as with Prendergast, most Irish readers of Thierry read him in the original before a second and better circulated English translation appeared in 1841.

concluded that despite all their oppressions, the independent spirit of the
natives had not yet been fully extinguished. On the face of it, it might seem
that this 'épopée des vaincus' had little consolation on offer to the Anglo-
Irish, for most of them were the descendants of one or another wave of conquerors. But there were other underlying elements within Thierry's theory
of conquest which supplied his *Norman Conquest* and its surrounding
polemical essays with far greater interest to the historically-minded among
the Irish generation of the 1840s than might have at first seemed evident.

For all his rhetoric about the brutality of the conquerors and the nobil-
ity of the conquered Thierry was realistic enough to recognize that conquest,
domination and dispossession were frequent and recurrent events in human
history, to be deplored but never denied. For the historian, however, the
interesting questions lay not in the event of conquest, but in what processes
had been set in train in the years after the initial act of conquest had been
accomplished. In raising this question there was an important comparative project at work in Thierry's book. For in studying the Normans in
England, Wales and Ireland, Thierry was also considering the Franks in
France, and in particular the effect of their conquest upon the subsequent
course of French history. Conceived within the repressive and defeatist
environment of Restoration France, the *Norman Conquest* was deliberately
intended as a reply to the central contentions asserted by the defenders of the
re-established old regime which were that the revolution initiated in 1789
had been from start to finish a catastrophe, that the appalling repressions,
wars and dictatorships that had ensued had been inherent in the revolutionary movement from the beginning. This denigration of the revolutionary
movement as a whole was something which Thierry, in company with a
significant number of other Liberal defenders of the 1789 revolution, was
determined to reject. And of crucial importance in this resurrection of the
ideals of 1789 was the defence of a key concept which had given so much
force and unity to that movement: the idea of the third estate.[48]

---

48   Among several studies of Thierry's ideological purposes and historical method see,
      Kieran Joseph Carroll, *Some aspects of the historical thought of Augustin Thierry (179–
      1856)* (Washington DC: The Catholic University of America Press, 1951); Stanley

For Thierry the third estate was made up of the solid gentry, the professional and commercial middle classes who were located in a place of independence midway between the idle exploitative and unproductive aristocracy and the benighted, oppressed and powerless peasant and labouring classes. But as an historical phenomenon the origin and character of the third estate was considerably more interesting. It represented in a very specific sense the essential and defining characteristic of French history in the days since the Frankish conquest. The imposition of government by force, the seizure of control over land and the establishment of the grounds for legitimizing this seizure represented only the first phases of a genuine conquest. The conquest's real test came next when the conquerors faced the challenge of how to consolidate, defend and build upon the accident of military success by developing a process of legitimation, a code and a set of practices and institutions which could sustain the gains of conquest long after the shock of the primal event of military victory and defeat had passed. Thierry, like Marx, had no illusions about the ideological origins and purposes of legal systems: the law was there to defend and extend the interests of the conqueror. But in practical terms, it followed that any legal system imposed by the conquerors must be possessed of an internal suppleness sufficient to retain its effectiveness amidst the unceasing, unanticipated and unpredictable complexes of intercourse between the descendants of the conquerors and the descendants of the conquered which would inevitably occur in the centuries to come. In particular it followed that the conqueror's law of property, regulating how realty and personalty were to be acquired, leased, sold, bequeathed, inherited and obtained in marriage settlements was capable of adapting to the challenges thrown up by unexpected and unavoidable political, social and economic change.

Mellon, *The Political Uses of History: A Study of Historians in the French Restoration* (Stanford: Stanford University Press, 1958); Rulon Nephi Smithson, *Augustin Thierry: Social and Political Consciousness in the Evolution of a Historical Method* (Geneva: Droz, 1972); Lionel Gossman, 'Augustin Thierry and Liberal Historiography', in Lionel Gossman, ed., *Between History and Literature* (Cambridge, MA: Harvard University Press, 1990), chapter 4.

No legal system, Thierry readily conceded, had been perfectly successful in meeting such a challenge. The processes of adaptation, moreover, were neither uniform, nor progressive; and history was filled with attempts of subsequent generations of conquerors either to concede to the conquered, or to roll back on those concessions when the opportunity arose. The Normans, for example, had by the very weakness of their grasp on rule in England proved remarkably adaptable. But the Franks, whose original conquest had been more complete, had been far less adaptable. Indeed, it was in the history of their attempts to escape from the unintended consequences of the system they had imposed that the third estate had emerged. Appearing first in the villages and towns of rural France and gradually taking their place at the national level in the eighteenth century as an agency for mediating between the conquerors and the conquered, the third estate was central in bringing about the agreed system of equitable, effective and enduring law represented in the constitution of 1791. It was here, in the examination of such undulating currents, that the true purpose and true value of historical research and interpretation lay. All history was the history of the attempts to develop or subsequently to overthrow a common ideology based on law which would transcend the profound and destructive conflicts arising from the recurrent accident of conquest.

The appeal of Thierry's conquest theory of history to Ireland's Anglo-Irish historians can now be seen to be far deeper than a sentimental attachment to old Irish songs. For there were several ways in which the Anglo-Irish conformed to Thierry's model of historical leadership. Pioneers of the first of several waves of English conquest, the Anglo-Normans, had served a crucial liaison function mediating between the natives and new conquerors, seeking to extend and to adapt the original accommodations they had reached to the particular conditions applying at the time. In this their role corresponded to that of the historical third estate in France as the engineers of a truly stable and just society through the amelioration of the worst consequences of conquest and exploitation. As with the third estate, of course, their success in this operation was far from perfect. And not infrequently they found themselves in direct conflict with the source of renewed movements of conquest, England. But the course of Irish history from the twelfth century on is a record of their repeated attempts to fulfil this specific historical role, whether it be in the days of Henry VIII, in the crisis times of the 1640s, under the Restoration, most particularly in the halcyon days of the late eighteenth-century Parliament. This Irish third estate, no more than its French prototype, was not constituted of one particular ethnic group. But its formations and reformations were none the less determined by the same fundamental operating mechanism: that is assimilation through family extension, miscegenation, marriage and sex.

The centrality of Thierry's conception of history to the specific history of the Anglo-Irish is neatly epitomized in poetic form in Davis's 'The Geraldines':

> — 'tis true, in Strongbow's van,
> By lawless force, as conquerors, their Irish reign began' but [...]
> not long our air they breathed;
> Not long they fed on venison, in Irish water seethed;
> Not often had their children been by Irish mothers nursed;
> When from their full and genial hearts an Irish feeling burst!
> The English monarchs strove in vain, by law, and force, and bribe,
> To win from Irish thoughts and ways this 'more than Irish' tribe;
> For still they clung to fosterage, to breitheamh, cloak, and bard:
> What king dare say to Geraldine, 'Your Irish wife discard'?[49]

But it was also an important influence in reinforcing Prendergast's and Lecky's understanding of the role of the Anglo-Irish as the historical leaders of the Irish people. Thus, rooted in a fierce sense of a special identity, separate both from government and the majority of the island's inhabitants, and now bolstered by the larger historical conceptualizations of French liberal historians, a powerful interpretative paradigm of Irish historical development came to be in the ascendant by the middle decades of the nineteenth century which was anti-Union in attitude, avowedly elitist in character and yet assured of its own historical role. The power of this conviction of political and cultural authority, coupled with a sense that such destiny, derailed by the Union, had still to be reaffirmed underlay the remarkable interpretative confidence displayed in Prendergast's and Lecky's

49 Thomas Davis, 'The Geraldines' in the *Nation*, June 1843.

writings in the 1860s. But it also explained their indifference to the trends in European historiography which were expressing a disillusion with the transformative pretensions of Romantic history writing and a drift toward the reconstitution of the genre as a modest but scientific discipline: for in Ireland the possibility of such a broad cultural transformation still seemed attainable and necessary.

It is the same remarkable confidence that serves, in part at least, to explain, the astonishing lack of reference to, or registering of, the major historical catastrophe of Ireland in the mid-nineteenth century, the Famine. In contrast to the enormous amount of debate couched in historical terms concerning the Act of Union, the silence in regard to the Famine in the history writing of the 1850s and 1860s is resounding. Though Prendergast was a land agent in Meath, one of the most gravely affected counties, he remained curiously unmoved by it. Privately, in an expansive autobiography that was remarkably candid in its revelations of his personal feelings Prendergast had hardly anything at all to say of his experiences in the Famine years.[50] Lecky, a landlord holding estates in another of the counties most deeply affected by the crisis (Carlow), was more expressive. But his understanding of the causes and consequences of the country's great catastrophe as revealed in *The Leaders* and elsewhere is disturbingly revealing. The roots of the Famine lay not in the evils of political economy, but in the backwardness of the people.[51] While the Famine may have been 'fearful', its net outcome was altogether for the good:

> before the famine [Ireland] was indeed such that it might well have made reasonable men despair. With the land divided into almost microscopic farms with a population multiplying rapidly to the extreme limits of subsistence, accustomed to the very

50   Charles Haliday, John Prendergast, *The Scandinavian kingdom of Dublin, by Charles Haliday. Ed. with some notice of the author's life by John P. Prendergast* (London: British Library, 2011), 58–60.
51   'Had that fearful famine, which in the present century desolated the land, fallen upon a people who thought more of accumulating subsistence than of avoiding sin, multitudes might now be living who perished by literal starvation', William Edward Hartpole Lecky, *The History of European Morals from Augustus to Charlemagne Vol. 1* (New York: Braziller, 1955), 153.

lowest standard of comfort, and marrying earlier than in any other northern country in Europe, it was idle to look for habits of independence or self-reliance, or for the culture which follows in the train of leisure and comfort. But all this has been changed [...] The population is now in no degree in excess of the means of subsistence [...] The greater part of Ireland has been changing from arable into pasture land, for which it is pre-eminently fitted; and this most important transformation, which almost convulsed English society in the sixteenth century [...] has been of late years effected in Ireland upon a still larger scale without producing any considerable suffering.[52]

Lecky's complacency is all the more remarkable for his refusal to engage with the fierce attack on *laissez-faire* liberalism mounted by the former Young Irelander, John Mitchel and (re)published in *The Last Conquest of Ireland (Perhaps)* (1861).[53] There was indeed an opportunity arising from the Famine, Mitchel asserted not for reform, but for conquest. No mere economic inevitability, the Famine was a political act: 'the Almighty indeed sent the potato blight, but the English created the Famine.'[54] It was moreover an act of calculated atrocity, as great as ever committed in history.[55] And its great political objective had at last been reached: 'the Conquest was now consummated – England, [...] had succeeded [...] in crushing out of sight the last agonies of resistance in a small, poor and divided island [...] "Now, for the first time in these six hundred

---

52 Lecky, *The Leaders of Public Opinion in Ireland*, x–xi. In this Lecky appears to have subscribed uncritically to the optimistic views first expressed in Robert Murray's 1847 tract *Ireland its present condition and future prospects* which argued that the Famine presented a marvellous opportunity for the introduction of social and economic reforms, in which the traditional leaders of Irish public opinion would take a prominent role.

53 Mitchel's *The Last Conquest of Ireland (Perhaps)* was first serialised in the *Southern Citizen* in 1858–9, before appearing in book form published by Cameron and Ferguson (Glasgow, 1861).

54 John Mitchel, *The Last Conquest of Ireland (Perhaps)*.

55 'No sack of Magdeburg, or ravage of the Palatinate ever approached in horror and desolation the slaughters done in Ireland by mere official red-tape and stationery and the principles of political economy', John Mitchel, *The Last Conquest of Ireland (Perhaps)*, 218.

years" said the London *Times*, "England has Ireland at her mercy and can deal with her as she pleases".[56]

A polemic against *laissez-faire*, Mitchel's book was also, as its title implies, an indictment of the Thierrean model of conquest so favoured by his Anglo-Irish contemporaries. For this time, Mitchel insisted, the conquest was by all appearances complete, aided by 'a powerful party on her side in Ireland itself'.[57] And any chance that it might not quite be so – as indicated by the title's parenthetical 'perhaps' – would come from sources outside Ireland and would be part of a far greater global upheaval which would consume the British Empire itself.[58]

Mitchel's was a powerful and unsettling voice. Yet its impact was decidedly uneven. Reasserted in his *History of Ireland from the Treaty of Limerick to the present time*,[59] it found a wider popular audience both in Ireland and especially in the United States. It clearly exerted some influence on Alexander Martin Sullivan's even more popular *The Story of Ireland*.[60] But among the Anglo-Irish historians it exerted little influence. The overtly polemical nature of *The Last Conquest* and the popular nature of *The History* rendered them both vulnerable to marginalization in scholarly discussion, while Sullivan's self-deprecating acknowledgement of his lack of original scholarship also facilitated dismissal. In time, the presentational strategies of polemic and deliberate popularization would prove to be far more subversive than they initially appeared. But in the 1860s and 1870s there seemed little to challenge the intellectual authority of the Anglo-Irish historical account of Irish history in Ireland.

56   John Mitchel, *The Last Conquest of Ireland (Perhaps)*, 210.
57   *Ibid.*
58   *Ibid.*, 220.
59   John Mitchel, *History of Ireland from the Treaty of Limerick to the Present Time* (2 volumes) (New York: D. &. Sadlier, 1869).
60   Alexander Martin Sullivan, *The Story of Ireland: A Narrative of Irish History, from the Earliest Ages to the Present Time* (Dublin: Sullivan, 1867).
     For the context and influence of Sullivan's popular history see Robert Fitzroy Foster, *The Irish Story: Telling Tales and Making It Up in Ireland* (London: Penguin, 2001), Chapter 1.

James Anthony Froude's challenge

It was ironic, therefore, that the first truly fundamental challenge to this interpretative hegemony arose not in Ireland, but from England and in the person of one who could never have been suspected of sympathy for radical movements in Ireland. This was the historian and man of letters, James Anthony Froude. Between 1872 and 1874, Froude, his reputation already established as the author of the *History of England from the Fall of Wolsey to the Defeat of the Armada*,[61] turned his attention to Irish history. In a general series of lectures on the course of Irish history since the twelfth century (delivered in America and widely published in Britain), and then in a deeply researched three-volume monograph entitled *The English in Ireland in the Eighteenth Century* (1872–4),[62] he developed an interpretation of Irish history which seemed deliberately designed to offend all interested parties. First, in accordance with the view of the vast majority of English commentators – and of Anglo-Irish historians – Froude asserted that the native Irish had proven themselves demonstrably incapable of self-government. Thus it had been England's historical and ethical duty to take charge of them. So far Froude would have alienated only Irish nationalist opinion. But the second half of his thesis was far more provocative. Given this historical responsibility, the English had failed: the English government, but even more signally the English colonists in Ireland, had by their greed and their neglect, their casual cruelties and their weak kindnesses ensured that the natural relationship of Ireland to England had never been established. Instead there had been chronic war and rebellion. The root of all of Ireland's sufferings throughout its history from the conquest through to the Famine lay not in the people themselves, but in their would-be conquerors. The colonists had perennially failed in the duty they had undertaken, and in the

61   James Anthony Froude, *History of England from the Fall of Wolsey to the Defeat of the Armada* (12 volumes) (Cambridge: Cambridge University Press, 1856–70).
62   James Anthony Froude, *The English in Ireland in the Eighteenth Century* (New York: Longmans, Green, 1874).

grossest of hypocrisies, had habitually re-presented their failure as an act of leadership, amidst a series of unnecessary calamities visited on Ireland throughout its modern history.[63]

In contrast to the silence with which they received the polemics of Mitchel and Sullivan, the response of the Anglo-Irish scholars to Froude was immediate and ferocious. Prendergast published more than a dozen intensely hostile reviews in Irish newspapers, combining unbridled personal abuse with acute evidential, factual and interpretative criticism. Lecky was more restrained in tone in two lengthy reviews he contributed to *Macmillan's Review* but no less damning. And other Anglo-Irish scholars, among many, the political economist, John Eliot Cairnes contributed to an assault seeking to reveal the inaccuracy, above all, the absurd malignity of Froude's attack.[64]

Froude was indeed perverse. No supporter of radical Irish national-ists, he aimed at an even stronger bond between Ireland and Britain. But the actual impact of his book was far different from his own intentions. Irish nationalists both at home and in the United States, Mitchel included, were naturally indignant at his characterization of the Irish people and Irish culture as retarded and incapable of self-rule.[65] But they were no less heartened by his sustained attack on the Anglo-Irish, as landlords, local officials, self-serving politicians, heedless capitalists and hypocritical church-men who were the real source of the country's woes. And for them Froude's indictment was all the more powerful because it issued from one who could

---

63   Ciaran Brady, *James Anthony Froude: an intellectual biography of a Victorian prophet* (Oxford: Oxford University Press, 2013), Chapter 9.

64   Donal McCartney, 'James Anthony Froude and Ireland: a Historiographical Debate', in Thomas Desmond Williams, ed., *Historical Studies VIII* (Dublin: 1977), 171–90.

65   James Anthony Froude et al., *Froude's Crusade.-Both Sides. Lectures by Very Rev. T. N. Burke...* (New York: J. W. O'Brien, 1873) collected the responses of many Irish nationalists including Mitchel. John Mitchel's expanded version of his critique shows a greater ambivalence, see his *Reply to the Falsification of History by James Anthony Froude, Entitled 'The English in Ireland' or The Crusade of the Period* (Glasgow: Cameron and Ferguson, 1875).

in no sense be seen as favourable to the nationalist cause, but also because it was based on extensive original research in Irish and British archives.

Nationalist Ireland was not, moreover, the only interest group to find support in Froude. For those more immediately interested in land reform in Ireland, Froude's revelations of the abuses of Irish ascendancy landlords supplied powerful ammunition to their cause. Thus Michael Davitt, a former Fenian who had no reason to appreciate Froude, publicly welcomed *The English in Ireland* as being among the most weighty contributions to the case for agrarian reform.[66] More significantly Charles Stewart Parnell, the radical new leader of the Irish Parliamentary Party, was delighted to use Froude in his re-orientation of the Party away from Repeal and toward radical land reform in 1880–1.[67] And most importantly of all, Prime Minister Gladstone read Froude enthusiastically and even quoted at length from *The English in Ireland* in Parliament and claimed him as a crucial witness in the case for radical Irish reform.[68] Froude's influence over the 1881 Land Act which Gladstone piloted though Parliament could be seen in two of its most radical and fateful elements: the establishment of a Land Commission, and the introduction of equity-based Land Courts for the settlement of disputes between landlords and tenants.[69] In time, these two innovations would be seen as the first in a series of policy initiatives which, ending in the Wyndham Act of 1903, would result in the destruction of the Irish landlord class. Already, by the early 1880s, both Lecky and Prendergast had foreseen the implications of Gladstone's Froudian inventions; and it was these more than any other factor that rapidly converted them from support for the modest, backward-looking Home Rule proposals as represented by

66   Michael Davitt, *The fall of feudalism in Ireland: or The story of the Land League revolution* (London: Harper & Brothers, 1906), 6.

67   Paul Bew, *Enigma: a New Life of Charles Stewart Parnell* (London: Gill & Macmillan, 2011), 190.

68   *Hansard Parliamentary Debates, House of Commons (16 April 1886, vol. 304, cols. 1782–6)*.

69   For Froude's advocacy of such measures see: *The English in Ireland*, vol. 3, 574.

Isaac Butt to outright hostility toward the radical post-land reform version
of Home Rule pioneered by Parnell.[70]

It was this combined threat to their cultural ascendancy presented
to the Anglo-Irish historians by Nationalists, Unionists, land reformers
and radical Home Rulers that at length forced them to respond. In this
strategic re-orientation the lead was taken, suitably enough, by the most
internationally renowned of their group, Lecky. Recognizing that bitter
and heated reviews exposing Froude's or Mitchel's errors and prejudices
were insufficient and in part counterproductive, Lecky began to develop
his own mode of representing Irish history which eschewed criticism or
even mention of his opponents, and concentrated instead on narrative.

The opportunity for the development of such a strategy was presented
to Lecky in the form of a commission to write a *History of England in the
Eighteenth Century*. Envisaged by the publishers (Longman's) as a con-
tinuation of Macaulay's great Whig monument which was cut short by
Macaulay's death around 1715, Lecky determined from early on to devote
a far greater amount of space to the history of Ireland than had ever been
featured in Macaulay. From volume two on, and in almost every subsequent
volume, Ireland received extensive independent discussion and amazingly,
having concluded his main English history in volume six, Lecky decided to
devote two entire further volumes to the history of Ireland in the 1780s and
1790s. An analysis of the eight volumes of the first edition of the *History*
reveals that in terms of pages alone the amount of space formally devoted
to a discussion of Irish affairs amounted to almost 40% of the entire book.
Even this, moreover, is something of an underestimate, for a search of those
volumes in which no separate chapters are devoted to Ireland reveals a very
high degree of reference. Thus in the survey chapters of volumes one and
three, reference to Ireland is made on more than forty occasions in both
cases. By contrast the history of Scotland which appeared in the earliest

70   Alan O'Day, *Reactions to Irish Nationalism, 1865–1914* (London: Hambledon Press,
     1987); D. George Boyce, Alan O'Day, *Defenders of the Union: A survey of British and
     Irish unionism since 1801* (London: Routledge, 2002); *Robert Brendan McDowell,
     Crisis and Decline: The Fate of the Southern Unionists* (Dublin: Lilliput Press, 1998).

pages of the work to be given fair attention fades almost completely, and no separate consideration is given to Wales. And finally when allowance is made for the attention given to the history of other countries in Lecky's several chapters on foreign affairs, notably France, Russia and Sweden, the disproportion between the discussion of Irish and English history is further diminished. Never before (or since) had any full-dress history of England devoted so much space to Ireland.

Lecky's powerful presentation of the history of Ireland as a subject of central importance could be read in sharply alternative ways. For Irish nationalists, many of whom reacted enthusiastically to his work, it was a magnificent demonstration of the intrinsic integrity and distinctiveness of Irish history.[71] Widely adopted, this was a perception that was reinforced by Lecky's willingness, in a twelve-volume cabinet edition (1892) of his *History*, to allow the Irish sections to be extracted and published in separate volumes – five Irish volumes against seven English ones (a division which incidentally confirmed the prominence of Ireland in the entire work). Yet Lecky himself, in the closing pages of the last volume, expressed a quite different view. Though the Union had, by and large, been forced on an unwilling nation, and though both the manner of its passage and the failure to honour the promises made during its passage were all deeply regrettable, it was now clear: 'that no Parliament, resembling Grattan's Parliament, could ever again exist in Ireland [...] The descendants of the members of Grattan's Parliament; the descendants of the volunteers; the descendants of that section of the Irish people among whom, in 1799 and 1800, the chief opposition to the Union was displayed, are now its staunchest supporters.'[72]

That this was so was due not to any particular benefit which the Union had brought, but rather to a 'whole chain of causes which have retarded the pacification of Ireland':

---

71   Donal McCartney, *W. E. H. Lecky: historian and politician, 1838–1903* (Dublin: Dufour, 1994), chapters 5 and 7.

72   William Edward Hartpole Lecky, *History of England in the 18th century* vol. 8 (London: Longmans, Green, 1980), 489.

a famine which exceeded in its horrors any other that Europe has witnessed during
the nineteenth century; the transformation [...] of the whole agricultural industry
of Ireland, through the repeal of the corn laws; the ruin of an immense portion of
the old owners of the soil; the introduction under the Encumbered Estates Act of
a new class of owners, often wholly regardless of the traditions and customs of Irish
estates; a period of land legislation which was intended to facilitate and accelerate this
change, by placing all agrarian relations on the strictest commercial basis [...] which
broke the most formal written contracts, deprived the owner [...] and established a
dual and a confused ownership which could not possibly endure.[73]

Such developments had destroyed the capacity of the Irish people for genuine self-rule:

the part which is incontestably the most diseased has the greatest proportionate
strength, while the soundest elements in Irish life are those which are least represented.
About a third part of the Irish people are fervently attached to the Union, and they
comprise the great bulk of the property and higher education of the country; the
large majority of those who take any leading part in social, industrial, or philanthropic
enterprise; nearly every man who is sincerely attached to the British Empire.[74]

Having once been unnecessary and undesirable, the Union was now
vital and in need of preservation at all costs. As a political position, this was
clear enough, and hardly different from any of the pro-Union sentiments
being expressed by the opponents of Parnell among the Irish landowning
classes as a whole. Yet it was rather more difficult to sustain as the conclusion of a long historical work. To understand how Lecky attempted to
achieve this, it is necessary to look a little more closely at the way in which
the Irish sections fitted into his whole historical scheme.

The very opening of Lecky's *History of England* signalled the manner
in which his approach would differ from Macaulay's in substantial ways.
Going far beyond the famous chapter 3, Lecky's first volume contained four
chapters only one of which had a strong narrative element. An introductory
chapter on themes and structures was followed by an analytic chapter on
the character of the Whig party; a narrative of Walpole's administration

73   Lecky, *History of England*, 480–1.
74   *Ibid.*, 481.

followed, but even this contained several thematic sections, and was followed by a final thematic survey on 'National tastes and manners' which included material similar to Macaulay's only effort in this direction. In subsequent volumes narrative sections became more frequent but they continued to be balanced and in some volumes surpassed by chapters offering surveys on the colonies, on 'The Religious Revival', on foreign policy, and on 'The Causes of the French Revolution'.

In structuring his *History* in this manner Lecky thus bedded his general narrative within the confines of structures which set its focus and its emphases.[75] In treating Ireland, however, Lecky's approach was markedly different. Though the opening chapters devoted to Ireland (chapters 6 and 7) are very largely thematic and comparative in character in keeping with the English sections, increasingly, direct chronological narrative begins to dominate. Thus in chapters 16 and 17, short introductory sections on the Whiteboys and the Volunteers give way to extensive chronological sections and thereafter from the next Irish chapter 'Ireland 1782–9' (chapter 24) right through to the concluding chapters of the entire book (chapters 25 to 32) the treatment is entirely chronological.

No less significant than the predominance of narrative in Lecky's specifically Irish sections, is the manner in which the narrative is organized. In the early sections the organizing principle is simply the succession of English viceroyalties which drive the narrative from 1767 down to the viceroyalty of Camden (1795–8). Then a different kind of narrative force begins to predominate in the bloody sequence of rebellion, repression and the bitter wrangling ending with the passage of the Act of Union. The narrational strategy espoused by Lecky is revealing of his overall but largely implicit interpretation of the underlying causes of that fateful historical event. Focussing on the several viceroyalties (no less than sixteen between 1767 and 1798) helped Lecky to emphasize the way in which the vagaries of English and imperial politics seriously affected and disrupted purely Irish domestic issues. The instability of the viceroys also nurtured a poisonous

---

75   The influence of the French positivist historians and of Buckle may be discerned in this aspect of his work.

indigenous tendency toward faction and place-seeking among the Irish political elite, reinforcing the worst tendencies of the Irish political system and for the most part inhibiting or paralysing urgently needed reforms. Such a nefarious matrix of forces not only stifled the Irish Parliament's capacity to act as a force of reform and progress, it drove 'the most intelligent and most energetic' patriots to find other forms of protest and agitation outside of Parliament. Repression further radicalized them, driving some into treasonous conspiracy. What followed was chaos which could only be clarified in detailed, austere, rigorously sequential narrative.

Lecky defended his departure from his English style in his Irish sections explicitly at the start of the final two volumes:

> It is a period which has been very imperfectly written, and usually under the influence of the most furious partisanship [...] It is also a period of great crimes and of great horrors, and the task of tracing their true causes, and measuring with accuracy and impartiality the different degrees of provocation, aggravation, palliation, and comparative guilt, is an extremely difficult one. In order to accomplish it with any success, it is necessary to bring together a much larger array of original evidence, drawn from the opposite camps, than would be required in dealing with a history of which the outlines, at least, were well established and generally admitted [...] It is only by collecting and comparing many letters, written by men of different opinions and scattered over wide areas, that it is possible to form a true estimate of the condition of the country, and to pronounce with real confidence between opposing statements. Such a method is, I believe, the one method of arriving at truth; it brings the reader in direct contact with the original materials of Irish history, and it enables him to draw his own conclusions very independently of the historian.[76]

Such a confident methodological statement obscured its darker implications. Did the existence of irreconcilable views necessarily imply the veracity of a judicious moderate middle? Was the authority of such a middle-ground validated by a claim simply to have surveyed more primary sources? Was the presentation of such a body of materials simply on the basis of chronological sequentiality either possible or demonstrably superior to alternative arrangements? Were the readers of such selective presentations made,

---

76   William Edward Hartpole Lecky, *History of England in the 18th century*, vol. 7, v.

as Lecky insisted, more independent judges by this strategy than by any other? And, if so, how? Above all how did the supply of waves of sequential contingent events of itself entail the suspension or indefinite deferral of moral judgement? Yet such critical hermeneutical questions remained happily buried under the reassurances of vast erudition, a rhetoric of scholarly detachment and a modest referral to all possible readers. And yet the appeal of such a diction, that was authoritative, reasoned, and yet, unlike that of all the polemicists from Mitchel to Froude, professedly moderate, was uniquely powerful and compelling.

So Lecky's subtle strategy for the rehabilitation of an Anglo-Irish history of Ireland became the template for many others seeking to construct a similarly exculpatory case for other periods in Irish history. Thus the three volumes of Richard Bagwell's *Ireland under the Tudors* were organized almost entirely on strict chronological grounds (with occasional separate chapters on Irish Church history) and he followed the same pattern in his *Ireland under the Stuarts*. This also was to be the format adopted by Goddard Henry Orpen in his *Ireland under the Normans*. In following Lecky's interpretative strategy, these younger Anglo-Irish historians echoed his justification. Rejecting any engagement with polemic which had traditionally disfigured Irish historical writing, both insisted that the best guarantee of their impartiality was their fidelity to the facts of history as they occurred in sequential order. It was the historian's duty, wrote Bagwell, simply 'to marshal all the material facts with just so much of comment as may enable his hearers to give them their due weight. The reading public is the jury'.[77] And Orpen was even more explicit, and revealing, in his own assertion of the historian's role:

> I have not thought it part of my duty to pass moral judgements on anybody [...]
> The most important function of an historian, after he has carefully ascertained the
> facts of a case, is to understand them in their relation to other facts, and to give an
> intelligible account of the whole. To understand an action he must regard it from
> the point of view of the actor and with reference to the circumstances in which the

---

77 Richard Bagwell, *Ireland under the Tudors* vol. 2 (London: Longmans, Green, 1890), v.

actor stood. When he has really done this he will seldom care to pass severe moral judgements. More often he will find that 'tout comprendre est tout pardonner'.[78]

There could have been no clearer statement of the exculpatory intent of the Anglo-Irish historical narrative.

Even as Orpen wrote, the vulnerabilities of this self-exculpatory narrative were becoming evident. Where did the narrative start? Why did it exclude pre-Conquest Irish history or the history of Gaelic Ireland in the centuries after the conquest? Such were the challenges being raised against the Anglo-Irish account of Irish history already being levelled by Gaelic scholars such as Eoin MacNeill and more radical critics such as Alice Stopford Green.[79] And why was the large, but entirely select group of English administrative, English language materials to be privileged above all other sources in the reconstruction of the Irish historical record? Before long the power of this nationalist critique would become irresistible.

But in the years immediately following the trauma of the Famine, the Anglo-Irish reconstruction of Irish history as a detailed complex sequence of contingencies in regard to which the attribution of blame was pointless and unscholarly had served its purpose. The dominant historians of late nineteenth-century Ireland may have eschewed the allure of professionalization and the related claim that their discipline could aspire to a scientific objectivity, but they had successfully refurbished an old kind of history which served more effectively than any pretension to scientific models to rebut the charges of their Froudian critics, exorcise their guilt, and reassert their claim to cultural leadership.

78   Goddard Henry Orpen, *Ireland under the Normans 1169–1216* vol. 1 (Nabu Press, 2011), x–xi.
79   Both MacNeill and Stopford Green independently launched critiques on the Anglo-Irish tradition of historiography, see Eoin MacNeill, *Phases of Irish History 1848–1929* (Dublin: Gill, 1920); Alice Stopford Green, *The Old Irish World* (Dublin: M. H. Gill & Son, 1914), chapter 1.

Notes on Contributors

BRIGITTE BASTIAT holds a PhD in Media and Communication Studies from the University of Paris 8. She teaches English at the University of La Rochelle and works with a research group on cinema based at the same university. She is an associate member of the Centre d'études irlandaises (Research Centre in Irish Studies) of the University of Rennes 2 and of the CRHIA (Research Centre for International Atlantic History) of the Universities of La Rochelle and Nantes. She has published on gender representations, Irish theatre and Irish, British and American cinema. She is currently involved in a research project dealing with the contemporary Northern Irish playwright Owen McCafferty. She co-translated into French one of McCafferty's plays, *Mojo Mickybo* (1998), which was premièred in French at the University of Tours in March 2012 and has been performed in various French cities since then. She is currently co-translating Owen McCafferty's *Quietly* (2012).

CARINE BERBÉRI is Senior Lecturer in British Studies at the University of Tours. Her research interests are principally in the field of British politics, with a particular emphasis on the relationship between Britain and Europe. She has published several articles and books about British attitudes towards the European Union and the Euro (*Le Parti travailliste et les syndicats face aux questions monétaires européennes*, 2005; *Le Royaume-Uni face à l'euro: de la prudence à l'hostilité*, 2012). Among her recent contributions on this topic are the articles 'Northern Ireland and the Euro: Changing Attitudes 2003–2013' (*Etudes Irlandaises*, 39 (1), Spring 2014) and 'Trade Unions and European Monetary Issues 1970–2013' (*GRAAT On-Line*, February 2015). She is also working on the impact of British devolution and the way devolution and European integration issues have been linked since the 1990s.

CIARAN BRADY is Professor of Early Modern History and Historiography in the School of Histories and Humanities at Trinity College Dublin. He is a Fellow of Trinity College Dublin and a member of the Royal Irish Academy. His latest book, *James Anthony Froude: An Intellectual Biography of a Victorian Prophet*, was published in 2013.

BERTRAND CARDIN, Professor of English at the Université de Caen Basse-Normandie, is the author of *Lectures d'un texte étoilé* (2009), a book combining six textual analyses with theoretically informed readings of a single short story by John McGahern, 'Korea'. He has also written a book on father-son relationships in the contemporary Irish novel entitled *Miroirs de la filiation. Parcours dans huit romans irlandais contemporains* (2005). He co-edited *Irlande, Ecritures et réécritures de la Famine* (with Claude Fierobe, 2007), *Ecrivaines irlandaises/Irish Women Writers* (with Sylvie Mikowski, 2014) and a special issue of the journal *Etudes irlandaises* entitled 'Contemporary Issues in Irish Studies: In Memoriam Paul Brennan' (with Alexandra Slaby, 40–1, Spring/Summer 2015). He also guest-edited a special issue of the *Journal of the Short Story in English* on 'The 21st-Century Irish Short Story' (63, Autumn 2014). He has published numerous articles about contemporary Irish novelists and short story writers.

CHANTAL DESSAINT teaches English in the Department of French Literature at the University of Lille 3. Her PhD thesis was entitled 'Memory and Writing in the Works of Nuala O'Faolain and Éilís Ní Dhuibhne'. She is an associate member of the CECILLE research centre in Lille 3, and her research deals with women's studies and the links between history, memory and autobiography.

CLAIRE DUBOIS lectures in Irish studies at the University of Lille 3. Since defending her PhD in 2006, she has been working mostly on the eighteenth and nineteenth centuries, particularly the history of ideas, the press and visual representations of Ireland. In 2015 she co-edited *The Foreignness of Foreigners: Cultural Representations of the Other in Britain* with Vanessa Alayrac-Fielding. Her recent publications also include 'The Representation of Ireland in Two Nineteenth-Century French Journals' in *Irish Studies in Europe*, 4; 'Visualising the Famine in the Nineteenth Century' in Yann Bévant (ed.), *La Grande Famine en Irlande* (2014); and 'Les voyageurs anglais en Irlande au dix-huitième siècle' in *La Revue Lisa* (2015).

MEHDI GHASSEMI teaches English at the University of Lille 1 and is preparing his doctoral dissertation for a joint PhD in Lille and Leuven under the supervision of Alexandra Poulain and Hedwig Schwall. His dissertation offers a Lacanian reading of 'precarious subjectivity' in the fiction of John Banville. He has previously published on Banville's relationship with deconstruction.

VIRGINIE GIREL-PIETKA is a research fellow in Irish drama at the University of Lille 3 and an associate lecturer in English, theatre and film studies at the Sorbonne Nouvelle. She completed her PhD on Denis Johnston's dramatic works in 2013, under the supervision of Alexandra Poulain. Her dissertation focused on the way Johnston's plays address modern man's identity crisis, the challenges they entail as far as stage language is concerned and the relationship between their content and their ever-changing form. She has published several articles on Johnston's works and is now reworking her dissertation into a monograph. She also maintains a Facebook page entitled 'Denis Johnston – Irish Playwright', where she shares information about research into Johnston's works.

NICHOLAS GRENE is Professor of English Literature at Trinity College Dublin, a Fellow of the College and a Member of the Royal Irish Academy. He was the founding director of the Synge Summer School (1991–2000) and is the chair of the Irish Theatrical Diaspora research network, for which he has co-edited three volumes: *Irish Theatre on Tour* (2005, with Chris Morash), *Interactions: Dublin Theatre Festival 1957–2007* (2008, with Patrick Lonergan) and *Irish Theatre: Local and Global Perspectives* (2012, with Patrick Lonergan). His books include *The Politics of Irish Drama* (1999), *Yeats's Poetic Codes* (2008) and *Home on the Stage* (2014). His childhood memoir, *Nothing Quite Like It*, was published in 2011.

FRANK HEALY is a lecturer in English for Academic Purposes at the University of La Rochelle. For many years his research was focused on the molecular basis of identity and he published extensively in this field. More recently, he has been working on assimilation of both the Irish in Scotland and North Africans in France. He is also involved in a research project examining the work of the contemporary Northern Irish playwright Owen

McCafferty. He co-translated into French one of McCafferty's plays, *Mojo Mickybo* (1998), which was premièred in French at the University of Tours in March 2012 and has been performed in various cities in France since then. He is currently co-translating Owen McCafferty's *Quietly* (2012).

MARIE-VIOLAINE LOUVET is a senior lecturer at the University of Toulouse 1 Capitole. She completed her PhD on Ireland and the Middle East crisis (1968–2013) in 2013 and she currently works on international advocacy networks between Ireland and Middle Eastern countries. Her research focuses on the framing of public discourse regarding the Arab–Israeli conflict in Irish civil society and historical connections between Ireland and the Middle East. She has published articles in *Études irlandaises* and *Irish Studies in International Affairs*. Her book *Civil Society, Postcolonialism and Transnational Solidarity: Ireland and the Middle East* will be published in 2016.

FABRICE MOURLON is a senior lecturer at the University of Paris 13 in the Applied Languages Department. He defended his PhD in 2009, with a thesis on the victims of the Northern Irish conflict between 1966 and 2006. His current research focuses on Northern Ireland and the model it offers for conflict resolution, looking at policies and local associations helping victims and at the role of memory in the reconciliation process. He has published articles on victims and survivors, policies, the role and value of testimonies and dealing with the past.

MARTINE PELLETIER is a senior lecturer in English and Irish studies at the University of Tours. She has published widely on Brian Friel, Field Day and contemporary Irish and Northern Irish theatre. Among her recent contributions are chapters in *Irish Drama: Local and Global Perspectives*, edited by Nicholas Grene and Patrick Lonergan (2012), *Drama Reinvented: Theatre Adaptation in Ireland (1970–2007)*, edited by Thierry Dubost (2012), *Adapting Chekhov: The Text and its Mutations*, edited by J. Douglas Clayton and Yana Merzon (2013) and *Preserving the Sixties: Britain and the 'Decade of Protest'*, edited by Trevor Harris and Monia O'Brien Castro (2014). She has also written prefaces to Alain Delahaye's ten French translations of Brian Friel's plays. Besides her teaching and research activities, she has been Vice-President in charge of Cultural Affairs for the University of Tours since 2003.

VALÉRIE PEYRONEL is Professor of Anglo-Irish Studies at the University of Paris 3 Sorbonne Nouvelle. Her research focuses on economic issues in Ireland and Britain, and economy, conflict and community relations in Northern Ireland. Her publications on these topics include *La crise financière et les économies du monde anglophone* (co-edited with Catherine Coron and Régine Hollander, 2010); *Les relations communautaires en Irlande du Nord: une nouvelle dynamique* (2003); and *Economie et conflit en Irlande du Nord* (2001). She is the director of CERVEPAS/CREW EA 4399 at Sorbonne Nouvelle.

AUDREY ROBITAILLIÉ specializes in Irish mythology and folklore in literature. She obtained her PhD in 2015 from Queen's University Belfast and the Université de Caen Basse-Normandie, working under joint supervision on the motifs of fairy abduction and the changeling in the folklore and literature of Ireland and its diaspora.

MICHEL SAVARIC spent several years in Belfast carrying out research for his PhD, 'The Question of Identity in Northern Ireland', which was submitted to the University of Toulouse-le-Mirail in 2001. Since 2002, he has been a lecturer at the University of Franche-Comté, where he is a member of the Centre de Recherches Interdisciplinaires and Transculturelles (CRIT). He has published articles on the representation of the conflict in cinema, visual arts and street murals as well as on the evolution of Northern Irish society. He recently contributed a chapter entitled 'Racism and Sectarianism in Northern Ireland' to *The Politics of Ethnic Diversity in the British Isles*, edited by Romain Garbaye and Pauline Schnapper (2014). He is currently researching the history of Northern Ireland.

NATHALIE SEBBANE lectures in British history and Irish studies at the University of Paris 3 Sorbonne Nouvelle. Her research focuses on gender studies, women's histories and relations between Church and State in Ireland, particularly the Industrial Schools, the Magdalen Asylums and feminism.

MATHEW D. STAUNTON is a printing historian currently teaching at the CELSA and the École Nationale Supérieure des Arts Décoratifs. His doctoral thesis (Paris 3, 2011) is a micro-history of the Sinn Féin Printing & Publishing Company. He has published articles and book chapters on Irish visual and material culture and is the editor of a series of monographs on printing, typography and writing systems. He was recently awarded a research fellowship by the Fondation Irlandaise and nominated an Associate Fellow of the Graduate School of Creative Arts and Media in Ireland. He has also curated several exhibitions at the Centre Culturel Irlandais in Paris. His research interests include book illustration, typography, cartography and the historiography of child abuse in Ireland.

Index

Reimagining Ireland

Series Editor: Dr Eamon Maher, Institute of Technology, Tallaght

The concepts of Ireland and 'Irishness' are in constant flux in the wake of an ever-increasing reappraisal of the notion of cultural and national specificity in a world assailed from all angles by the forces of globalisation and uniformity. Reimagining Ireland interrogates Ireland's past and present and suggests possibilities for the future by looking at Ireland's literature, culture and history and subjecting them to the most up-to-date critical appraisals associated with sociology, literary theory, historiography, political science and theology.

Some of the pertinent issues include, but are not confined to, Irish writing in English and Irish, Nationalism, Unionism, the Northern 'Troubles', the Peace Process, economic development in Ireland, the impact and decline of the Celtic Tiger, Irish spirituality, the rise and fall of organised religion, the visual arts, popular cultures, sport, Irish music and dance, emigration and the Irish diaspora, immigration and multiculturalism, marginalisation, globalisation, modernity/postmodernity and postcolonialism. The series publishes monographs, comparative studies, interdisciplinary projects, conference proceedings and edited books.

Proposals should be sent either to Dr Eamon Maher at eamon.maher@ittdublin.ie or to ireland@peterlang.com.

Vol. 1   Eugene O'Brien: 'Kicking Bishop Brennan up the Arse':
          Negotiating Texts and Contexts in Contemporary Irish Studies
          ISBN 978-3-03911-539-6. 219 pages. 2009.

Vol. 2   James P. Byrne, Padraig Kirwan and Michael O'Sullivan (eds):
          Affecting Irishness: Negotiating Cultural Identity Within and
          Beyond the Nation
          ISBN 978-3-03911-830-4. 334 pages. 2009.

Vol. 3   Irene Lucchitti: The Islandman: The Hidden Life of Tomás
          O'Crohan
          ISBN 978-3-03911-837-3. 232 pages. 2009.

Vol. 69   Michel Brunet, Fabienne Gaspari and Mary Pierse
           (eds): George Moore's Paris and His Ongoing French
           Connections
           ISBN 978-3-0343-1973-7. 279 pages. 2015.

Vol. 70   Carine Berbéri and Martine Pelletier (eds): Ireland: Authority
           and Crisis
           ISBN 978-3-0343-1939-3. 296 pages. 2015.

Vol. 71   David Doolin: Transnational Revolutionaries: The Fenian
           Invasion of Canada, 1866
           ISBN 978-3-0343-1922-5. 292 pages. 2015.

Vol. 72   Terry Phillips: Irish Literature and the First World War:
           Culture, Identity and Memory
           ISBN 978-3-0343-1969-0. 297 pages. 2015.

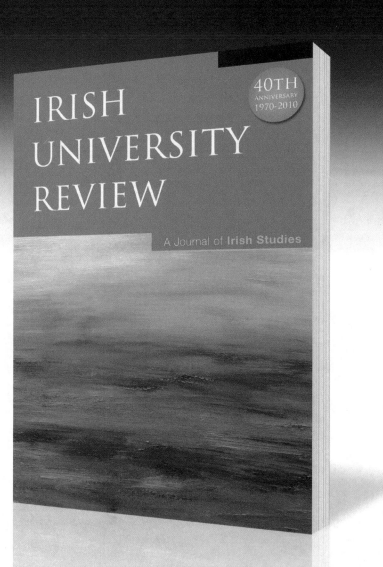

Established in 1970, the **Irish University Review** is the leading journal of Irish literary studies. It publishes the best current criticism and scholarship, an extensive review section, and the IASIL annual bibliography of Irish Studies.

The 'special issues', published annually, and devoted to the work of a particular author, or a topic of current interest in Irish Studies, have shaped and defined the field.

To find out more, and for details of how to subscribe, please visit our website.

www.irishuniversityreview.ie